Electronic Payment Systems

For a complete listing of the *Artech House Computer Science Library,*
turn to the back of this book.

Electronic Payment Systems

Donal O'Mahony
Michael Peirce
Hitesh Tewari

Artech House
Boston • London

Library of Congress Cataloging-in-Publication Data
O'Mahony, Donal, 1961–
    Electronic payment systems / Donal O'Mahony, Michael Peirce, Hitesh Tewari.
        p.   cm. — (The Artech House computer science library)
    Includes bibliographical references and index.
    ISBN 0-89006-925-5 (alk. paper)
        1. Electronic funds transfers.   2. Data encryption (Computer science).
3. Internet (Computer network)   I. Peirce, M. A. (Michael A.)   II. Tewari,
Hitesh.   III. Title.   IV. Series.
    HG1710.045   1997
    332'.0285—dc21   97-9405
                                                              CIP

British Library Cataloguing in Publication Data
O'Mahony, Donal, 1961–
    Electronic payment systems
    1. Electronic funds transfers
    I. Title. II. Peirce, Michael, 1961–   III.Tewari, Hitesh
    332.1'0285

    ISBN 0-89006-925-5

Cover design by Jennifer Makower

International Standard Book Number: 0-89006-925-5
Library of Congress Catalog Card Number: 97-9405

10 9 8 7 6 5

Contents

Chapter 4

Chapter 7

Micropayment systems   191

Preface

The study of diverse techniques for making payments across networks has occupied researchers in cryptography for many years; however, it was not until the public began to connect to the Internet in large numbers that the topic became urgent. In the space of two years or so, a measured hum of activity in universities and research institutes developed into a frantic search for what was seen as the missing link in the burgeoning area of electronic commerce. This search was characterized by the development of many different proposals for making electronic payments. New companies emerged, some of which were floated on the world's stock markets in a blaze of publicity. Older companies formed alliances and made bold announcements to demonstrate the fact that they intended to be key players in this new area of commerce.

Around this time, the authors of this book were engaged in research work involving electronic payments at Trinity College Dublin. Writing a textbook in a field where the ground is continually shifting is a daunting prospect, but we felt that with a concerted team effort we could capture a useful snapshot. What you are now reading is the result of these efforts, and we hope that, regardless of when you read it or how much the field has changed in the intervening time, you will still find it illuminating.

The book is written as a guide to the field for those who will deal with electronic payments in their professional lives. This covers a spectrum from researchers interested in advancing the state of the art to technical advisors for businesses engaging in network-based commerce. Bankers, financial service providers, and those involved in implementing current payment techniques will be interested in this book as a means of providing a glimpse of the future direction of this industry and to help them in making choices between the new technologies on offer. We have not assumed any knowledge of cryptography, and tutorial material is included where necessary.

The authors would like to thank Kate Hawes of Artech House for her guidance from proposal stage to the final manuscript. We are also indebted to Judith Grass for her helpful criticisms on the draft copy.

Chapter 1

Motivation for electronic payment

Everything . . . must be assessed in money; for this enables men always to exchange their services, and so makes society possible.

Aristotle (384–322 B.C.)

THE IDEA of paying for goods and services electronically is not a new one. All around us we see evidence of transactions taking place where at least part of the process is carried on electronically. Since the late 1970s and early 1980s, a variety of schemes have been proposed to allow payment to be effected across a computer network. Few of these schemes got beyond the design stage since they were of little use to those who were not connected to a network.

The arrival of the Internet has removed this obstacle to progress. This network of networks has grown dramatically from its inception in the late 1970s to today's truly global medium. It is not known how many people make regular use of the Internet, but Figure 1.1 shows a graph of the number of host computers [1] connected at different points in its history.

By January of 1997, after a period of exponential growth, the number of

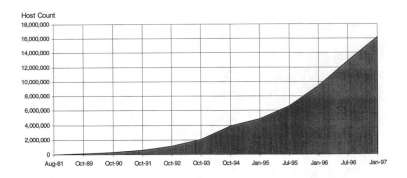

Figure 1.1   Count of host computers connected to the Internet over time.

machines hooked up to the network had grown to more than 16 million. If each host computer is used by 10 individuals (a popular assumption), this means that there are 160 million people around the world who have access to services on the Internet. Much of this growth has been driven by the availability of World Wide Web (WWW) technology that allows information located on machines around the world to be accessed as a single multimedia linked document with simple point-and-click interactions.

Many forecasters predict that every household in the developed world will have access to an Internet connection by the end of the century. Surveys of Internet users [2] suggest that the profile is changing from the original university-centered user base to a more broadly based residential population with a high spending power. These facts are not lost on commercial organizations wishing to offer goods and services for sale to a global consumer audience.

Goods and services began being traded on the network, without the use of any supporting technology. Consumers could select the goods using WWW-based catalogs and when the payment phase of the transaction was reached a variety of ad-hoc mechanisms were used. These ranged from sending unencrypted credit card numbers across the network to the use of telephone or fax to transfer sensitive payment information.

At the same time, a wide variety of new secure network payment schemes were being developed in universities and research institutes as well as by commercial organizations and the banking sector. Some of these schemes are still at the concept stage while others have already undergone extensive testing in pilot schemes. The mainstream banks have also been keen to adapt their card-based payment schemes to work across a network.

This book attempts to present the technology involved in the more influential of the payment systems currently available to network users. Since payment technology is undergoing major upheaval, this account will necessarily be a kind of snapshot of the current state of play.

The following chapter will look at the ways in which the world's population currently pays for goods and services in order to gain a good appreciation for the context in which the new systems are being introduced. Since most of the new schemes rely on cryptographic techniques for their security, Chapter 3 provides the necessary background information on cryptography required for a thorough understanding of how the new schemes operate.

Chapters 4, 5, and 6 survey the principal schemes used to effect payment electronically in a manner that is most similar to credit card, check, and cash, respectively, while Chapter 7 looks at micropayments, a new form of payment that has no counterpart in conventional commerce. We conclude with a look at what lies ahead for payment systems in the years to come.

REFERENCES

[1]   Internet Host Count maintained by the Network Wizards, Menlo Park, California, January 1997, http://www.nw.com

[2]   Kehoe, C., and J. E. Pitkow, "Surveying the Territory: GVU's Five WWW User Surveys," *The World Wide Web Journal*, Vol. 1, No. 3, http://www.cc.gatech.edu/gvu/user_surveys/papers

Chapter 2

Characteristics of
current payment systems

PAYMENT in its most primitive form involves barter: the direct exchange of goods and services for other goods and services. Although still used in primitive economies and on the fringes of developed ones, this form of payment suffers from the need to establish what is known as a *double coincidence of wants*. This means, for example, that a person wishing to exchange food for a bicycle must first find another person who is both hungry and has a spare bicycle! Consequently, over the centuries, barter arrangements have been replaced with various forms of money.

The earliest money was called *commodity money*, where physical commodities (such as corn, salt, or gold) whose values were well known were used to effect payment. In order to acquire a number of desirable properties including portability and divisibility, gold and silver coins became the most commonly used commodity money, particularly after the industrial revolution in the 1800s.

The next step in the progression of money was the use of tokens such as paper notes, which were backed by deposits of gold and silver held by the note issuer. This is referred to as adopting a *commodity standard*. As an economy becomes highly stable and governments (in the form of central banks) are trusted, it becomes unnecessary to have commodity backing for notes that are issued. This is referred to as *fiat money* since the tokens only have value by virtue of the fact that the government declares it to be so, and this assertion is widely accepted.

Cash payment is the most popular form of money transfer used today, but as amounts get larger and security becomes an issue, people are less inclined to hold their wealth in the form of cash and start to avail of the services of a financial institution such as a bank. If both parties to a payment hold accounts with the same bank, then a payment can be effected by making a transfer of funds from one account to another. This essential mechanism is at the root of a wide variety of payment schemes facilitated by the financial services industry today. The following sections will look at some of these and how they compare with traditional cash payment.

2.1   Cash payments

On first examination, payment by cash appears to be the simplest and most effective of all of the alternatives. It is easily transferred from one individual to another. In paper form, it is quite portable and large amounts can be carried in a pocket or briefcase. There are no transaction charges levied when a payment is made, which makes it very suitable for transactions with a low value, and no audit trail is left behind. This last attribute makes cash payment a favorite payment method for those engaged in criminal activity.

But contrary to appearances, cash is not *free*. There is a huge amount of cash in circulation. As of late 1995, it was estimated that $410 billion in U.S. currency [1] is in the hands of the public. This currency wears out—a $1 bill has a life expectancy of 15–18 months, while the less common $50 bill usually lasts about 5 years. Each year, around 10 billion notes are destroyed and replaced with newly printed ones. Regardless of the denomination, each note costs some 4¢ to produce, and this cost is ultimately borne by the tax payer. A similar situation exists in every country in the world.

Once the cash has been produced, it must then be transferred to and from banks or companies under very high security. Vaults must be built to store it, and heavy insurance premiums paid to cover losses due to theft. All of these costs are eventually passed on by a variety of indirect means to the cash user. With recent advances in color photocopying techniques, the risk from counterfeiters is also growing at an alarming rate.

Nevertheless, cash is the most commonly used form of payment, accounting for about 80% of all transactions. As an example, U.S. statistics and estimates [2] suggest that in 1993, nearly 300 billion cash transactions took place in the American economy with a total dollar value of some $3,400 billion. The fact that this yields an average transaction value of around $11 reflects the fact that cash is mostly used to buy low-value goods.

One of the factors that has allowed cash to remain the dominant form of payment is the development of automated teller machines (ATMs), which allow consumers much easier access to money in cash form. The banking industry, which acts as the distributor of cash in the economy, has been attempting for many years to wean consumers off cash and into electronic bank mediated payments and in recent years is beginning to have some success.

2.2 Payment through banks

Where both parties have lodged their cash with a bank for safekeeping, it becomes unnecessary for one party to withdraw notes in order to make a payment to another. Instead, they can write a check, which is an order to their bank to pay a specified amount to the named payee. The payee can collect the funds by going to the payer's bank and cashing the check. Alternatively, the payee can lodge the check so that the funds are transferred from the account of the payer to that of the payee.

2.2.1 Payment by check

If the parties hold accounts with separate banks, then the process gets more complicated. The cycle begins when A presents a check in payment to B. What happens next is shown in Figure 2.1. Party B lodges the check with his bank (referred to as the *collecting bank*), who will collect the funds on his behalf. In most cases, a credit is made to B's account as soon as the check is lodged, but this *immediate funds* availability is not always the case. All checks lodged with bank B over the course of a day will be sent to the *clearing department*, where they are sorted in order of the banks on which they are drawn. The following day, they are brought to a *clearing house*, where a group of banks meet to exchange checks. The check in question will be given to bank A and (usually) one day later bank A will verify that the funds are available to meet the check and debit A's account for the sum involved.

If funds are not available, the signature on the check does not match with samples, or any other problem occurs, then the check must be returned to the

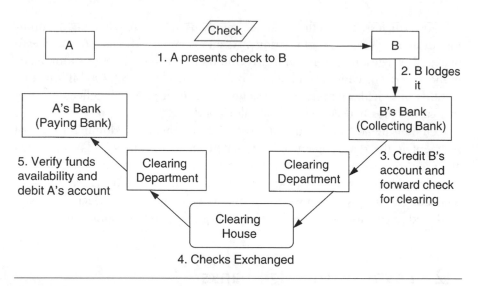

Figure 2.1   The check-clearing process.

collecting bank together with some indication as to why it could not be processed. Bank A must attend to this promptly, usually within one working day. These so-called *returned items* are the major problem with the check as a payment instrument in that their existence introduces uncertainty, and the fact that they need individual attention from banking staff means that they are very expensive to process. The principal loser in this situation is B, who finds himself in possession of a dishonored check with hefty bank charges to pay. In general, however, the bank's changes are seldom high enough to cover their processing expenses.

If funds are available to meet the check, then the following day the banks that are part of the clearing arrangement will calculate how much they owe to or are owed by the group of clearing banks as a whole. This amount is then *settled* by making a credit or debit from a special account usually maintained by the central bank.

The clearing of paper checks is a major operation, and in the United Kingdom over 3 billion items went through the system in 1995, with a value £1,000 billion [3]. Volumes have declined by between 2% and 4% per year since 1991. The cost to the member banks of operating the clearing system is very high and in the United Kingdom has been estimated at over £1.5 billion per year. One way to reduce the costs is to keep the check at the collecting bank and forward the transaction details electronically through the clearing system. These may be accompanied by a scanned image of the check to allow signatures to be verified. This process is known as *truncation*, and has been implemented in many countries since the early 1970s, but was forbidden by law in some jurisdictions. The United Kingdom, for example, until May 1996, required that a check be physically presented at the bank branch on which it was drawn.

2.2.2 Payment by giro or credit transfer

The "returned items" problem is the single biggest drawback with checks as a payment method. This problem is eliminated using a credit transfer or giro payment. A giro is an instruction to the payer's bank to transfer funds to the payee's bank. As Figure 2.2. shows, the processing of a giro is similar to a check, with the main difference being that the transaction cannot be initiated unless A has the funds available. This eliminates any uncertainly and extra cost imposed by the need to process returned items. It is an easier process to conduct electronically since the correct processing of the payment does not require sending the signed document through the clearing system.

This form of payment is quite popular in many European countries where national post offices rather than banks tend to operate the system. The payment method is not used in paper form in the United States, but credit transfers in electronic form are possible.

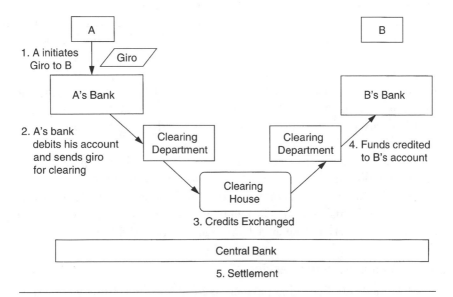

Figure 2.2 Payment by credit transfer or giro.

2.2.3   Automated clearing house (ACH) payments

From their inception, paper-based payments (checks and giros) grew in popularity and as the task of carrying out paper-based clearing grew, the banks began to look for more automated ways to make payments. In 1968, a group of Californian bankers came together to form the Special Committee on Paperless Entries (SCOPE), which led to the formation in 1972 of the California Clearing House Association, the first regional automated clearing house (ACH) in the United States. In the United Kingdom, similar moves were happening, and an automated clearing center was established in 1968, which was incorporated in 1971 as the Bankers Automated Clearing Service (BACS).

The ACH system operates in a similar way to paper clearing except that the payment instructions are in electronic form. In the early days of ACH, banks prepared magnetic tapes of these transactions that were transported to the ACH, sorted by destination bank, and distributed in much the same way as paper checks and giros, but increasingly this method is being replaced by real-time transactions sent on telecommunications links.

In the United States ACH system, the first message to be used was a corporate cash disbursement (CCD) message consisting of a 94-character message to identify the payee, amount, and any other details. In more recent years, more message formats have been added, and message formats have been changing from proprietary formats to ones that comply with open standards defined by the electronic data interchange (EDI) community [4].

The system is now used extensively by employers to pay wages directly into workers' bank accounts, to implement standing orders, direct debits, and direct credits. In the United Kingdom in 1995, BACS processed 2.2 billion transactions to the value of £1,055 billion. In the United States, usage of ACH has been growing at between 9% and 22% per year and in 1995 processed 3.4 billion transactions with a value of $11.1 trillion. More than half of the recipients of Social Security use it for direct deposit, and nearly half of the private sector receive their wages by ACH.

The ACH systems in different countries have evolved separately in the same general direction. In general, there is no compatibility between the messages used in the individual countries. Indeed, international transfers are generally achieved by using a third format using a service operated by the Society for Worldwide Interbank Financial Transactions (SWIFT).

2.2.4   Wire transfer services

The ACH method of effecting payment is ideal for mid- to low-value transactions. In 1993, for example, the average value of an ACH payment in the United

Table 2.1   Volumes and Values of Noncash Payments in the United States in 1993

Payment Instrument	Transaction Volume	Transaction Value	Average Value
Check	80%	13%	$1,150
Credit card	16%	0%	$45
Credit transfer (Giro)	2%	1%	$2,300
ACH	2%	1%	$5,000
Wire transfer	0%	85%	$4,100,000

States was $5,000. Where the value of payments is considerably higher, the risk level rises and different procedures involving more scrutiny are required. These high-value payments are referred to as wire transfers.

In the United States, the Federal Reserve (central bank) operates the Fedwire payment system, and a private sector organization called the Clearing House Interbank Payment System (CHIPS) is also in operation. Typically, these systems handle payments between corporations and banks and to and from government. In 1993, the average wire transfer payment was worth $4.1 million. As Table 2.1 (taken from [5]) shows, while wire transfers do not register in terms of the proportion of transactions that take place, they account for 85% of the value transferred.

2.3   Using payment cards

The idea of payment using cards first arose in 1915, when a small number of U.S. hotels and department stores began to issue what were then referred to as "shoppers plates" [6]. It was not until 1947 that the Flatbush National Bank issued cards to its local customers. This was followed in 1950 by the Diners Club, which was the first "travel & entertainment" or charge card, and eight years later the American Express card was born.

Over the years, many card companies have started up and failed, but two major card companies, made up of large number of member banks, have come to dominate this worldwide business. These are VISA International and MasterCard.

Credit cards are designed to cater for payments in the retail situation. This means that payments can only be made from a cardholder to a merchant who has preregistered to accept payments using the card. The card companies themselves do not deal with cardholders or merchants, but rather license member organizations (usually banks) to do this for them. A bank that issues cards to their customers is called a card-issuing bank. This means that they register the cardholder, produce a card incorporating the card association's logo, and operate a card account to which payments can be charged.

Merchants who wish to accept payments must also register with a bank. In this case, the bank is referred to as the *acquiring bank* or simply the acquirer. In a paper-based credit card payment, a merchant prepares a sales voucher containing the payer's card number, the amount of the payment, the date, and a goods description. Depending on policy, the transaction may need to be authorized. This will involve contacting an authorization center operated by or on behalf of the acquiring bank to see if the payment can go ahead. This may simply involve verifying that the card does not appear in a blacklist of cards, or it may involve a reference to the card-issuing bank to ensure that funds are available to meet the payment. Assuming it can be authorized, the payment completes.

At the end of the day, the merchant will bring the sales vouchers to the acquiring bank, which will clear them using a clearing system not unlike that used for paper checks and giros but operated by or on behalf of the card associations. The merchant's account is credited, the cardholder's is debited, and the transaction details will appear on the next monthly statement.

In recent years, the card associations and their member banks have made great efforts to eliminate paper from credit card transactions. This has meant that sales vouchers with the cardholder's signature only come into play when a dispute arises, and most of the information flows in Figure 2.3 are entirely electronic.

All the costs associated with a credit card transaction are borne by the merchant involved. The cardholder will see only the amount of the transaction on her statement, but the merchant typically pays over a small percentage of the transaction value with some associated minimum charge that is divided between the acquiring bank and the card association. For this reason, credit cards are not worthwhile for transactions where the amount is below a certain threshold (typically around $2).

The reason why a credit card is so named is that the balance owing on a cardholder's account need not necessarily be paid at the end of the monthly period. The cardholder can pay interest on the outstanding balance and use the card for credit. Other arrangements are possible, for example, if the balance must be paid in full at the end of the period, it is called a *charge card*.

Another possibility is to link the card to a normal bank account, and to

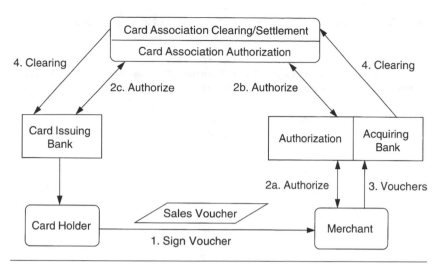

Figure 2.3   Stages in a credit card payment.

process the transaction in real time. This means that at the time the transaction takes place, the amount is transferred from the customer to the merchant bank account. This arrangement is called a *debit card*.

One final way to use a payment card is to incorporate a storage facility into the card that can be loaded with cash from the cardholder's bank account. This *electronic purse* facility will be fully discussed in Chapter 6. Bankers often classify payment cards into three types: pay before (electronic purse), pay now (debit cards), and pay later (credit cards).

2.4   Consumer preferences in payment systems

The sections above have described most methods commonly used to effect payment today. The degree to which they are used differs between countries for a variety of reasons including the level of development of the country and the state of the banking system.

Consumers in all countries use cash for some 80% of their day-to-day transactions. For the most part, these transactions are low in value. Table 2.2 (extracted from [6]) shows how the remaining 20% of payments are made for a number of different countries. It can be seen that of the developed countries, the United States is unusual in that checks are the most popular with almost no use of Giros or direct debits. The picture in Europe shows considerably less check usage, with a more even spread of payment options. In

Table 2.2   Consumer Preferences in Noncash Payment Methods by Country in 1992

Country	Use of Checks	Use of Credit Transfers (Giros)	Payment Cards	Direct Debits
U.S.	81%	2%	17%	1%
Netherlands	12%	61%	3%	24%
U.K.	45%	21%	19%	15%
Germany	9%	50%	2%	39%
India	99%	0%	1%	0%
Thailand	26%	7%	65%	2%

less developed countries such as India and Thailand, the picture changes yet again.

This represents the starting position before the electronic payment methods discussed in this book are introduced. All other things being equal, one would expect that an electronic payment method that was check-like would be popular in the United States, but may not have the same appeal in European countries. It would also be unlikely that an electronic payment scheme based on credit cards would find a ready market in India. Of course, the market share of network payment methods may depart radically from the above in the event of one electronic payment scheme being immensely superior to others.

2.5   Regulatory framework

Payment systems are crucial to the efficient functioning of any economy, and consequently governments are keen to exert some control and regulation over how these systems operate. Conventional payment instruments have, in the past at least, been operated by banks who are subject to regulation by their national central bank. Typically, a bank must be licensed to operate, and in the course of obtaining this license will subject itself to scrutiny. This will include a test to ensure that the individuals representing the bank are "fit and proper" individuals, that the bank has a minimum level of capital, and that it meets the needs of some section of the community. These tests are mainly aimed at ensuring that consumers are protected from the consequences of bank failure. Indeed, in many countries banks are required to take out insurance to cover such an eventuality.

All conventional payment methods involving banks have been the subject of central bank regulation in the past. The newer electronic payment methods described in this book have only just started to attract the scrutiny of the central bank regulators. Many of the newer methods of payment are, to a certain extent, electronic extensions of existing bank-operated payment methods and thus can be covered by minor adjustments to existing regulations. For example, in the United States, the electronic funds transfer act of 1980 as implemented by the Federal Reserve Regulation E covers a variety of banking transactions including electronic bill payment, payment at the point of sale, and many others. It limits consumers' liability for unauthorized electronic withdrawals, provides procedures for resolving errors, and requires institutions to provide terminal receipts and account statements. This represents a good starting point for regulating any form of electronic payment.

The payment method that has caused most concern is the preloaded stored-value card. In Europe, a working group consisting of representatives of central banks from all countries in the European Union convened in 1993 and produced a report [7] detailing what changes in policy would be required to cope with the electronic purse. Their concerns would apply equally to any of the electronic cash schemes described later in this book. They distinguished between single-purpose electronic purses (e.g., cards for pay phones or public transport) and multipurpose cards. In the case of the latter, they recommended that only *credit institutions* (meaning financial institutions that are already subject to central bank regulation) should be allowed to issue such cards. It further suggested that central banks may wish to discourage some electronic purse initiatives if they were worried about the adequacy of the security features of the scheme. A more recent study [8] undertaken by the Bank for International Settlements reviewed the issues raised by electronic money but stopped short of making any definite recommendations.

In the United States, the policy on the new forms of payment has been to adopt a "wait-and-see" attitude. A landmark speech by Alan Blinder, a vice chairman of the Federal Reserve Board of Governors [9], in 1995 stated as follows: "*The present is, we believe, an appropriate time for public debate and discussion, a poor time for regulation and legislation.*" At the time of writing, considerations [10] are ongoing as to whether the existing Regulation E should be extended to cover the new forms of payment. Current thinking is that they should not apply to electronic purses, where the maximum stored amount is less than $100.

Another area where concern could be expected is in the area of monetary policy. If the government is the only issuer of cash in an economy, it can keep a tight rein on the amount of cash in circulation. Operators of stored-value cards or other electronic cash systems could, in principle, affect this balance, decreasing the amount of control a government can exert. This possibility is dismissed [10] by the U.S. Federal Reserve members who believe that the impact of electronic payment systems on the money supply will be insignificant in the short to medium term.

There are, of course many other issues relating to electronic payment that governments may wish to regulate. These would include the question of the levying of taxes on transactions that take place electronically, protection against money laundering, and many others. It seems that both in Europe and the United States, the authorities have only begun to consider the issues involved.

REFERENCES

[1]   Federal Reserve Bank of New York, *Fedpoint 1: How Currency Gets into Circulation*, 1996, p. 3, http://www.ny.frb.org/pihome/fedpoint/fed01.html

[2]   Miller, R., and D. VanHoose, *Modern Money and Banking*, 3rd ed., New York: McGraw-Hill International, 1993.

[3]   Association for Payment Clearing Services (APACS). *Yearbook of Payment Statistics*, London, APACS Statistical Unit, 1995.

[4]   O'Hanlon, J., *Financial EDI - Closing the Loop*, London: Banking Technology Ltd., April 1993.

[5]   Humphrey, D., *Payment Systems: Principles, Practice, and Improvements*, World Bank Technical Paper Number 260, 1995, 104 pp.

[6]   Members of the Bankers Clearing House, *Payment Clearing Systems : Review of Organisation, Membership and Control*, London, Banking Information Service, 1984.

[7]   *Report of the Working Group on EU Payment Systems*, European Monetary Institute, Frankfurt, 1993.

[8]   Bank for International Settlements, Implications for Central Banks of the Development of Electronic Money, Basle, October 1996, http://www.bis.org/publ/bisp01.pdf.

[9]   Blinder, A., *Statement by Vice Chairman of the Board of Governors of the Federal Reserve System before the Subcommittee on Domestic and International Monetary Policy, U.S. House of Representatives*, October 1995.

[10]   Kelley, E., *Remarks by Edward W. Kelley, Jr., Member of the Board of Governors of the Federal Reserve System at the CyberPayments '96 Conference*, Dallas, TX June 18, 1996, http://woodrow.mpls.frb.fed.us/info/speeches/s960618.html

Chapter 3

Cryptographic techniques

THE PAYMENT SYSTEMS outlined in the previous chapter rely on a number of different mechanisms for establishing the *identity* and *intent* of the various parties involved in a payment-related transaction. The most often-used method is the application of a human signature to a document that will serve as the legal basis for the transaction. The identity of the signer can be confirmed by comparison with a stored sample signature or, in case of subsequent dispute, a handwriting expert may later testify to its authenticity.

The essential elements of these mechanisms can be replicated across computer networks through the use of cryptographic techniques. In addition, cryptography is useful in protecting against a wide variety of other attacks on the communications between two parties. In this chapter we will give a basic introduction to the essential cryptographic techniques necessary to understand how electronic payment systems function. Readers who are already familiar with this material may skip ahead to Chapter 4 and refer back as required.

3.1 Encryption and decryption

A message in human readable form is referred to in cryptographic terms as *plaintext* or *cleartext*. The process of disguising a message in such a way as to hide its substance is called *encryption* and the resulting message is referred to as *ciphertext*. As Figure 3.1 shows, the reverse process (*decryption*) takes ciphertext as input and restores the original plaintext.

Plaintext is denoted by P, whereas ciphertext is denoted by C. The encryption function E operates on P to produce C:

$$E(P) = C$$

In the reverse process, the decryption function D operates on C to produce P:

$$D(C) = P$$

A cryptographic algorithm, also called a *cipher*, is a mathematical function used for encryption and decryption. All modern encryption algorithms use a *key*, denoted by K. The value of this key affects the encryption and decryption functions, so that they can now be written as:

$$E_K(P) = C$$

$$D_K(C) = P$$

Historically, the primary purpose of cryptography has been to keep the plaintext hidden from adversaries. *Cryptanalysis* is the science of recovering the plaintext message without knowledge of the key. One can categorize attacks on a cryptosystem as being of a number of different forms:

1. Ciphertext-only attack: In this attack, the cryptanalyst has the ciphertext of several messages, all of which have been encrypted using

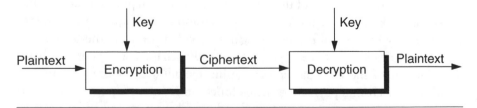

Figure 3.1 Encryption and decryption using a key.

the same encryption key. From this the cryptanalyst attempts to derive either the plaintext or the key.

2. Known-plaintext attack: The cryptanalyst has access not only to the ciphertext of several messages but also to the corresponding plaintext. From this she may be able to derive the key used for encrypting the messages.

3. Chosen-plaintext attack: The cryptanalyst has access to the ciphertext and associated plaintext for several messages and she can gain access to ciphertext corresponding to plaintext that she has chosen. These blocks could be chosen to yield more information about the key or to pursue a particular line of attack.

Any cryptosystem may be *broken* by the "brute force" method, which simply involves testing all possible key values until the correct one is found. With the rapid increases in computer processing power, coupled with the development of special-purpose encryption hardware, this form of attack deserves more attention than it had merited in the past. This theme will be explored further in later sections.

3.2 Symmetric encryption

As the name suggests, symmetric encryption implies that both parties to a communication must first possess a copy of a single secret key as shown in Figure 3.2. The most widely used algorithm in this category is the Data Encryption Standard (DES).

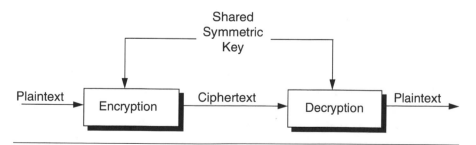

Figure 3.2   Operation of a symmetric cryptosystem.

3.2.1   Data Encryption Standard (DES)

In January 1977, a standard encryption method was adopted by the U.S. government, called the Data Encryption Standard [1,2]. Its origins lay in an internal IBM project to develop an algorithm codenamed *Lucifer* that could not be broken, even by the fastest machines available at the time. The terms of the Federal Information Processing Standard (FIPS) under which it was adopted were that it should be used for sensitive, but not classified, information. Though the algorithm used is complex, it is easily implemented in hardware, and software implementations are widely available. The American National Standards Institute (ANSI) approved DES as an industry standard [3], calling it the Data Encryption Algorithm (DEA).

3.2.1.1   Algorithm

DES is a *block cipher*. This means that it operates on a single chunk of data at a time, encrypting 64 bits (8 bytes) of plaintext to produce 64 bits of ciphertext. The key length is 56 bits, often expressed as an 8-character string with the extra bits used as a parity check. The algorithm has 19 distinct stages. The first stage reorders the bits of the 64-bit input block by applying a fixed permutation. The last stage is the exact inverse of this permutation. The stage penultimate to the last one exchanges the leftmost 32 bits with the rightmost 32 bits. The remaining 16 stages (called "rounds") are functionally identical but take as an input a quantity computed from the key and the round number. Figure 3.3 shows the overall process

At each iteration, the algorithm takes in two 32-bit inputs and produces two 32-bit outputs. The left output is simply a copy of the right input. The right output is an exclusive OR (XOR) of the left input and a function of the right input and the key for the stage K_i. All the complexity lies in the function f, which does a number of substitutions and permutations using simple hardware elements called S-boxes (for substitution) and P-boxes (for permutation). Decryption in the DES algorithm uses the same sequence of steps, but the keys used at each of the 16 stages (K_1 to K_{16}) are applied in reverse order.

In addition to the fundamental DES algorithm, the standards [4] specify a number of different modes of operation. These include electronic codebook, cipher block chaining, output feedback, and cipher feedback. The electronic codebook mode is that outlined in Figure 3.3 and is the most widely used (because of its simplicity), but it is also the most vulnerable to attack. We shall briefly discuss the cipher feedback mode.

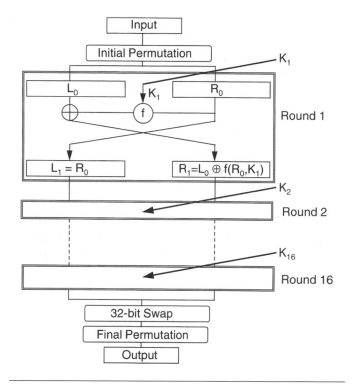

Figure 3.3 The DES algorithm.

3.2.1.2 DES cipher feedback (CFB) mode

Another way to make cryptanalysis of DES much harder is to operate it as a so-called *stream cipher*. Stream ciphers treat the plaintext as a continuous stream of information, where the ciphertext produced depends on the entire history of the stream. When using stream cipher mode, both sender and receiver operate their DES chips in encryption mode. Figure 3.4 shows this process in action. Each DES chip has a 64-bit input register, which operates as a shift register, and a 64 bit output register, which does not. When a plaintext character arrives, it is XORed with 8 bits of output register O_1. The ciphertext thus created is both transmitted to the receiver and shifted into the input register, pushing I_8 off the end. The chip is then activated and the output computed for the new input.

At the receiving end, the incoming character is first XORed with O_1. This will reverse the effect of the XOR operation applied by the sender,

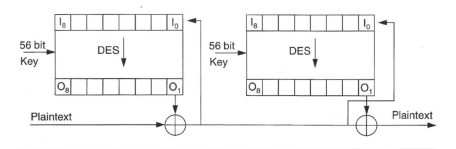

Figure 3.4   DES stream encryption.

yielding the plaintext. The arriving ciphertext is simultaneously shifted into I_1 so that the input registers at both ends of the link are synchronized. If the sender and receiver start out with identical registers, they should remain identical forever.

3.2.1.3   Cracking DES & U.S. export restrictions

All encryption algorithms can theoretically be broken using the so-called "brute-force" attack. This form of attack involves simply applying every possible key until the correct one is found. When DES was first conceived, the idea of breaking a cipher by making 2^{56} attempts was not considered practical, but machines have become considerably faster since then, and the availability of even greater computing power can be expected in the future.

In 1996, using application specific integrated circuits (ASICs), a single chip can be produced that is capable of testing 30 million DES keys per second [5]. Estimates are that a determined government agency that was willing to spend \$300 million on building a massively parallel array of such chips could recover a single DES key in 12 seconds. In light of these facts, designers of cryptographic protocols need to ensure that the safety of their schemes cannot be compromised by successful brute-force attacks.

In terms of attacks other than brute force, DES has proved to be highly resilient. Using a technique known as differential cryptanalysis, Biham and Shamir [6] mounted an attack on 16-round DES that was somewhat more effective than a brute-force attack. A related technique known as linear cryptanalysis was applied by Matsui [7] to some effect. Neither attack has caused too much concern to those using the DES algorithm.

The U.S. government, mindful of the fact that cryptographic techniques can be used against the American national interest, has taken steps to ensure crytographic products are treated in much the same way as munitions for export purposes. The International Traffic in Arms Regulations (ITAR) states that products involving cryptography must be individually licensed before they can be exported from the United States. Applicants for export licenses have found that, in general, licenses will not be granted where a software or hardware product uses strong algorithms to encrypt the message content, whereas using cryptography to assure message integrity is not a problem. Exceptions to the above are frequently made where the encrypted data is purely concerned with financial data.

In 1992, under an agreement with the American Software Publishers Association (SPA), the State Department eased the restrictions on two algorithms, RC2 and RC4 (described below) provided the key length was 40 bits or less. It was clear that this would leave products using these small keys open to brute-force attacks. In January 1996, a group of eminent cryptographers produced a report [5] that stated that 40-bit keys offer "virtually no protection" against such attacks. They went on to state that cryptosystems that expect to protect information adequately for the next 20 years should use keys that are at least 90 bits long. The government responded to this in October 1996 by permitting the export of software using 56-bit keys on condition that the companies involved produced a plan to implement some form of key-escrow scheme that would allow government agencies to gain access to such keys in accordance with national policies.

3.2.2   Triple DES

Triple DES [8] is a possible successor to DES and is appealing in that it requires no new algorithms or hardware over and above conventional DES. Figure 3.5 shows three 56-bit DES keys being used as input to an array of three DES chips (or software blocks). The pattern used for the encryption step is encrypt-decrypt-encrypt (EDE) with a DED pattern being used to reverse the process. In one variation of triple DES, $K1$ is set to be equal to $K3$ giving a 112 bit key length. This latter mode is sometimes referred to as "2 key triple DES," as opposed to "3 key triple DES" when $K1$, $K2$, and $K3$ are distinct.

Its greatest appeal will be for the very large number of financial institutions that have an installed base of equipment with DES hardware.

3.2.3   IDEA

Like DES, the International Data Encryption Algorithm (IDEA), is a block cipher, using secret-key symmetric encryption. It is defined in [9] and a good description is given in [10]. It was originally developed in Zurich by Massey

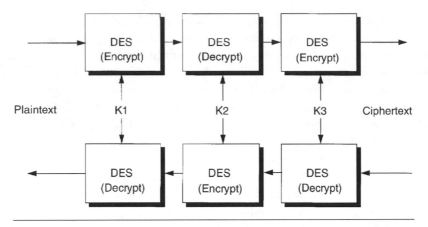

Figure 3.5 The triple DES algorithm.

and Lai in 1990 [11]. It was strengthened against Biham and Shamir's *differential cryptanalysis* attack to become IDEA in 1992.

IDEA uses a 128-bit key to operate on 64-bit plaintext blocks. The same algorithm is used for both encryption and decryption and consists of eight main iterations. It is based on the design concept of "mixing operations from different algebraic groups." The three algebraic groups whose operations are being mixed are

- XOR;
- Addition, ignoring any overflow (addition modulo 2^{16});
- Multiplication, ignoring any overflow (multiplication modulo $2^{16} + 1$).

As shown in Figure 3.6, these operations operate on 16-bit sub-blocks, making the algorithm efficient even on 16-bit processors. IDEA runs much faster in software than DES.

3.2.3.1 Cracking IDEA

IDEA's key length is 128 bits, over twice as long as DES, which means that trying out half the keys would take 2^{127} encryptions. This is such a large number that breaking IDEA by brute force is obviously out of the question.

However the algorithm is still too new for any definitive cryptanalytic results. Biham and Shamir have been examining the IDEA cipher for weaknesses without success. As many formidable academic and military cryptanalyst groups still attempt to attack it, confidence in IDEA is growing. To

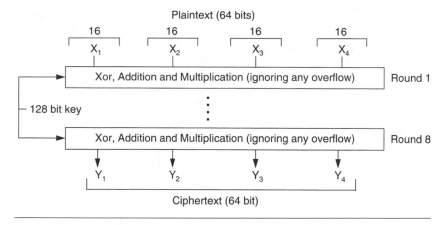

Figure 3.6   The workings of the IDEA cipher.

date, it appears IDEA is significantly more secure than DES. The algorithm is covered by patents in both the United States and Europe, and license fees must be paid if it is to be used commercially.

3.2.4   RC2, RC4, and RC5

In anticipation of the demise of DES, Ron Rivest, a noted cryptographer, has been developing a family of ciphers for RSA Data Security Inc., that might be used to replace it. Unofficially, RC stands for Ron's Code, but officially it is an abbreviation of "Rivest Cipher." It appears as though RC1 never got beyond the design stage, and RC3 was broken before it was released. RC2, however, was released and is used in a number of commercial products. It is a 64-bit block cipher with a variable-length key. RC4 can also use a variable-length key, but operates as a stream cipher. A commodity export license was obtained for 40-bit versions of RC2 and RC4, and the latter was used as the stream cipher in the first secure WWW browsers that became available in 1995. No patents have been applied for and the details of the algorithms are only available subject to a nondisclosure agreement with RSA Data Security Inc. In September 1994, however, code to implement RC4 was posted to a network newsgroup and implementations can now be easily obtained. This knowledge was used in late 1995 [12] to mount a successful brute-force attack against a single ciphertext message encrypted with 40-bit RC4.

The final algorithm in the series is RC5 [13], which is a totally para-metrized system. Among the items that may be changed are the block size, the key length, and the number of rounds. The basic algorithm is a block cipher, but stream versions [14] are also defined. The details of this algorithm are published, the name RC5 is trademarked, and patents have been applied for. It is likely that this algorithm will play a role in new payment system protocols.

3.3 Message digesting or hashing

When the symmetric algorithms above are applied to a message, they provide two main services. First, the message contents are kept confidential from eavesdroppers, who cannot unscramble the encrypted message, and second, the integrity of the message is assured. This can be guaranteed since no alteration can be made to the message unless one is in possession of the key.

In many cases, a check on the message integrity is all that is required, and time spent in providing message confidentiality is wasted. In many business applications, users are not concerned with attackers eavesdropping on the message, but would be very worried if their contents could be altered in transit. Export restrictions applied by the U.S. government are primarily concerned with the ability of law enforcement agencies to intercept the contents of messages. If a system uses encryption strictly for message integrity checks only, then exportability is assured.

One way to provide integrity without confidentiality is to use a device known as a message digest. This involves applying a digesting or hash algorithm to the (long) message to produce a (short) message digest. The secret key can be applied to this hash and the result sent with the message across the network. Figure 3.7 shows how the hashing algorithm is first applied to the complete message. The hash is then encrypted to become a message integrity check (MIC), which is appended to the message before transmission. Since the encryption is only being applied to a very small quantity, and message digesting is very much faster than encryption, this process can be considerably faster than encrypting the entire message.

When the message arrives, the receiver computes a hash of the message using the same algorithm. If this matches the decrypted MIC that came with the message, then the message has not been tampered with.

A good hash function will have two properties. Firstly, it will be difficult to invert. This means that attempting to produce a message that would yield a given hash should be completely infeasible. It should also be resistant to collision, which means that there should be a low probability of finding two messages with the same hash.

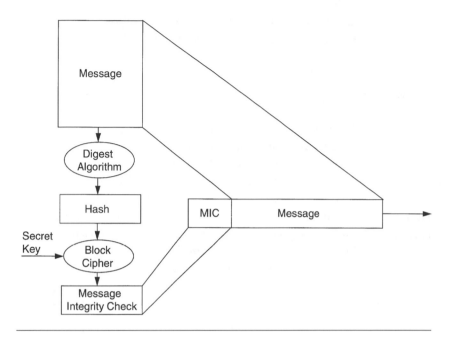

Figure 3.7   Computing a message integrity check (MIC).

Two well-known hash functions that have found a place in payment protocols are MD5 and SHA.

3.3.1   MD5

The MD5 algorithm [15] is one of a series (including MD2 and MD4) of message digest algorithms developed by Ron Rivest. It involves appending a length field to a message and padding it up to a multiple of 512-bit blocks. Each of these 512-bit blocks is then fed through a four-round process involving rotation and a range of Boolean operations producing a chaining value that is input into the processing of the next 512-bit block. The hashed output is the 128-bit chaining value produced in processing the last block of the message.

3.3.2   The Secure Hash Algorithm (SHA)

The U.S. National Institute of Standards and Technology (NIST) released a series of cryptographic standards in 1993, one of which [16] specified the secure hash algorithm. It is based quite heavily on the work of Ron Rivest in the MD series of algorithms. The message is first padded as with MD5, and then fed through four rounds, which are more complex than those used in MD5. The chaining value passed from one round to the next is 160 bits in length, which means that the resulting message digest is also 160 bits.

3.4 Kerberos

Using just the symmetric encryption algorithms outlined above together with message digest algorithms, some quite sophisticated security protocols can be devised. One such protocol is Kerberos, which provides message authentication and confidentiality facilities for communicating parties and is used as the basis for a number of payment systems outlined in later chapters. It is based on the trusted third-party model presented by Needham and Schroeder [17]. The Kerberos authentication service was developed at the Massachusetts Institute of Technology (MIT) for Project Athena and the following discussion is based on version 5 of the protocol [18]. Kerberos allows a client to prove its identity to a third-party server without sending any sensitive information across the network and also encrypts the channel between the two. This section presents an overview of the protocol from the payment systems point of view.

3.4.1 Overview of Kerberos model

Network services that require authentication are required to register with Kerberos, as are the clients that wish to use those services. The Kerberos model consists of a Kerberos server (A), which securely stores the keys of each principal on the network. These shared keys are symmetric keys that are established out-of-band and have a long lifetime. It is also responsible for generating session keys that are used to exchange messages between two principals with a lifetime limited to the duration of a single communication session.

Two types of credentials are used in Kerberos: *tickets* and *authenticators*. A ticket is used to authenticate a client (C) to a server (S) when used in conjunction with an authenticator. A ticket consists of two parts, one encrypted and the other in plaintext. A Kerberos ticket has the form:

$$T_{CS} = [S, K_S[C, \text{Addr}, \mathcal{N}, \text{Validity}, K_{CS}]]$$

A ticket contains

- The name of the server (S) in plaintext;
- The name of the client (C);
- The network address of the client (Addr);

- A timestamp in the form of a nonce (N) to prevent replays;
- The period of validity of the ticket;
- A session key (K_{CS}) that will be used to secure dialogues between the client and the server.

A ticket is only valid for a single server and a single client. The secret part of the ticket is encrypted with the key of the server (K_S) for which the ticket is issued. Once a ticket has been issued, it may be used multiple times by the named client to gain access to the named server until the ticket expires.

An authenticator contains additional information which when compared with against that in the corresponding ticket proves beyond doubt that the client presenting the ticket is the same one to whom the ticket was issued. An authenticator has the form:

$$\text{Auth}_c = \{C, \text{Addr}, \text{Timestamp}\}\, K_{CS}$$

It contains

- The name of client (C);
- The network address of the client (Addr);
- A timestamp in the form of a nonce to prevent replays.

The authenticator proves that the client has knowledge of the session key (K_{CS}) included in the ticket.

Figure 3.8 shows an overview of the Kerberos authentication protocol. A

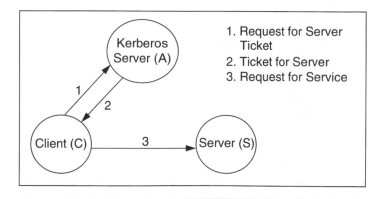

Figure 3.8 Overview of the Kerberos authentication protocol.

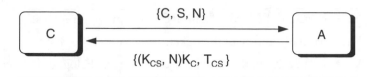

Figure 3.9   Request for ticket.

client initiates the protocol by requesting the Kerberos server (A) to generate a ticket for a specific server (S). The Kerberos server responds by returning a ticket encrypted with the key of the server. The client presents this ticket to the server along with an authenticator. Assuming that each of the above steps is successful, the client will gain access to the service.

3.4.2   Obtaining a ticket

When a user requires a service, she sends a request (see Figure 3.9) to the Kerberos server requesting it to grant the user a ticket for a server. The user sends an identity (C), the name of the server (S) for whom the ticket is required, and a nonce (N).

The Kerberos server checks that it knows about the identity of the client and generates a session key (K_{CS}) and another nonce. It encrypts these two fields with the *secret key* (K_C) of the user, which it obtains from its secure database.

It then creates a ticket for the end-server (T_{CS}) that includes the session key (K_{CS}). The contents of the ticket are encrypted using the shared key of the end-server (K_S) that the Kerberos server obtains from its secure database. The Kerberos server sends the ticket along with a copy of encrypted the session key back to the client. Once the response has been received by the client, she uses her key (K_C) to decrypt it.

3.4.3   Service request

Once the client has obtained a ticket for a specific service, it builds an authenticator containing the name of the client, the network address of the client, and a timestamp. The authenticator is encrypted with the session key (K_{CS}) obtained as part of the procedure above.

As Figure 3.10 shows, the client sends the encrypted authenticator and the

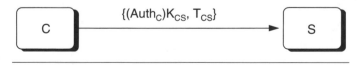

Figure 3.10   Service request.

service ticket to the server. The server decrypts the ticket using its key (K_S) and recovers the session key (K_{CS}). It then decrypts the authenticator (Auth$_C$) and matches the fields contained within the authenticator to that in the ticket (T_{CS}). If all the fields match, then the server allows the request to proceed. Optionally, a client can request a server to verify its identity. The server adds one to the timestamp sent by the client in the authenticator, encrypts the result with the session key (K_{CS}), and returns it to the client.

3.5 Asymmetric or public-key encryption

The greatest problem with the use of symmetric cryptosystems is that before any communication can occur, both parties must somehow acquire a shared, common key. For closed applications (e.g., within a single company), this problem can be addressed using protocols such as Kerberos or by employing human couriers to distribute the keys. A special *key distribution key* may also be employed, which is used only to distribute new values for the more frequently used working key.

The problem is much more severe in an open network, where parties that have never before had any kind of relationship may wish to enter into a spontaneous communication. A good example of this is where a user wishes to buy goods across a network from a merchant to whom she is completely unknown.

Public-key cryptography was first proposed in 1976 by Whitfield Diffie and Martin Hellman [19] in order to solve the key management problem highlighted above. In public-key cryptography, each person gets a pair of keys, called the *public key* and the *secret key*. The public key is published and widely distributed while the secret key is never revealed. The need for exchanging secret keys is eliminated as all communications only involve public keys. No secret key is ever transmitted or shared.

Thus when user Alice wishes to send an encrypted message to Bob, she looks up Bob's public key (PK$_B$) in a public directory or obtains it by some other means, uses it to encrypt the message, and sends it off to Bob (see Figure 3.11). Bob then uses his secret key (SK$_B$) to decrypt the message. Anyone who has access to Bob's public key can send him an encrypted message, but no one else apart from Bob can decrypt it.

3.5.1 Properties of a public-key cryptosystem

Assume PK is the encryption key and that SK is the decryption key. A public-key cryptosystem will have the following general properties:

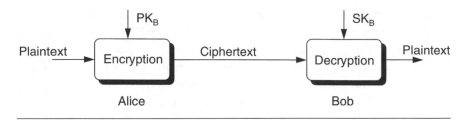

Figure 3.11 Public-key cryptosystem.

1. Encipherment (applying the algorithm with the encryption key) followed by decipherment of a message M results in M:

$$SK\,(PK\,(M)) = M$$

2. Both PK and SK are easy to compute.
3. By publicly revealing PK, the user does not reveal an easy way to compute SK.

A function satisfying properties (1) to (3) above is known as a "trapdoor one-way function" and fulfills the basic criteria for public key cryptosystems. If, in addition, the system can operate in reverse (i.e., if a message M is first deciphered and then subsequently enciphered), M is the result:

$$PK\,(SK\,(M)) = M$$

This is then known as a "trapdoor one-way permutation" and can be used to implement *digital signatures*. This process will be described below.

3.5.2   One-way functions

The notion of *one-way functions* is central to public-key cryptography. A one-way function is a function that is relatively easy to compute in one direction, but (apparently) very difficult to compute in the other direction. As they stand, they are not of much use for encryption purposes since it would be impossible to decrypt the resulting ciphertext. For encryption, we need something called a *trapdoor one-way function*. They are called "trapdoor" functions since the inverse function is easy to compute once certain private trapdoor information is known.

3.5.3 Using public-key cryptosystems for authentication

Authentication is the process whereby the receiver of a digital message can be confident of the identity of the sender. If Bob receives a message that purports to come from Alice, he may like to have some means of proving the message's authenticity (i.e., a check that the message was indeed sent by Alice).

One way to achieve this is for Alice to apply her secret key (SK_{Alice}) to the message before it is sent. The resulting ciphertext can be read by anyone (including Bob) by simply obtaining and applying Alice's public key, but the only person capable of producing it is the person who possesses Alice's secret key (i.e., Alice).

3.6 Digital signatures and enveloping

The examples above have shown how public-key systems can be used for two purposes: encrypting a message with the recipient's public key to achieve confidentiality, or encrypting a message with the sender's secret key to achieve message authentication. Both of these involve applying the public-key algorithm to the entire message. The public-key algorithms in use today are computation-intensive, and with large messages they may be too expensive or too slow for the application, but alternative solutions are available.

If message authentication is the focus of attention, a simple way to achieve this is to compute a message digest using an algorithm such as MD5 or SHA, and apply the sender's secret key to this. The resulting quantity can be thought of as a digital signature and be appended to the message before it is transmitted.

Figure 3.12 shows this process. At the destination, the receiver uses the same hashing algorithm to produce a message digest, and using the sender's public key verifies that the computed digest matches the decrypted signature. In the case of a match, he can be assured that the message emanated from the purported sender and that it has not been altered in transit.

If message confidentiality is what is required, then the message can be *enveloped*. To achieve this, the sender can invent a key at random and use this message key in conjunction with a (fast) symmetric encryption algorithm to encrypt the message. As shown in Figure 3.13, this will protect the message from eavesdroppers. In order to transport this message key to the recipient, it is encrypted with the recipient's public key and included with the message that is transmitted.

When the message arrives, the recipient uses his secret key to unlock the content encryption key thus allowing him access to the message in plaintext.

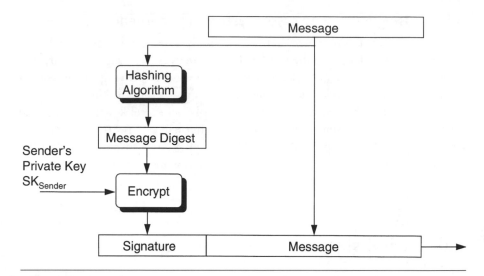

Figure 3.12   Appending a digital signature to a message before transmission.

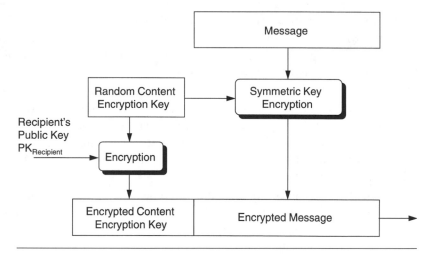

Figure 3.13   Enveloping a message for a recipient.

3.7 RSA

The de-facto standard algorithm for implementing public-key cryptography can be used for both encryption and authentication and is called the RSA algorithm. It is named after its inventors, Rivest, Shamir, and Adleman [20], who developed it in 1978 while working at MIT. Its security is based on the difficulty of factoring very large numbers. The basic algorithm is outlined below. Firstly, the public and matching secret key must be generated. This is done in the following manner:

1. Choose two large distinct primes, p and q.
2. Compute the product(modulus) $n = pq$.
3. Randomly choose encryption key e, such that e and $(p - 1)(q - 1)$ are relatively prime.
4. Finally use Euclid's algorithm to compute the decryption key, d such that $e \cdot d = 1 \ (mod \ (p - 1) \cdot (q - 1))$.

Note that, d and n are also relatively prime. The numbers e and n are the public key. The number d is the secret key. The two primes p and q are never needed again. They should be discarded and never revealed.

To encrypt a message M, we first break the message into a series of blocks and represent each block as an integer. The block size is chosen to ensure that this integer will be smaller than n. We then raise it to the power of e modulo n:

$$C = M^e \bmod n$$

To decrypt the resulting ciphertext C, we raise to another power d modulo n:

$$M = C^d \bmod n$$

Thus with RSA, each owner of a key pair holds d secret, and issues e and n as her public key. The owner does not need to know about p and q, although knowledge of these factors may be used to speed up calculations. The security of RSA depends on the problem of factoring large numbers. As an example, for a human to factor the number 29,038 by hand would take perhaps an hour, but confirming that the factors are indeed 127 and 229 takes only about a minute. The disparity between the effort required to compute the factors and that required to confirm them gets wider as the size of the numbers is increased.

The size of key used in RSA is completely variable, but for normal use a key size of 512 bits is typically used. In applications where key compromise would have very serious consequences or where the security must remain valid for many years into the future, key lengths of 1,024 and 2,048 bits are used. Note that performing exponentiation with numbers of this size is expensive in terms of computing resources. A typical software implementation of a symmetric encryption algorithm (e.g., DES) would be around 100 times faster than RSA, while hardware implementations would be between 1,000 and 10,000 times as fast.

3.8 Public-key management

Public-key cryptography is based on the idea that an individual will generate a key pair, keep one component secret, and publish the other component. Other users on the network must be able to retrieve this public key, associate it with an identity of some sort, and use it to communicate securely with, or authenticate messages from, the user claiming that identity.

If an attacker can convince a user that a bogus public key is associated with a valid identity, then the attacker can easily masquerade as the person with that identity. The simplicity of this attack demonstrates that public-key cryptography can only work when users can associate a public key with an identity in a trusted fashion.

3.8.1 Certificates

One way to form a trusted association between a key and an identity is to enlist the services of a trusted third party (TTP). This is an individual or organization that all users of a system can trust. In an identification scheme, it could be a government organization; in a payment system, it is likely to be a financial institution. As Figure 3.14 shows, the TTP will construct a message, referred to as a *certificate,* that contains a number of fields, the most important of which are a user identity and the associated public key. The TTP signs this certificate using its private key, in the process guaranteeing that the public key is associated with the named user.

Subject (Identity of User)	Public Key	Validity Period	Issuer (Identity of TTP)	Other fields	Signature of TTP

Figure 3.14 Typical set of fields found in a certificate.

This guarantee is made subject to a defined security policy. This could be quite lax and involve the user forwarding the public key to the TTP for certification, or it could be an involved process requiring the physical presence of the user together with the presentation of multiple forms of identification.

The certificate is used when a message recipient wishes to gain access to the sender's public key. The recipient can either consult some online directory service to obtain this or, alternatively, the sender may append their certificate to the message. It is assumed that every user in the system is first equipped with the public key of the TTP. Using this, the signature on the certificate can be verified, and if it passes the test, the public key contained in the certificate can be trusted.

3.8.2   Certification authorities

TTPs that issue certificates are referred to as certification authorities (CAs), and when the population of users becomes large, it is unlikely that a single CA can serve the entire user base. This means that either each user must acquire the public keys of each independent CA or the CAs can organize into a hierarchy.

The root of the hierarchy is a CA that issues certificates only to other CAs, which then certify users of the system. There may, of course be, more levels than this, but the principles are the same. Each user of the system need only hold the public key of the root CA, and when sending a message they include a copy of all certificates in the path between them and the root.

Figure 3.15 shows a simple certification hierarchy where Alice has been certified by CA1 and Bob by CA2. The two CAs use a common root CA that has issued certificates for both CA1 and CA2, and all users of the system are equipped with the public key of this root CA. When Alice sends a message to Bob, she includes her own certificate, signed by CA1 and CA1's certificate signed by the root CA. When Bob receives this message, he uses the PK_{Root} to verify PK_{CA1}, PK_{CA1} to verify PK_{Alice}, and PK_{Alice} to authenticate the message. This is called traversing the trust chain of certificates, and a similar process can be undergone for messages in the reverse direction.

In cases where the certification hierarchy is extensive, including all certificates with each message can be a substantial overhead. This can be alleviated by each user keeping a copy of the certificates they receive. Rather than including the certificates in the message, the sender includes a message digest of the certificate, called a "thumbprint," in its place. The receiver compares this

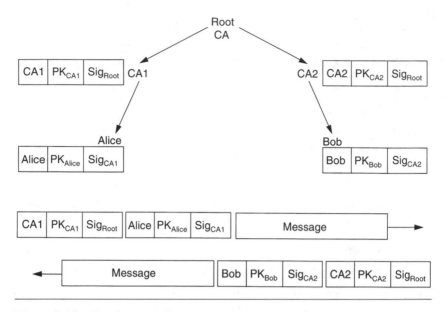

Figure 3.15   Certification hierarchy in action.

thumbprint with a digest of each certificate that it has a copy of, and if it cannot find a match, it will ask the sender to forward a copy.

If a user's secret key becomes compromised, then the certificate associated with the public key must be revoked. CAs keep certificate revocation lists (CRLs) that are available for users of the system. In order to completely trust the authenticity of the message, the CA for each certificate in the trust chain must be contacted to check that none have been revoked since they were issued. The extent of this problem will depend on two things: firstly, the number of compromised keys, and secondly, the normal period of validity of a certificate.

3.9 Transport of security information

The above sections have outlined a number of different security algorithms and techniques. If these techniques are to be implemented across a global network, then they will involve communication between a wide diversity of machine architectures and software development environments. This is particularly the case in the area of electronic payments, where the machines participating in dialogues will range from handheld personal machines to large transaction-processing mainframes in financial institutions. For this to work, there must be a standardized means of representing cryptographic information before it is sent across the network.

3.9.1 Abstract syntax notation (ASN.1)

The problem of communicating between heterogeneous computer systems is twofold. Firstly, there must be some means of agreeing on what information is to be communicated. Ideally, this information could be specified in a machine-independent manner. Second, there is a need for a standard means of representing this information as it flows through the network. This means that a machine receiving such a stream should be able to make sense of the information that arrives and relate it to the machine-independent specification.

The approach adopted by the International Standards Organization (ISO) to this was to define an abstract syntax notation (ASN) in which data could be described in just such a machine-independent fashion. The first such notation to be developed was called ASN.1 [21] and although some changes have been made to the original document, it has not been necessary to create an ASN.2 thus far.

The notation contains some built-in types such as INTEGER and OCTET STRING to describe a whole number (of any size) or an arbitrary string of bytes, respectively. There are also structuring mechanisms such as SEQUENCE to denote an ordered grouping of basic fields or SET where no order is defined.

One of the more novel basic types is called an OBJECT IDENTIFIER. This is a sequence of numbers that is used to uniquely identify something. The numbers are the path through a naming tree, where the owner of each node has naming authority from that point in the tree downwards.

Figure 3.16 shows the naming tree for the object identifier that uniquely identifies the MD5 message digest algorithm. The first-level branches of the tree are under the control of the ISO and CCITT standards bodies. ISO has defined branch number 2 for national standards bodies and branch 840 of that to the United States. The national naming body for the United States has assigned branch number 113549 to RSA Data Security Inc., who can assign as many globally unique object identifiers as they wish, beginning with the prefix 1.2.840.113549. They have built a subtree for digest algorithms and assigned branch 5 of this to represent the MD5 algorithm. Figure 3.16 also shows how this is specified in ASN.1 notation.

Figure 3.17 shows a hypothetical example of how two communicating parties may define a hashed message to be sent across a network. The new type

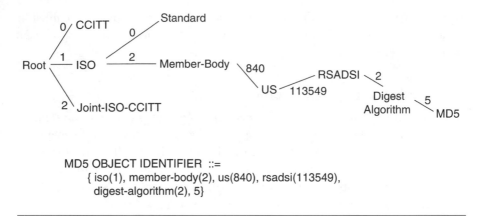

MD5 OBJECT IDENTIFIER ::=
    { iso(1), member-body(2), us(840), rsadsi(113549),
    digest-algorithm(2), 5}

Figure 3.16   The object identifier for MD5 in ASN.1 and naming tree form.

will have three fields: *contents* is an arbitrary length string of bytes containing the message itself, *digestAlgorithm* will identify which algorithm is used to create the message digest, and *digest* will hold the output of the designated algorithm.

When it comes to expressing this or any other ASN.1 specified data stream as a sequence of bytes, an encoding scheme must be chosen. The scheme most commonly used with ASN.1 is called the basic encoding rules (BER) [22], but this is unsuitable for cryptographic applications as it allows for more than one way to encode some of the basic types. Where cryptography is used, a constrained subset of the BER called the distinguished encoding rules (DER) is used instead. Each element of an ASN.1 data type is encoded as three fields: a tag identifying the data type involved (e.g., INTEGER, OCTET STRING, SEQUENCE, etc.), a length, and the value of the data element. In this way, the receiver of the information stream can reconstruct a data element of arbitrary complexity.

```
HashedMessage ::= SEQUENCE
            { contents  OCTET STRING,
            digestAlgorithm  OBJECT IDENTIFIER,
            digest  OCTET STRING }
```

Figure 3.17   Example definition of a new ASN.1 data type.

Using ASN.1 as the specification mechanism, it is possible to define payment protocols that can be implemented by many different organizations across the world on a variety of machine architectures and still have a very high probability of successful interworking.

3.9.2 The X.509 directory authentication framework

In payment protocols, it is often a critical requirement that various parties to a payment establish their identity. Since we are dealing with entities such as people, payment servers, and so forth that may be distributed across many different countries, it is important that we have some scheme for assigning globally unique names to people and processes.

In 1988, the CCITT—an organization representing the operators of the world's telephone networks—produced a series of recommendations [23] that described how to build a global distributed database containing details on people and processes. This database was to be called the X.500 directory. The CCITT has now been superseded by the International Telecommunications Union Technical Standards (ITU-TS), which is now responsible for X.500, and the standards are also co-issued by the International Standards Organizations (ISO) [24].

The X.500 recommendations are based on the idea of a single global distributed database containing objects representing people and processes. The objects are arranged in a tree structure that at the top level would hold a single object for each country in the world together with objects representing organizations of global standing (e.g., the United Nations). The countries are identified by a standardized two letter code (e.g., US (United States), GB (Great Britain, FR (France), JP (Japan)). Under each country, there would be objects representing significant organizations at a national level together with objects representing each main region in a country, and this hierarchy would continue as required. At each level, one attribute of each object must give a name that is unique at that level. For example, at the global level, there can only be one country with a country attribute having the value FR (c = FR). This attribute is used to distinguish that object at that level and is called the relative distinguished name (RDN). If all the RDNs on the path from the root to a particular object are concatenated, the result globally identifies an object and is called a distinguished name (DN).

Figure 3.18 shows a part of the global X.500 information tree. An organization (o) named "Universal Export" is registered under the Great Britain country object and under it is registered a "person" object whose common name (cn) attribute is "James Bond." The X.500 DN for this entity would be

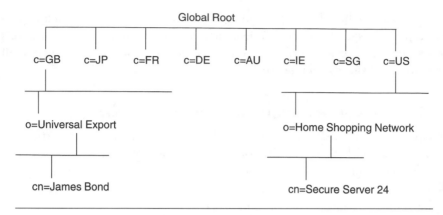

Figure 3.18   The X.500 directory hierarchy.

the concatenation of these: c = GB, o = Universal Exports, cn = James Bond. Similarly, the server number 24 operated by the Home Shopping Network in the United States could be identified as c = US, o = Home Shopping Network, cn = Secure Server 24. The X.500 scheme also allows for individuals to be named relative to the locality in which they reside and to have two or more entries in the directory tree.

3.9.2.1   X.509 certificates

Earlier in this chapter, we discussed how an identity could be linked to a public key by using a certificate. The X.509 recommendation specifies the exact syntax for a certificate that can link a public key to an X.500 DN where the trusted third party is also identified by an X.500 DN.

Figure 3.19 shows a fragment of ASN.1 adapted from the X.500 standards. The *certificate* data element is defined with the most important fields in italics. Using a macro capability of ASN.1, the entire data unit is defined as having a signature appended to it. The meaning of the certificate is to bind the entity identified by SUBJECT with the public key held in the SUBJECTPUBLICKEY-INFO field for a period specified by VALIDITY. This binding is certified by the entity identified by ISSUER. At the time of writing , the latest version of this standard was X.509 version 3, and in it the EXTENSIONS field has been added to provide much more information related to the policy governing the certified binding.

Many of the payment systems outlined in later chapters will employ X.500 DNs to identify entities, with X.509 certificates being used to link these identities with the corresponding public keys. The availability of the ASN.1 speci-

```
Certificate ::= SIGNED SEQUENCE {
              version  Version,
              serialNumber  CertificateSerialNumber,
              signature  AlgorithmIdentifier,
              issuer  Name,
              validity  Validity,
              subject  Name,
              subjectPublicKeyInfo  SubjectPublicKeyInfo,
              issuerUniqueID [1] IMPLICIT UniqueIdentifier  OPTIONAL,
              subjectUniqueID [2] IMPLICIT UniqueIdentifier  OPTIONAL,
              extensions [3] Extensions  OPTIONAL}


Validity ::= SEQUENCE {
              notBefore  UTCTime,
              notAfter  UTCTime}


Name ::= RDNSequence

RDNSequence ::= SEQUENCE OF RelativeDistinguishedName
```

Figure 3.19   The specification for an X.509 certificate in ASN.1.

fication means that developers of diverse software will be able to exchange certificates without the need for bilateral agreement.

3.9.3   PKCS cryptographic message syntax

Another family of quasi-standards that are of interest for payment system applications are the "Public Key Cryptography Standards" [25]developed by RSA Laboratories. These are a group of documents defining in ASN.1 how a variety of cryptographic exchanges that commonly occur should be performed. One of the series that is of particular interest is PKCS#7 [26], which describes how signed and enveloped data should be transferred across networks.

The simplest data type defined in the standard is SignedData, and an excerpt from the ASN.1 is shown in Figure 3.20. This allows multiple signers (each described by an individual SignerInfo) to sign a message held in the ContentInfo field in parallel. Fields are present to determine what digest algorithms have been used by each signer. Optional fields are included to enclose such certificates and certificate revocation lists as are necessary to verify the signatures.

Enveloping is specified in a similar manner. Figure 3.21 shows how an arbitrary chunk of data (EncryptedContent) can be encrypted using a symmetric

```
SignedData ::=SEQUENCE {
                version  Version,
                digestAlgorithms  DigestAlgorithmIdentifiers,
                contentInfo  ContentInfo,
                certificates [0] IMPLICIT ExtendedCertificatesAndCertificates
                        OPTIONAL,
                crls [1] IMPLICIT CertificateRevocationLists  OPTIONAL,
                signerInfos  SignerInfos}
```

Figure 3.20   The PKCS#7 specification for sending signed data across a network.

cipher with the key chosen at random. For each recipient of the data, a RecipientInfo field is constructed that contains the symmetric key encrypted with the public key of the recipient.

The PKCS#7 standards also include much ancillary information necessary to fully construct the data elements described above, and also to define a SignedandEnvelopedData type that combines both security functions into one type.

```
EnvelopedData ::= SEQUENCE {
                    version  Version,
                    recipientInfos  RecipientInfos,
                    encryptedContentInfo  EncryptedContentInfo }


EncryptedContentInfo ::= SEQUENCE {
                    contentType  ContentType,
                    contentEncryptionAlgorithm
                            ContentEncryptionAlgorithmIdentifier,
                    encryptedContent [0] IMPLICIT EncryptedContent
                            OPTIONAL}

EncryptedContent ::= OCTET STRING

RecipientInfo ::= SEQUENCE {
                    version  Version.
                    issuerandSerialNumber  IssuerandSerialNumber,
                    keyEncryptionAlgorithm  KeyEncryptionAlgorithmIdentifier,
                    encryptedKey  EncryptedKey }

EncryptedKey ::= OCTET STRING
```

Figure 3.21   The PKCS#7 specification for sending enveloped data across a network.

3.10 Dual signatures

Digital signatures are used to link an identity with the content of a particular message. In order to verify the message, the recipient must also be able to access the message content. In protocols involving three parties, such as a credit card transaction, a cryptographic technique that is sometimes employed is the dual signature. This provides a link between a message and an identity, without the need to be able to see the message contents. As the name implies, it is used in applications where two related messages are being sent. Whenever a payment is made, a separation can be made between financial details required to effect the transaction and the details of what is being purchased. These can be separated into two distinct messages.

Figure 3.22 shows how a dual signature is constructed. Firstly, the two related messages are individually hashed using some message digest algorithm. Next, the two digests are concatenated and a new digest computed, which is then signed with the sender's private key.

If Alice had two such messages and wanted to send Message1 to Bob and Message2 to Carol while assuring both Bob and Carol that a second linked message existed, she could send Message1, Digest2, and the dual signature to Bob with Message2, Digest1 and the dual signature going to Carol. When Bob receives this data, he can apply the hash algorithm to Message1, concatenate this with Digest2, hash the result, and check that this matches the dual signature. Thus, although he can only see the contents of Message1, he can be confident that a Message2 exists that hashes to Digest2 and that

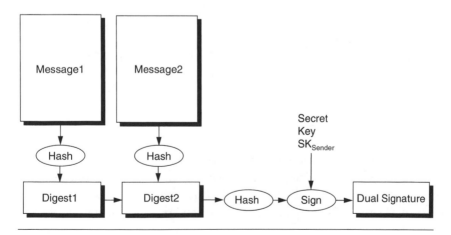

Figure 3.22   Constructing a dual signature on a pair of messages.

the dual signature links these two documents. Carol is in a similar position in that she can only see Message2, but can verify that the dual signature links this to Message1. As an additional benefit, the sender need only compute one dual signature for the pair of messages, which saves some computing resources.

The use of this technique in a payment application will be demonstrated in later chapters.

3.11 Nonces

When using cryptographic protocols, a form of attack that is often neglected is the so-called *replay attack*. This type of attack does not attempt to break the cryptographic algorithms used; rather, it records valid messages and plays them back in a different context. A classic example is the recording of messages from an automated teller machine. An attacker can record the (crytographically protected) dialogues that occur when a withdrawal is made and then replay these repeatedly at a later time to make multiple unauthorized withdrawals.

This can be guarded against by including a quantity in each message that will never be used again in subsequent messages. Such a quantity is called a *nonce*. A simple nonce would be an ever-increasing integer, where the party contacted could keep track of the numbers that had been used to date. A more general system would involve including some form a timestamp (expressed as time since some epoch) together with a randomly generated quantity. Nonces containing timestamps can also be used to limit the period of validity of the message. For example, participants could agree that a message is only valid for a fixed period beyond the timestamp.

Many of the payment systems outlined in later chapters will make extensive use of nonces.

3.12 Blind signatures

The use of blind signatures is a method for allowing a person to sign a message without being able to see its contents. The method has been used for implementing voting and digital cash protocols. Blind signatures were first proposed by David Chaum [27], who also developed their first implementation [28] using the RSA algorithm.

The process of blinding a message can be thought of as putting it in an envelope along with a piece of carbon paper. Nobody can read the message through the envelope. A blind signature is made by signing the outside of the envelope. The signature goes through the carbon paper and onto the message as well. When the message is taken out of the envelope, it will be signed, and the signer will not have known what she has signed. This blind signature analogy is shown in Figure 3.23.

In the steps below, a user Alice uses the blind signature protocol to get another user, Bob, to sign a message without knowing its contents.

1. Alice takes the message and multiplies it by a random value, called a blinding factor. This blinds the message so its contents cannot be read.

2. Alice sends the blinded message to Bob.

3. Bob digitally signs the blinded document and returns it to Alice.

4. Alice divides out the blinding factor, leaving the original message now signed by Bob.

For this to work, the signature function and the multiplication function should be commutative. The properties of blind signatures are the following.

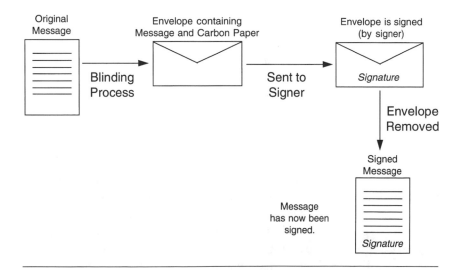

Figure 3.23   Blind signature analogy.

1. The signature on the document after it has been unblinded is a normal valid digital signature. It has the same properties of any digital signature.

2. It can't be proved in any way that the digital signature was placed on the message using the blind signature protocol. If a record is kept of every blind signature made, given an unblinded signed message, it cannot be linked to any of the signing records.

Mathematically, the blind signature protocol works as follows. Bob has a public key e, a private key d, and a public modulus n. Alice wants Bob to blindly sign message M.

1. Alice chooses the blinding factor, k, as a random value between 1 and n. Then M is blinded by computing

$$T = Mk^e \bmod n$$

2. Bob signs T:

$$T^d = (Mk^e)^d \bmod n = M^d k \bmod n$$

3. Alice unblinds T^d by computing

$$S = \frac{T^d}{k} = \frac{M^d k \bmod n}{k}$$

4. The result is

$$S = M^d \bmod n$$

This result is the message encrypted (signed) with Bob's secret key. In essence, this scheme demands that Bob sign a message without knowing anything of its contents. Blind signatures are generally applied using a special-purpose key that is only used for signing one kind of document. A specific example is given in Chapter 6, where a digital quantity may be signed by a bank with its $1 secret key. The resulting signed quantity can be only be used to represent a $1 bill regardless of the message contents.

3.13 Chip cards/smart cards

All of the techniques that have been described so far in this chapter have centered on software implementations of algorithms or protocols. In many applications, particularly in payment, secure hardware devices can play an important role. One of the most important secure hardware devices is the chip card (popularly referred to as a *smart card*), which is a portable data storage device with intelligence and provisions for identity and security. It most often resembles a traditional credit or bank card in size and dimensions, and embedded within the card is a customized integrated circuit. The physical characteristics of a chip card are defined by [29,30].

By demanding that the user provide a password, usually in the form of a personal identification number (PIN), before making any meaningful response, a chip card is equipped to identify positively its authorized bearer on each occasion. Second-generation chip cards are characterized by the presence of a magnetic stripe, as shown in Figure 3.24(a). In addition, an *active* or *super* smart card may consist of a keyboard, a liquid crystal display, and an onboard power supply, as shown in Figure 3.24(b). Such devices are also referred to as *electronic wallets* in the context of electronic payment systems.

Such a card allows a user to enter his PIN directly on the card and further limits the chance of an adversary gaining knowledge of the user's PIN. All data passing between the card and the external system (which may be local or at the end of a network link) may be encrypted to render all transmissions unreadable to any intruders attempting to intercept sensitive material.

3.13.1 Card types

There are a number of card types in use today, namely:

- *Magnetic stripe cards:* This type of card most resembles the credit card of today. It has a magnetic stripe at the back of the card that holds the details about the user, such as name, the card number, and so forth. Anyone with an appropriate card reader device can read the information stored on the card.

- *Memory cards:* These are used for simple applications such as the prepaid telephone card, which has a chip with 60 or 120 memory cells, one for each telephone unit. Each cell can be switched on/off. A memory cell is cleared each time a telephone unit is used. Once all the memory units are used, the card becomes useless and is thrown away.

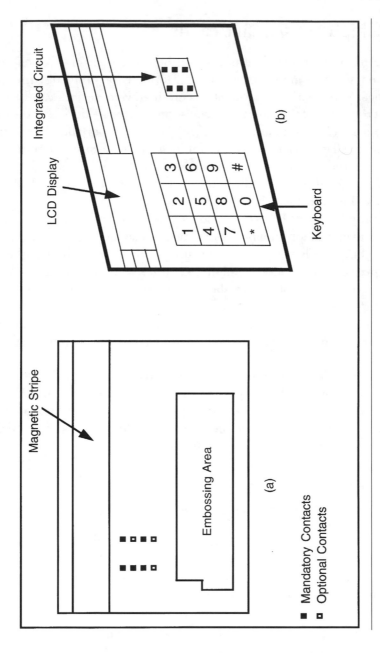

Figure 3.24   (a) Smart card with magnetic stripe card and (b) third-generation super smart card.

The hard-wired security provides enough protection for relatively low-value applications.

- *Processor cards:* Processor cards are characterized by the presence of a microprocessor onboard that controls access to information on the card. It operates under the control of an operating system also housed on the chip (a chip card operating system is usually unique to the chip and the card supplier). The microprocessor card increases protection against fraud and can be used in high-value or security-critical applications. An example application could be storage of cryptographic keys, and the chip card would act as a secure hardware device. Processor cards can be further classified as:

  1. Contact cards: The integrated chip (IC) on the card requires an external power source and clock to drive the chip and an input/output path for the transmission of data. The card achieves this through a direct connection to an external device, such as a card reader. The IC on the chip is connected to a contact plate on the surface of the card, which is the interface presented to the outside world. When the card is placed on the card reader device, the contact plate comes in contact with its opposite number and the circuit is complete.

  2. Contactless cards: This type of card provides added flexibility in the sense that the user's card does not need to come into direct contact with a third-party external device (e.g., a card reader device). The card uses some form of electrical coupling to communicate with a card reader device. Generally, contactless chip cards have to be placed in close proximity to the reader. There is ongoing research to extend the distance between the two devices. One application has been in a toll system, where each driver carries a contactless chip card in the car, which can be used to automatically pay the toll charge. Some forms of contactless cards use radiowave energy to operate over longer distances.

3.13.2 Memory types and capacity

Processor and nonprocessor chip cards contain data storage or memory as shown in Figure 3.25. This comes in the following forms:

- *ROM:* Read-only memory (ROM) is memory programmed by means of masks and is integrated at the time the chip is manufactured. The data contained in it can subsequently be read by the microprocessor, but not altered. Into this memory is put the card operating system (COS), the input/output routines, routines for data logging, and basic functions such as algorithms for PIN checking and authentication.

- *EPROM:* An electrically programmable read-only memory (EPROM) can generally be erased with ultraviolet light after it has been programmed. In order to do this, normal EPROM chips have a small window which, when placed under an ultraviolet light source for about half an hour, erases the information contained within the chip. Since a chip card has no window, it is not possible to erase this type of memory. For this reason, an EPROM contained in a chip card can only be programmed once (i.e., data can only be written to it). The first thing to be written here is personalization information. This includes data specific to the card and to certain applications. When the card is used, other data is stored here such as transaction monitoring or error data. Since it is not possible to erase the data, an increasing amount of memory space is written to until such time as the memory is full and the card becomes unusable.

- *EEPROM:* Unlike the EPROM, an electrically erasable programmable read-only memory (EEPROM) allows memory cells to be erased electrically. This has considerable advantages for the chip card, as it removes virtually all limitations on the use of the card. The memory cells can be reprogrammed at least 10,000 times. Data can be retained in the memory for at least 10 years. The EEPROM also offers advantages in the realm of security.

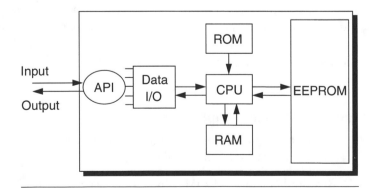

Figure 3.25   Basic chip card configuration.

- *RAM:* Random access memory (RAM) serves as high-speed working storage for the processor. It is used as a scratch pad by the microprocessor. The amount of RAM has a lot of influence on the overall performance of the card. If more RAM is available, larger blocks of data can be exchanged in one single message between the card and the external world, reducing communication overheads.

3.13.3 Physical specifications

There is considerable variation in the specification of the microprocessors and memory technology used in contact cards by the various vendors. Below is a typical specification for a chip card:

- Clock rates: 1 to 5 MHz;
- EPROM: 8 to 16 KB (for data storage, nonvolatile);
- RAM: 256 to 500 bytes (for operating system computation);
- EEPROM: 2 to 8 KB (nonvolatile).

An EPROM usually takes up a lot less physical storage space than an EEPROM. Since a chip card that conforms to the ISO standard [29] can only use a single storage chip that cannot be greater than 20 mm^2, this limits the amount of EEPROM memory that a chip card may contain. Current chip card architectures may use both EPROM and EEPROM memories.

3.13.4 Security

There are two types of security associated with a chip card, logical security and physical security:

- *Logical security:* The chip card is designed such that no single function or a combination of functions can result in disclosure of sensitive data except as allowed by the security procedures implemented in the card. This can be achieved by internal monitoring of all operations perfomed by the card user and by imposing an upper limit on the number of function calls that can be made within a time period [31]. Recent advances made by researchers at Bellcore [32] cast some doubt on this security. Their attack was based on heating the card to induce it to produce an incorrect output. By examining this output, attacks on the key became easier.

- *Physical security:* Chip cards incorporate not only logical but physical security features as well. Special layers of oxide over the chip protect against analysis of the contents of the memory. Even if the protective layers were removed and the silicon exposed, further difficulties make analysis virtually impossible. Another barrier protecting the contents of the memory against unauthorized reading results from the fact that the electrical charges at the memory gates of an EEPROM are very small. This means that they are lost if a probe is put close to them, thus making any attempt to probe the memory contents impossible. Although it is theoretically possible to analyze the memory contents of a secure chip, the enormous effort involved is out of proportion to any possible advantage to be gained.

3.13.5 Public-key processing capabilities

Asymmetric cryptography is fast becoming the norm in the cryptographic world today as it alleviates key distribution problems associated with symmetric key cryptosystems. On the other hand, public-key cryptosystems require far greater processing capabilities. At present, the predominant architecture in the chip card world is 8-bit, which does not have the processing power to run public-key algorithms in an acceptable time. Hence the need to move to 32- or even 64-bit architectures. Early developments in the area concentrated on generating a 512-bit signature in less than a second. This was later revised to three signatures in less than one second.

3.13.6 Multiservice capability

Multiservice or multiapplication capability in essence means the capability to take a chip card hosting one or more different applications and to be able to add another application without reference to those existing on the card and without disturbing them. This capability will help in reducing the overall number of cards in the consumer's hands.

3.13.7 Observers

An interesting concept that has been proposed by David Chaum [33,34] of DigiCash is the idea of observers. Each chip card, in addition to having a microprocessor, also has an embedded IC, the observer module. As shown in Figure 3.26, the observer is a trusted entity of the bank or organization that issued the chip card. The central idea behind the protocol for observers is that

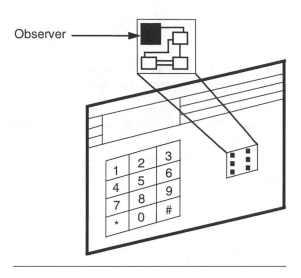

Figure 3.26   Observer module.

the observer does not trust the chip card hardware in which it has been placed and the chip card does not trust the observer module.

The observer acts on behalf of the issuing organization, ensuring that the chip card cannot deviate from the prescribed protocols or change any information in its database. The chip card can freely communicate with the outside world without the knowledge of the observer, but honest organizations will only accept messages that have been approved by the observer. If the chip card follows all the prescribed protocols, then it is impossible for the observer to send or receive any unauthorized information from the outside world without the knowledge of the chip card. This implies that if the issuing organisation places a malicious observer in the chip card, there is no way that it can divulge any information about the owner.

Thus the interests of both the cardholder and the card issuer are protected.

REFERENCES

[1]   National Bureau of Standards, *Federal Information Processing Standard (FIPS) Publication 46: The Data Encryption Standard*, 1977.

[2]   National Institute of Standards and Technology (NIST), *Federal Information Processing Standard (FIPS) Publication 46-1: Data Encryption Standard*, Jan.1988.

[3]   American National Standards Institute (ANSI), *ANSI X3.92 - Data Encryption Algorithm*, 1981.

[4]   National Bureau of Standards, *Federal Information Processing Standard (FIPS) Publication 81: DES Modes of Operation*, December 1980.

[5]   Blaze, M., et al., *Minimal Key Lengths for Symmetric Ciphers to Provide Adequate Commercial Security: A Report by an Ad hoc Group of Cryptographers and Computer Scientists*, Jan. 1996,
http://www.cs.ust.hk/~gray/archive/cryptologists.html
ftp://coast.cs.purdue.edu/pub/doc/cryptography/Symmetric-Cipher-Keylength.ps.Z

[6]   Biham, E., and A. Shamir, "Differential Cryptanalysis of the Full 16-round DES," *Advances in Cryptology - CRYPTO '92, 12th Annual International Cryptology Conference Proc.,*Lecture Notes in Computer Science, Vol. 740, Berlin: Springer-Verlag, 1993, pp. 487–496.

[7]   Matsui, M., "Linear Cryptanalysis Method for DES Cipher," *Advances in Cryptology -EUROCRYPT '93 Proc.,*Lecture Notes in Computer Science, Vol. 765, Springer-Verlag, 1994.

[8]   American National Standards Institute (ANSI), *ANSI X9.17-1985: Financial Institution Key Management*, 1985.

[9]   Lai, X., *On the Design and Security of Block Ciphers*, ETH Series in Information Processing, Vol. 1, Konstanz, Hartung-Gorre Verlag, 1992.

[10]   Schneier, B., *Applied Cryptography: Protocols, Algorithms, and Source Code in C*, 2nd ed., New York, NY: John Wiley and Sons, Inc., 1996, p. 145.

[11]   Lai, X., and J. Massey, "A Proposal for a new Block Encryption Standard," *Advances in Cryptology - EUROCRYPT '90, Workshop on the Theory and Application of Cryptographic Techniques Proc.*, Lecture Notes in Computer Science, Vol. 473, Berlin: Springer-Verlag, 1991, pp. 389–404.

[12]   Doligez, D., *Account of the successful breaking of the SSL Challenge*, INRIA, Aug.1995, http://pauillac.inria.fr/~doligez/ssl/

[13]   Rivest, R., "The RC5 Encryption Algorithm," *Dr. Dobbs Journal*, Iss. 225, Jan.1995, pp. 146–148.

[14]   Baldwin, R., and R. Rivest, *The RC5, RC5-CBC, RC5-CSC-Pad, and RC5-CTS Algorithms*, MIT Laboratory for Computer Science and RSA Data Security Inc., Internet Draft: draft-rsadsi-rc5-00.txt, March 1996, ftp://ftp.rsa.com/pub/rc5/

[15]   Rivest, R., *The MD5 Message-Digest Algorithm*, RFC 1321, Internet Activities Board, April 1992, ftp://nic.ddn.mil/rfc/rfc1321.txt

[16] National Institute of Standards and Technology (NIST), *Secure Hash Standard*, May 1993.

[17] Steiner, J. G., B. Clifford Neuman, and J. I. Schiller, "Kerberos: An Authentication Service for Open Network Systems," *Proc. Usenix Conference*, Dallas, TX, Feb.1988, pp. 191–202, http://nii.isi.edu/info/kerberos/documentation.html

[18] Khol, J., and B. Clifford Neuman, *The Kerberos Network Authentication Service: Version 5 Protocol Specification*, RFC 1510, Sept.1993, ftp://nic.ddn.mil/rfc/rfc1510.txt

[19] Diffie, W., and M. Hellman, "New Directions in Cryptography," *IEEE Trans. on Information Theory*, No. 22, 1976, pp. 644–654.

[20] Rivest, R., A. Shamir, and L. Adleman, "A method for obtaining Digital Signatures and Public-Key Cryptosystems," *Communications of the ACM*, Vol. 21, No. 2, 1978, pp. 120–126.

[21] ISO/IEC, *Information Processing - Open Systems Interconnection -Specification of Abstract Syntax Notation One (ASN.1)*, IS 8824, 1987.

[22] ISO/IEC, *Information Processing - Open Systems Interconnection -Specification of Basic Encoding Rules for Abstract Syntax Notation One (ASN.1)*, IS 8825, 1987.

[23] International Telegraph and Telephone Consultative Committee, *X.500 -The Directory -Overview of Concepts, Models and Service*, 1988.

[24] ISO/IEC, *Information Technology - Open Systems Interconnection - The Directory: The Models*, IS 9594-2, 1995.

[25] Kaliski, B., *An Overview of the PKCS Standards*, RSA Laboratories, Nov. 1993, ftp://ftp.rsa.com/pub/pkcs/doc/overview.doc

[26] RSA Laboratories, *PKCS #7: Cryptographic Message Syntax Standard*, Nov. 1993, ftp://ftp.rsa.com/pub/pkcs/doc/pkcs-7.doc

[27] Chaum, D., "Blind Signatures for Untraceable Payments," *Advances in Cryptology: Proceedings of CRYPTO '82*, Plenum, NY, 1983, pp. 199–203.

[28] Chaum, D., "Security without Identification: Transaction Systems to make Big Brother Obsolete," *Communications of the ACM*, Vol. 28, No. 10, Oct. 1985, pp. 1030–1044.

[29] ISO/IEC, *Identification Cards - Physical Characteristics*, ISO Central Secretariat, Geneva, IS 7810 1985.

[30] Europay International S.A., MasterCard International Incorporated, and VISA

International Service Association, *EMV '96: Integrated Circuit Card Specification for Payment Systems*, June 1996, http://www.mastercard.com/emv/

[31]   Europay International S.A., MasterCard International Incorporated, and VISA International Service Association, *EMV '96 : Integrated Circuit Card Terminal Specification for Payment Systems*, June 1996, http://www.mastercard.com/emv/

[32]   Boneh, D., R. DeMillo, and R. Lipton, *On the Importance of Checking Computations*, Bellcore, Sept. 1996, http://www.bellcore.com/SMART

[33]   Chaum, D., and T. Pedersen, "Wallet Databases with Observers," *Advances in Cryptology - CRYPTO '92, 12th Annual International Cryptology Conference Proc.*, Lecture Notes in Computer Science, Vol. 740, Berlin: Springer-Verlag, 1993, pp. 89–105.

[34]   Chaum, D., "Achieving Electronic Privacy," *Scientific American*, Vol. 267, No. 2, Aug. 1992, pp. 76–81, http://www.digicash.com/publish/publish.html

Chapter 4

Credit card–based systems

CREDIT CARD schemes have been in use as a payment method since the early 1960s and the two major international brands, VISA and MasterCard, are household names all over the world. The VISA brand grew from a scheme launched by the Bank of America, which was subsequently licensed by Barclaycard in the United Kingdom in 1966. By the middle of 1995, this organization, owned by its 18,000 member financial institutions, had issued more than 420 million cards and is now accepted by more than 12 million merchants in 247 countries.

Its principal competitor, MasterCard, is of comparable size with 13 million merchants in 220 countries and 22,000 member organizations. As Table 4.1 shows, they collectively account for a total of amost 800 million cards issued and nearly (U.S.) $1,300 billion of sales each year.

Since their inception, the introduction of more payment options has led to the development of a number of different *payment card* schemes. These include the following:

- *Credit cards*, where payments are set against a special-purpose account associated with some form of installment-based repayment

Table 4.1   Usage of Two Main Branded Credit Cards in 1995

Region	VISA		MASTERCARD	
	Sales Volume billions of dollars (U.S.)	Number of Cards (millions)	Sales Volume billions of dollars (U.S.)	Number of Cards (millions)
U.S.	358.4	228.1	202.4	174
Europe	262.4	81.2	not available	53.5
Asia-Pacific	91.6	73	116.2	72.5
Canada	36.8	18.6	not available	not available
Middle East, Africa	5.6	2.3	5.5	2
Latin America	23.6	21.4	19.1	21.2
Totals	778.4	424.7	470	338.7
Combined	US $1248.4B Sales		763.4 million cards	

scheme or a revolving line of credit. Cards typically have a spending limit set by the card issuer and the interest rate levied on unpaid balances is typically many times the base lending rate.

- *Debit cards* are linked to a checking/savings account. Normally, a payment cannot be made unless there are funds available to meet it. In effect, this type of payment can be considered a paperless check.

- *Charge cards* work in a similar way to credit cards in that payments are set against a special-purpose account. The principal difference is that the entire bill for a charge card must be paid at the end of the billing period. Often, there is no associated spending limit.

- *Travel and entertainment cards* are charge cards whose usage is linked to airlines, hotels, restaurants, car rental companies, or particular retail outlets.

With the exception of debit cards, where funds transfer takes place at the moment of payment, the above schemes all operate in a similar fashion. Figure 4.1 shows the actors involved. Banks that belong to the card association may act as *card issuers* to their personal or business clients. This will

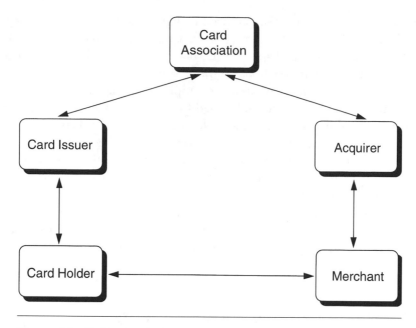

Figure 4.1   Entities involved in a conventional credit card transaction.

involve the provision of a card and maintenance of a credit card account for that individual, to which transactions can be posted as they occur.

Another or the same bank will act as an *acquirer* for clients of theirs who wish to accept credit card payments. This will usually involve providing equipment and/or software to process payments at the merchant's premises. Arrangements to perform online verification of transactions, as well as the policy for requiring online verification, is set by the acquirer. This may involve the setting of a *floor limit*, where any transaction exceeding this limit requires an online check as to the card status.

In a typical purchase, a merchant will capture the cardholders details at the point of sale. Depending on the policy in force, the transaction may be completed straight away or an online check may be made. Batched transactions are later sent to the acquirer for processing.

4.1 Mail order/telephone order (MOTO) transactions

For many years now it has been possible to make payments with credit cards without requiring the buyer and merchant to be colocated. Credit card companies have for some time allowed orders to be taken either by post or by telephone. These orders are referred to as mail order/telephone order (MOTO) transactions, and special rules have been imposed by the card companies on how these transactions are processed.

Normally, cardholders are asked to supply additional information, such as their name and address, that can be used to verify their identity. If goods that require physical delivery are being ordered, they must be dispatched to the address associated with the card. This gives limited protection against bogus orders. Since there is no cardholder signature involved, the processing rules allow the buyer to opt out of any transaction if they claim that they did not agree to the purchase. Clearly, this increases the risk borne by merchants.

Although there are more possibilities for fraud associated with this type of ordering, it is still a very popular form of payment, and it is clear that the benefits outweigh the fraud risks involved.

4.2 Unsecured network payments

Using credit cards to make payments across computer networks has similar associated risks as are experienced with MOTO transactions. Attackers eavesdropping on network traffic may intercept messages and capture credit card details as well as any associated verification information (e.g., name and address). Because of the distinctive structure of credit card numbers, with their inbuilt check digits, programs can be written to scan a data stream for occurrences of such patterns. The data stream could be either an intercepted transmission, a file on disk, reclaimed disk space on a shared system, or even the stream of keystrokes produced by someone typing at their workstation.

What makes the risks considerably higher than MOTO transactions is the speed with which transactions can be conducted. If merchants are processing orders electronically, then fraudsters can generate vast numbers of orders before the fraud is detected. The global scope of the network means that transactions can be carried out at locations that are far removed from where the card was issued. Thus the gap between the card details being intercepted and blacklist notifications reaching all relevant merchants can be very significant.

Despite the increased risk, the absence of commonly accepted network payment schemes in a period when the Internet was rapidly expanding meant that many people resorted to this method of effecting payment. Some buyers adopted simple security measures such as spelling out the numbers of the credit card, or splitting the number across multiple messages. At the merchant end, the orders were processed in the same way as a MOTO transaction, using existing point of sale clearing systems.

4.3 First Virtual

One of the earliest credit card–based payment systems launched for the Internet was the product of a company called *First Virtual Holdings, Inc.* In October 1994, the company commenced operation of a payment system called the VirtualPIN that did not involve the use of encryption. The goal was to allow the selling of low-value information items across the network without the need for special-purpose client software or hardware to be in place. The system is not entirely fraudproof, but in the context of its target market this is not of such great importance.

Both merchants and buyers are required to register with First Virtual (FV) before any transactions can take place. The First Virtual server also has an involvement in every transaction and at intervals will lodge the proceeds to the merchant's bank account.

A buyer registering with FV forwards his credit card details and electronic mail address to FV and in exchange will receive a pass phrase, called a VirtualPIN. The initial part of this exchange can take place across the network, with the user filling in a WWW form and inventing a pass phrase. FV acknowledges this and adds a suffix to the pass phrase to form the VirtualPIN. The next step involves the buyer making a telephone call to FV to tender his credit card number. This allows FV to establish a link between the VirtualPIN and the credit card without ever using the credit card number on the network.

Merchants must go through a similar registration process where they give their bank details to FV and are given a merchant VirtualPIN. The normal method of transferring the bank details is to send a conventional check drawn on the bank account associated with the merchant. FV takes all account identifier information from the check itself. Once this is done, the merchant can request FV to process transactions from registered FV customers and, after deducting a per-transaction charge, deposit the funds in the merchant's bank account using the conventional bank automated clearing house (ACH) service.

Figure 4.2 shows a buyer using FV to make a purchase. Initially, the buyer browses the FV InfoHaus(FV Web server) or another Web server, where a FV merchant is selling goods. The buyer selects the item she wishes to purchase. The buyer is asked to enter her FV account identifier (Virtual PIN), which is forwarded to the merchant. The merchant checks that this account identifier is

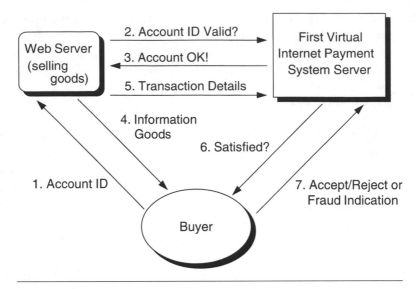

Figure 4.2   Buying with First Virtual.

valid by querying the FV server. This can be done in a number of ways, ranging from manual queries to automated dialogues with an FV server. If the Virtual-PIN has not been blacklisted, then the merchant will deliver the information to the buyer, either by e-mail, WWW reply, or other means.

The merchant forwards information about the transaction, including the buyer's VirtualPIN, to the First Virtual Internet payment system server. No payment has yet been made, since the system is based on a "try before you buy" philosophy. Accordingly, the next step is for the FV server to send electronic mail to the buyer asking if the information was satisfactory.

There are three possible replies to this request:

- *Accept*, in which case the payment proceeds;
- *Reject*, indicating that the goods either were not received or that the buyer is not happy to pay for them;
- *Fraud*, which means that these goods were not ordered by the buyer. Upon receipt of this message, the FV server will immediately blacklist the VirtualPIN.

At the end of every 90 days, the buyer's credit card account is billed for the charges that have accumulated during the time period. The merchant's checking accounts are then credited with payments for items sold. FV performs the accounting for both the buyer and merchant, taking a percentage of the transaction as commission.

It is quite clear that if a VirtualPIN becomes compromised by attackers eavesdropping on network traffic, bogus purchases can be made from then until such time as the VirtualPIN is blacklisted. Since payment authorization requests are sent to the buyer by e-mail, this time period could range from a few minutes to perhaps a day or so. Also, denial of service or masquerade attacks on the e-mail system could prolong this period quite substantially.

In addition, a stolen credit card number could be used to set up Virtual-PINs associated with e-mail addresses controlled by the attacker, which may also allow long periods where bogus transactions can be carried out.

The exposure to fraud outlined above is of lesser importance if the payment system is used for information items. In this context, although a fraud has been committed, the seller will have lost a sale rather than incurring a large financial loss. Experience with the first year of operation of the system has shown a very low fraud rate. The overall model of how credit card payments work has been modified somewhat by the FV system. From the card company's point of view, FV takes on the role of merchant in that they are the ones that establish the relationship with the acquirer, and the value of all transactions is credited to their account in the first instance before being distributed using ACH bank transfers.

Perhaps the major advantage of the FV system is its simplicity. Since it makes no use of encryption, there are no export problems, and the simple exchanges that make up the protocol mean that no special software is needed at the front end, and the backend software is not complex.

Its major disadvantage is that before either merchants or buyers can use the system, they must preregister and have either a bank account (in the case of a merchant) or a credit card (in the case of a buyer). There are, however, no other qualifications demanded of merchants, in contrast with the stipulations typically made by credit card acquirers, and this makes the system more attractive for merchants who are likely to have limited turnover.

4.4 Collect all relevant information (CARI)

CARI [1] is a unique and simple system that allows hard goods to be ordered by credit card through the World Wide Web. It was designed by a team of technologists at Information Technology Partners (ITP), Milford, CT, USA. Like the FV system described above, credit card numbers are not present on the Internet. The CARI designers believe that consumers are reluctant to transmit their credit card numbers over the Net, regardless of the security or encryption provided. For this reason, the real credit card information is obtained by telephone using a "voice robot."

4.4.1   Virtual credit cards

To use the system, a consumer must first obtain and activate a virtual credit card (VCC). This is simply a random number assigned by CARI that will map to a consumer's real credit card number and details, as shown in Figure 4.3. It serves much the same purpose as the VirtualPIN used by FV. The virtual credit card is protected by a short personal identification number (PIN) that prevents entering another user's VCC number by accident during a purchase.

Once the virtual credit card has been set up, it can be used to order goods at a merchant's shop on a "CARI-connected" Web server. A CARI-connected Web server is one that can pass details from the Web server to the CARI system, as shown in Figure 4.4. The VCC and PIN are passed to the merchant in a normal Web form at the time of purchase. This allows CARI to work with all Web browsers and Web server software.

4.4.2   Setting up a virtual credit card

To obtain a virtual credit card number, the user enters some personal details using a Web form at the CARI-connected Web server. This usually includes

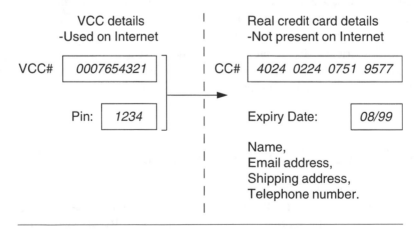

Figure 4.3   The virtual credit card mapping.

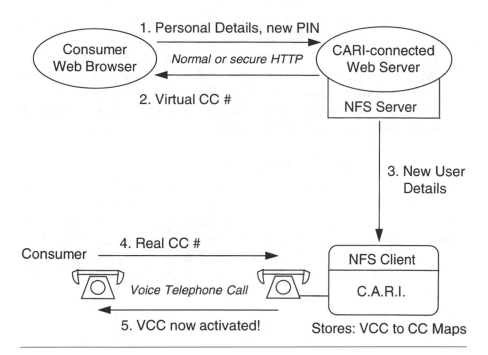

Figure 4.4 Setting up a virtual credit card.

their name (to match the one on the real credit card), e-mail address (for confirmation of purchases), shipping address (to send goods to), and telephone number. Having chosen a PIN, they are then assigned a virtual credit card number as shown in Figure 4.4. Normally, none of this information is encrypted since normal HTTP is used. However, provided both parties had secure HTTP capabilities (such as SSL, described later), where the Web's HTTP connection is encrypted, the information could be protected.

The new user details are now automatically transferred to the CARI machine, a PC-compatible system not accessible from the Internet. CARI obtains the information from the Web server using NFS [2], a network filesystem protocol. The new user details are placed in a file on the NFS exported drive, from which CARI collects them. Since NFS is not a secure protocol [3], some of the user details are encrypted so that only the CARI machine will be able to decrypt them. The Web server, or any other Internet host, cannot access any information on the CARI machine.

NFS is used to provide a simple one-way only link between the CARI machine and the Web server. Any other file exchange protocol such as ftp could have been used to obtain the user details from the Web server. The CARI designers found NFS to be the most suitable for the task.

To activate the VCC, users must give their real credit card details to CARI by telephone. A voice robot (basically a sophisticated telephone answering system) obtains the information by telephoning the user's number or by awaiting a call from that user. Once the real card is verified, the matching VCC is activated and the user can start shopping.

4.4.3   Independent CARI systems

In a typical CARI system configuration there will be a single Web server from which the CARI PC can obtain orders and new user registration details. Many merchant storefronts may appear as individual pages on this Web server. Each merchant's Web page will be capable of accepting orders using a virtual credit card. New-user registration for a virtual credit card will be performed through the same Web server. A single VCC is usable at all merchants in the same CARI system; that is, on the same CARI-connected Web server. In this setup, virtual credit cards are usually free to consumers, and merchants only pay for the Web space on the server. NetResource [4] offer this service.

Alternatively, a large organization with a high order volume may wish to purchase the CARI system for use with their own Web server. This solution does not scale very well since VCCs are valid only within one independent CARI system. There is no mechanism for CARI PCs to communicate with each other to exchange account details.

4.4.4   A virtual credit card purchase

A user places an order by sending the VCC, PIN, and order details to the Web server where the merchant's shop resides, using a Web form, as shown in Figure 4.5. CARI then collects the order from the Web server and verifies it. The order information, including the customer's real credit card number, is then forwarded to the merchant via fax, secure ftp, encrypted e-mail, or a dial-up line. The merchant system must have the ability to process the credit card purchase. Typically, this will require a merchant agreement with a credit card company.

If the HTTP connection between the buyer's Web browser and the Web server is not encrypted, an attacker can intercept the virtual credit card number and PIN. However, since goods must be sent to the shipping address associated with the VCC, the damage an attacker can do is limited to causing merchandise that has not been ordered to arrive at the real user's home. To help prevent this, e-mail confirmation can be required from the user before shipping, much like in the FV system.

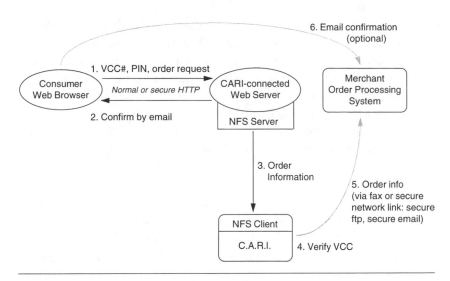

Figure 4.5 Purchasing using a virtual credit card.

CARI is best suited for selling hard goods (physical goods) that are actually sent to a user's address. Due to the one-way NFS link between the Web server and CARI, information cannot be returned easily via the Web to the user. However, once a merchant has received and processed a valid order she may be able to provide purchased information or services to the user via e-mail.

In the future, it is planned for the CARI system to work with bank account details rather than credit card information to provide a payment instrument equivalent to an electronic check.

4.5 The secure socket layer (SSL)

Both FV and CARI effect payment using the transfer of a semisecret quantity (VirtualPIN or VCC) without the use of cryptography. An alternative approach is to securely transfer the credit card details across the network and then treat the transaction in the same way as a mail order/telephone order (MOTO) transaction.

For this to occur, two basic security services are required. First, some means must be found to encrypt the buyer-to-merchant communications link so that attackers cannot intercept the credit card details. Second, the merchant must be authenticated in some way to prevent attackers posing as merchants in order to capture card details. Although, it would be desirable for the merchant to have some assurance that the person tendering the card details is in fact the cardholder, this is not strictly necessary in a MOTO type of transaction.

The security services alluded to above can be provided using the secure socket layer (SSL) [5,6] which is a general-purpose protocol designed to be used to secure any dialogue taking place between applications communicating across a "socket" interprocess communications mechanism, though its primary use to date has been to enable secure credit card transactions on the WWW. The protocol was developed by staff at Netscape Corporation in late 1994 and progressed as an Internet draft standard late the following year. At the time of writing, it has reached version 3.0 and is being progressed as an Internet standard. It is in widespread use by merchants selling goods across the Internet to buyers using credit cards with no preregistration required. A protocol called Private Communications Technology (PCT) [7], offering the same facilities and having many similarities, is proposed by Microsoft Corporation. It is not yet clear whether either one of these proposals or some form of hybrid will succeed in becoming an Internet standard.

Parties to an SSL exchange identify themselves by producing certificates that link their *name* to a public key. No trust hierarchy is specified, so software agents taking part in SSL dialogues must be initialized with the certificates of certification authorities that are trusted. Much network commerce taking place today uses a product called Netscape Commerce Server, which can establish HTTP dialogues secured by the SSL with Netscape World Wide Web client software. Merchants using the commerce server will apply for a certificate from one of a small number of certification authorities whose public keys are preconfigured into all Netscape WWW clients. This enables them to authenticate themselves to clients in advance of payments being made.

The SSL protocol is transparent to the application using it. Once both sides are equipped with an SSL implementation, application data should pass through the secure socket in the same way as it would a normal (insecure) socket. Secured applications can exist side by side with normal applications. For example, calls to port 80 of a machine running a WWW server can expect to have a dialogue with a WWW server in an unsecured fashion, whereas calls to port 443 of the same machine will talk to the server over a secure socket connection.

Figure 4.6 shows the major components of the SSL protocol. When a socket connection is being set up, the *handshake* protocol does some initial work to establish the identities of the parties and negotiate cryptographic parameters for the session. Thereafter, application data is manipulated in accordance with these parameters and sent in *Application_Data* packets across

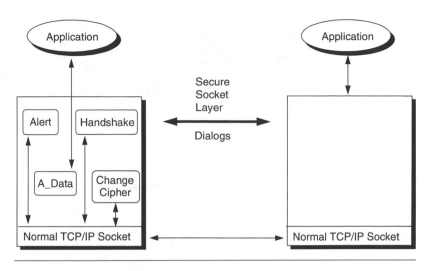

Figure 4.6 The main protocol components of the secure socket layer (SSL).

the underlying socket connection. If the need arises to change the parameters midsession, then the *Change_Cipher* primitives come into play. Similarly, any problems that may occur are dealt with by the *alert* protocol.

Within the *Handshake* protocol, there are a wide variety of options depending of whether the client, the server, or both are to be authenticated, and which encryption and key-exchange algorithms should be used. In the following description, we will concentrate on the one most commonly used to effect electronic payment. In this configuration, only the server side is authenticated and subsequent payment dialogues must be encrypted.

Figure 4.7 shows a typical handshake process. When the client application initiates a connection to the server, the SSL layer emits a Client_Hello message. This contains 28 bytes of data generated by a secure random number generator in addition to a list of client-supported cryptographic and compression methods listed in order of preference. A unique session ID is also established that can be used to allow this session to be resumed later in a subsequent connection.

The server picks a cipher suite and a compression method from those offered and sends this back to the client in the Server_Hello message. The server also generates a random value that must be different from, and independent of, that included in the Client_Hello message. This is sent as part of the Server_Hello message. Following this, the server sends a Certificate message that contains a list of X.509 version 3 certificates beginning with the it's own certificate and including all certs as far as the root of the certification hierarchy. This part of the exchange is terminated with a Server_Hello_Done message.

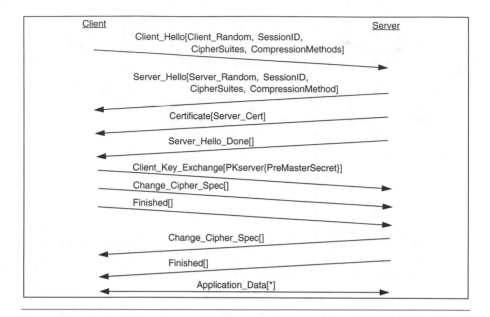

Figure 4.7   The main exchanges in the handshake protocol.

Using the certificate path, the client can now extract the public key of the server and verify it's authenticity by following the trust path as far as the root. It computes a quantity called the *PreMasterSecret*. This is 48 bytes long and consists of 2 bytes giving the protocol version and 46 bytes of randomly generated data. The client encrypts this with the server's public key and sends it in a Client_Key_Exchange message. This PreMasterSecret contains all of the information necessary to secure the SSL dialogue, and after this message is sent, both the client and server perform an identical set of computations (given below) on it to generate the *MasterSecret:*

$$
\begin{aligned}
\text{MasterSecret} = \ & \text{MD5(PreMasterSecret} + \text{SHA}('A' + \text{PreMasterSecret} + \\
& \text{ClientHello.Random} + \text{ServerHello.Random})) + \\
& \text{MD5(PreMasterSecret} + \text{SHA}('BB' + \text{PreMasterSecret} + \\
& \text{ClientHello.Random} + \text{ServerHello.Random})) + \\
& \text{MD5(PreMasterSecret} + \text{SHA}('CCC' + \text{PreMasterSecret} + \\
& \text{ClientHello.Random} + \text{ServerHello.Random}))
\end{aligned}
$$

This computation combines the PreMasterSecret with the random quantities sent in the Client_Hello and Server_Hello messages using concatenation

(+), the message digest algorithm MD5, and the secure hash algorithm (SHA). Once the MasterSecret has been generated, a similar computation, shown below, is performed repeatedly to generate a stream, called a KeyBlock, until sufficient material has been generated for the partitioning process that follows:

KeyBlock = MD5(MasterSecret + SHA('A' + MasterSecret + ServerHello.Random +
  ClientHello.Random))
  + MD5(MasterSecret + SHA('BB' + MasterSecret +
  ServerHello.Random + ClientHello.Random))
  +MD5(MasterSecret +
  SHA('CCC' + MasterSecret + ServerHello.Random +
  ClientHello.Random)) + [...]

Depending on the cipher suite agreed to in the negotiating process, key lengths for signing and encryption will vary. Figure 4.8 shows the sequence in which these are extracted from the KeyBlock. The first two quantities (client and server Write_MAC_Secret) will be used to generate message authentication codes (MACs) for messages. The remaining material is used to provide the encryption key (Write_Key) and initialization vector (IV) for whatever symmetric algorithm is used for bulk encryption of the dialogue. If there is material remaining after all keys have been generated, it is simply discarded.

At this point, both sides are equipped with all the necessary quantities to implement the agreed cryptographic regime. The client signals this by first

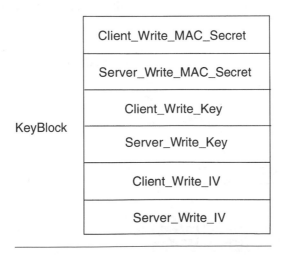

Figure 4.8 Partitioning the KeyBlock to obtain the individual keys.

sending a Change_Cipher_Spec message to indicate a changeover to the specification that has just been negotiated. This is followed by a Finished message, which is sent under this new specification. To signal its agreement, the server sends a similar Change_Cipher_Spec and Finished message pair.

At this point, the handshake protocol has terminated, the client and server application processes will be informed that a socket connection has been initiated, and they will start to exchange user data. This data is encapsulated in Application_Data units that vary in form depending on the cipher specification in force.

Figure 4.9 shows how user data to be sent on the secure socket is fragmented first into fragments of up to 2^{14} bytes (16 KB) in size. If both ends have agreed to use compression, then this fragment is passed through the agreed upon algorithm before proceeding. Depending on the cipher specification in force, the sender of data will want to do one of two things. Either she will want to produce a GenericStreamCipher unit sending the data in cleartext with a MAC appended, or a GenericBlockCipher will be produced where the data is fully encrypted as well as having a MAC appended. The length of the MAC field will depend on which algorithm is used to generate it. Similarly, the PAD fields included in the GenericBlockCipher serve to bring the size of the overall data unit up to some multiple of the block size associated with the ciphering algorithm.

The cipher suites that can be used in an SSL connection are given names that are of the form:

SSL_KeyExchangeAlg_WITH_BulkCipherAlg_MACAlgorithm

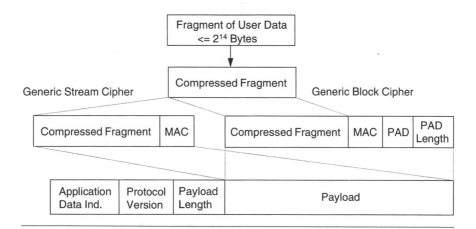

Figure 4.9 Encapsulating user data into application data protocol data units.

where the algorithms used for key exchange, bulk enciphering, and generation of message signatures are individually specified. Some examples include

SSL_RSA_WITH_NULL_MD5
SSL_RSA_EXPORT_WITH_RC4_40_MD5
SSL_RSA_WITH_IDEA_CBC_SHA
SSL_DHE_RSA_WITH_3DES_EDE_CBC_SHA
SSL_DH_ANON_EXPORT_WITH_DES40_CBC_SHA
SSL_FORTEZZA_DMS_WITH_FORTEZZA_CBC_SHA

It can be seen from the above that a large number of different algorithms are catered for in the SSL version 3.0 specification. At the time of writing, the bulk of electronic payment is being carried out using the predecessor (version 2.0) of this protocol, and in this situation, the RSA algorithm is used for the KeyExchange phase (Client_Key_Exchange message). WWW clients used within the United States use 128-bit RC4 to encrypt the messages, while export versions of the same software use a 40-bit variant of the same algorithm.

When SSL is used to effect payment, the merchant operates an SSL-enabled WWW server loaded with a certificate signed by an authority trusted by the WWW client software. The client software will request a WWW page whose address begins with *https* rather than the usual *http*. This indicates that SSL is to be used to secure the http dialogue. The server first authenticates itself, bulk encryption parameters are established, and the buyer's credit card details are sent in a WWW form to the server, where they can be decrypted and processed. Eavesdroppers will be unable to access the encrypted network traffic, and the merchant processes the credit card details in the same way as for a MOTO order.

4.6 CyberCash

CyberCash, Inc., [8] of Reston, VA, USA, was founded in August 1994 to provide software and service solutions for secure financial transactions over the Internet. The CyberCash Secure Internet Payment System, which uses special wallet software, enables consumers to make secure purchases using major credit cards from CyberCash-affiliated merchants. The CyberCash payment system was launched in April 1995, and by mid 1996 over half a million copies of the wallet software were in circulation. The system is used mainly by merchants to sell hard goods.

CyberCash intends to provide a complete solution for all types of Internet payments. Its CyberCoin electronic cash system is covered in Chapter 5, and as this book goes to press, a *PayNow* electronic check scheme has been launched.

The description below is limited to the credit card payment system initially deployed.

Figure 4.10 gives an overview of the CyberCash system. A gateway server links to the existing financial infrastructure. It is connected to the Internet on one side and to many banks and bank card transaction processors on the other side. Purchase messages containing a consumer's credit card details are forwarded through this gateway from a merchant at the time of purchase. The actual credit card purchase is authorized and captured in the existing banking network. The results of the transaction are forwarded back through the Cyber-Cash gateway to the merchant. If the transaction was successful, the merchant can then ship the goods to the consumer. CyberCash is not an acquirer, issuer, or bank, but provides the gateway as a means of securely passing messages between the Internet and the banking networks and vice versa.

Much like other credit card payment systems, the CyberCash payment protocol [9] is concerned only with payment messages and not other electronic commerce protocols such as shopping.

4.6.1   CyberCash wallet

The CyberCash wallet is the application software used by a consumer to make purchases with their credit card. It aims to make purchases as transparent as possible to the user by hiding the details of the payment steps and messages during a purchase. The wallet software runs alongside any Web browser software.

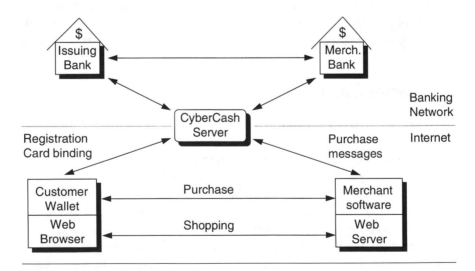

Figure 4.10   CyberCash model.

The software uses 56-bit DES and 768-bit RSA for protecting the card details stored on the user's hard drive and in the CyberCash payment protocol. Since the encryption is only used to protect the financial data, the software has been approved for international export from the United States. This allows CyberCash to be global, and no U.S. banking presence is needed to use the system. Both CheckFree, CompuServe, and America Online have adopted the CyberCash software to provide Internet payment solutions to their customers. While their versions of the wallet may differ slightly, the payment protocols and security used are identical to the original CyberCash wallet.

4.6.2 CyberCash persona

Every CyberCash user chooses a unique CyberCash ID and pass phrase. This ID is registered with the CyberCash payment server and maps to the user's public/private key pair.

The ID and pass phrase are used to unlock the wallet, where the card data and secret keys are stored in encrypted form. The ID also acts as a mapping between an identified user and that user's public key within the system, much like in a certificate except that there is no third-party authorization signature. Finally, the ID and pass phrase can be used to perform an "emergency close-out" in the case of fraud. Any further attempted purchases using the consumer's credit cards are blocked once the close-out has been initiated by contacting CyberCash with the correct pass phrase.

4.6.3 A CyberCash purchase

Having completed shopping at a merchant's Web site, the consumer clicks on the "Pay" button at that site. The merchant returns a summary of the item, price, and a transaction ID through the consumer's Web browser. This message causes the CyberCash wallet to be launched on the consumer's machine, and it is passed the purchase details.

The buyer chooses the credit card that he wishes to use to pay with from those cards which he has already registered with the software (described in a later section). Having agreed with the order details presented, he then clicks on the wallet's Pay button. This initiates the CyberCash payment protocol. The card details are securely sent to the merchant. The merchant authorizes and clears the payment with the financial network via the CyberCash payment server. The merchant returns an unsigned receipt to the buyer.

Figure 4.11 shows the payment steps in more detail. The financial data is always encrypted and the merchant never sees the card data, thereby eliminating

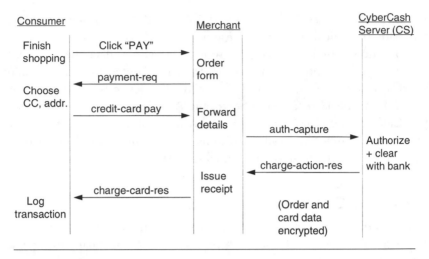

Figure 4.11   Payment steps in a CyberCash purchase.

some risk of merchant fraud. Digital signatures are used by all three parties (the cardholder, merchant, and payment gateway) for authentication and nonrepudiation during a purchase. Each message in the payment process is now briefly examined.

4.6.3.1   Payment-Req (PR)

This is the message initially sent from the merchant to the cardholder to launch the CyberCash wallet software. It contains a summary of the order signed by the merchant. The signature is verified later by the CyberCash server and not by the actual cardholder.

4.6.3.2   Credit card payment (CH1)

This is the payment message from the cardholder to the merchant. It includes the card data encrypted with the public key of the CyberCash server (PK_{CS}) and signed by the buyer. It also contains a hash of the order to show agreement with the merchant without revealing what the order is and the forwarded merchant's initial signature.

4.6.3.3   Auth-Capture

The merchant forwards the encrypted card data and order to the gateway. The gateway verifies the cardholder signature on the card details, and the forwarded merchant's signature on the order details. The gateway verifies that both the customer and merchant agree on the order.

4.6.3.4   Charge-Action-Response

Having authorized and captured the purchase in the banking network, the gateway returns unsigned receipts for the merchant and buyer to the merchant.

4.6.3.5   Charge-Card-Response (CH2)

The merchant forwards the unsigned receipt from the gateway to the cardholder.

4.6.4   CyberCash messages

The CyberCash messages are transport-independent so that they can be sent over the Web's HTTP, the SMTP protocol of electronic mail, or any other transport protocol. An example CyberCash message is shown in Figure 4.12. It consists of four parts:

- *Header:* This identifies the start of a CyberCash message.

- *Transport:* This is the plaintext part of the message. It can contain the order information in a purchase, transaction ID, date, and the identifier of the key used to encrypt the opaque part. The key identifier allows the receiver to know which key to select to decrypt the opaque part.

- *Opaque:* The encrypted part of a message. Typically, this will contain the encrypted financial data if it is present.

- *Trailer:* Used to indicate the end of the CyberCash message. It also contains a transmission checksum to allow the receiver to check that the entire message was received intact. This checksum is implemented

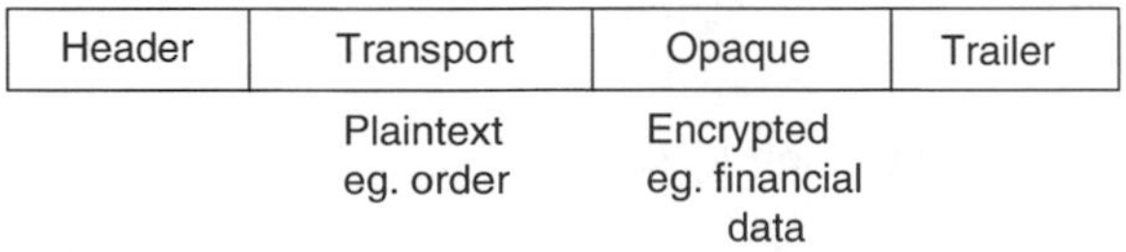

Header	Transport	Opaque	Trailer
	Plaintext eg. order	Encrypted eg. financial data	

```
$$-CyberCash-1.0-$$
id: MIKE-50
transaction: 918273645
date: 199712250955
cyberkey:CC1001
opaque:
  GpOJvDpLH62z+eZlbVkhZJXtTneZH32Qj4T4IwJqv6kjAeMRZw6nR4f0OhvbTFfPm+GG
  aXmoxyUlwVnFkYcOyTbSOidqrwOjnAwLEVGJ/wa4ciKKl2PsNPA4sThpV2leFp2Vmkm4
  elmZdS0Qe350g6OPrkC7TKpqQKHjzczRRytWbFvE+zSi44wMF/ngzmiVsUCW01FXc8T
  9EB8KjHEzVSRfZDn+IP/c1nTLTwPrQ0DYiN1lGy9nwM1ImXifijHR19LZIHlRXy8=
$$-End-CyberCash-End-jkn38fD3+/DFDF3434mn10==-$$
```

Figure 4.12   CyberCash message structure.

as an MD5 hash of the first three message parts (header, transport, and opaque parts).

4.6.5   Binding credit cards

A cardholder must register or bind the cards she wishes to use to her CyberCash persona. The card details are validated through the CyberCash gateway server before being stored securely in the wallet software. The messages used to do this are shown in Figure 4.13. By binding the credit cards to a persona, those card details can only be used in a purchase where the payment request has been signed by the private key corresponding to that persona. Also, in the binding process, the issuing bank will be asked whether this card may be used on the Internet. These precautions help reduce the risk of fraud.

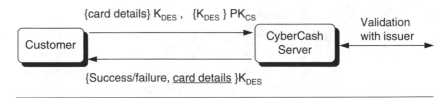

Figure 4.13   Binding a credit card.

4.6.6   Software updates

In the CyberCash system, software is informed if it is out of date automatically. Figure 4.14 shows the method of securely getting the location of new software. Such software migration is useful since CyberCash plans to update their payment protocol to be SET-compatible.

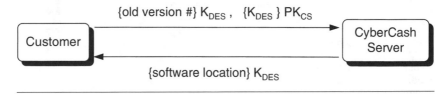

Figure 4.14   Automatic software updating.

4.7   *i*-Key protocol (*i*KP)

*i*KP [10] (where $i = 1, 2, 3$) is a family of secure payment protocols developed at IBM Research Labs in Zurich and Watson Research Center in the United

States. The *i*KP protocols are based on public-key cryptography and differ from each other based on the number of parties that possess their own public-key pairs. This number is indicated by the name of the individual protocols: 1KP, 2KP, 3KP. The greater the number of parties that hold public-key pairs, the greater the level of security provided. The 1KP protocol is based on what security infrastructure already exists today. The 2KP and 3KP protocols can be phased in gradually to achieve full multiparty payment security as a more sophisticated certification infrastructure is put into place. This allows for gradual deployment of the system.

The current emphasis of the protocols is on credit card payments as this is envisaged to be the most popular form of payment in the near future due to a large user base in place already. The entities involved in the system are the customer, the merchant, the customer's bank, and the merchant's bank. In the context of credit card systems, the merchant's bank is known as the *acquirer* because it acquires paper charge slips from the merchants. The customer's bank is known as an *issuer* because it issues credit cards to users. In the *i*KP protocols, the acquirer acts as a gateway between the Internet and the existing financial networks that support transactions between banks. The *i*KP protocols deal with *payment* transactions only (i.e., the solid lines in Figure 4.15). Therefore, the main parties involved in the transaction are the Customer (C), the Merchant (M), and the Acquirer gateway (A).

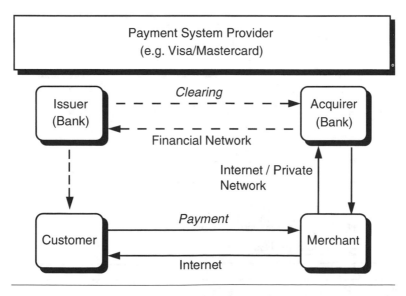

Figure 4.15 Payment protocol.

An important point to note is that the *i*KP suite of protocols are not a *shopping protocol* (i.e., the protocols do not provide encryption of the order information and assume that the order and price details have already been agreed upon by the customer and the merchant). Their sole function is to *enable* payment transactions between the various parties involved. This allows the protocols to be compatible with different browsing mechanisms.

4.7.1 Framework of *i*KP protocols

Each of the protocols consists of the seven basic steps shown in Figure 4.16. The contents of these steps may differ in each case:

1. *Initiate:* The customer initiates the protocol flow.
2. *Invoice:* The merchant responds by providing an invoice.
3. *Payment:* The customer generates a payment instruction and sends it to the merchant.
4. *Cancel:* The merchant can refuse to further process the transaction.
5. *Auth-Request:* The merchant sends an authorization request to the acquirer.
6. *Auth-Response:* The acquirer uses existing networked clearing systems to obtain the authorization and returns an authorization response.

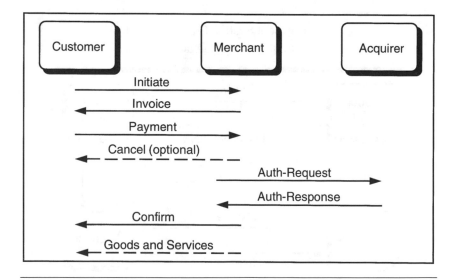

Figure 4.16 Overview of *i*KP protocol exchanges.

7.   *Confirm:* The merchant forwards the acquirers signed response and any other additional parameters to the customer.

Table 4.2 lists a number of fundamental data elements that are exchanged in the course of an *i*KP transaction. Table 4.3 lists a number of fields that are formed by combining one or more of the atomic fields listed in Table 4.2. The quantities surrounded by square brackets are either optional or may occur in individual *i*KP protocols.

4.7.2   1KP

The 1KP protocol is the most basic of the protocols. Only the acquirer needs to possess and distribute its public-key certificate CERT$_A$. Public-key encryption

Table 4.2   Quantities Occuring in the *i*KP Protocols

Item	Description
CAN	Customer's account number (e.g. credit card number)
ID$_M$	Merchant ID. Identifies merchant to acquirer
TID$_M$	Transaction ID. Uniquely identifies the transaction
DESC	Description of the goods. Includes payment information such as credit card holder's name and bank identification number
SALT$_C$	Random number generated by C. Used to randomize DESC and thus ensure privacy of DESC on the M to A link
NONCE$_M$	Random number generated by a merchant to protect against replay
DATE	Merchant's current date/time
PIN	Customer's PIN which, if present can be optionally used in 1KP to enhance security
Y/N	Response from card Issuer. Yes/No or authorization code
R$_C$	Random Number chosen by C to form CID
CID	A customer pseudo-ID which uniquely identifies C. Computed as CID = H(R$_C$, CAN).
V	Random number generated in 2KP and 3KP by merchant. Used to bind the Confirm and Invoice message flows.

Table 4.3   Composite Field

Item	Description
Common	Information held in common by all parties: PRICE, ID_M, TID_M, DATE, $NONCE_M$, CID, H(DESC, $SALT_C$), [H(V)]
Clear	Information transmitted in the clear: ID_M, TID_M, DATE, $NONCE_M$, H(Common), [H(V)]
SLIP	Payment Instructions: PRICE, H(Common), CAN, R_C, [PIN]
EncSlip	Payment instruction encrypted with the public key of the acquirer: PK_A (SLIP)
$CERT_X$	Public key certificate of X, issued by a CA
Sig_A	Acquirer's signature: $SK_A[H(Y/N, H(Common))]$
Sig_M	Merchant's signature in Auth-Request: $SK_M[H(H(Common), [H(V)])]$
Sig_C	Cardholder's Signature: $SK_C[H(EncSlip, H(Common))]$

is required from the customer only, while decryption is required from the ac-quirer only. Both customer and merchant are required to verify the signature generated by the acquirer. Each entity participating in the protocol is assumed to possess some starting information.

Table 4.4 lists the starting information for each of the entities in the system.

Table 4.4   Starting Information

Actor	Information Items
Customer	DESC, CAN, PK_{CA}, [PIN], $CERT_A$
Merchant	DESC, PK_{CA}, $CERT_A$
Acquirer	SK_A, $CERT_A$

It is assumed that the customer and merchant have agreed on the description of the goods (DESC) prior to initiating the protocol (i.e., DESC is not carried within any *i*KP flow). It is also assumed that both the cardholder and merchant are in possession of the public key of the CA and the acquirer's certificate from which they can extract its public key.

All parties in 1KP must perform certain public-key computations. Each cardholder has a customer account number (CAN). This is normally the customer's credit card number and is kept secret from the merchant. The following sections describe each of the steps shown in Figure 4.17.

4.7.2.1 Initiate composition

1. The customer forms a one-time cardholder ID (CID) that uniquely identifies him. It is computed as the hash of the customer's account number (CAN), and a random value R_C. CID = $H(R_C, \text{CAN})$. (This avoids revealing the CAN to the merchant).

2. Generates another random number SALT_C that will be used by the merchant to randomize the goods' description information to avoid revealing it to the acquirer.

3. The customer transfers the two quantities to the merchant as part of the Initiate message.

Initiate: (SALT_C, CID)

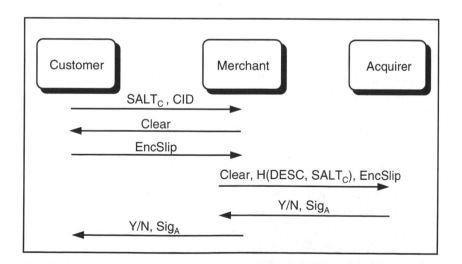

Figure 4.17 1KP protocol flows.

4.7.2.2   Initiate processing and invoice composition

1. The merchant generates NONCE_M and DATE. This allows the acquirer to uniquely identify an order. She also chooses a transaction ID (TID_M) to identify the context.

2. Computes $H(\text{DESC}, \text{SALT}_C)$ and is now in a position to form Common. The merchant then computes $H(\text{Common})$ (see Table 4.3).

3. Sends Clear in the Invoice flow to the customer. (The fields in Clear are sent as cleartext.)

Invoice: $(\text{ID}_M, \text{TID}_M, \text{DATE}, \text{NONCE}_M, H(\text{Common}))$

4.7.2.3   Invoice processing

1. The customer already has DESC and SALT_C as part of his starting information and computes $H(\text{DESC}, \text{SALT}_C)$. This quantity is included in Common by the merchant and is used by the customer to form Common in the next step.

2. Computes $H(\text{Common})$ and verifies that this matches the value of $H(\text{Common})$ in Clear generated by the merchant. This confirms that the customer and merchant agree upon the contents of Clear.

3. Generates a payment instruction (SLIP). He also includes the random number R_C, which was used to create the CID. This allows the acquirer to check that the CID given to the merchant corresponds to the CAN in the Payment message, but not the merchant to recover the customer's account number. He then encrypts the SLIP using the acquirer's public key.

4. Transfers the encrypted SLIP (EncSlip) to the merchant as part of the payment flow.

Payment: $(\text{PK}_A(\text{SLIP}))$

4.7.2.4   Payment processing

1. If for some reason the merchant decides not to further process the message, she sends a Cancel message to the customer.

2. The merchant now performs an authorization. She forms an Auth-Request message. The merchant includes Clear and $H(\text{DESC}, \text{SALT}_C)$ along with EncSlip, which she received as part of the payment instruction. This allows the acquirer to form Common

and verify H(Common) generated by both the merchant and customer.

$$\text{Auth–Request: (EncSlip, Clear, } H \text{ (DESC, SALT}_C))$$

4.7.2.5   Auth-Request processing

1. The acquirer extracts from Clear the value H(Common) as computed by the merchant. This is referred to as h_1. It also checks for replays using the values ID_M, TID_M, DATE, and $NONCE_M$.

2. Decrypts EncSlip and extracts H(Common) from Slip as computed by the customer. This is referred to as h_2.

3. Checks that $h_1 = h_2$. This ensures that both customer and merchant agree on the order information.

4. Reforms Common from the various fields it receives in the Auth-Request and ensures that H(Common) $= h_1 = h_2$. In short, Common consists of a number of fields and H(Common) allows each of the participants in the protocol to verify that they all agree on the details (e.g., the price and description of the goods) of the transaction. However, quantities such as the description information (DESC) and the cardholder's account number (CAN) are disguised/salted in such a manner that only the parties that need to know that information are given access to it.

5. The acquirer then contacts the card issuer and obtains clearance for the transaction.

Upon receipt of a response from the issuer, the acquirer computes a digital signature on the response (Y/N) and H(Common) and sends the Auth-Response to the merchant. (Note that both the merchant and customer are already in possession of H(Common) and thus it is not sent as part of the Auth-Response message flow.)

$$\text{Auth–Response: } (Y \mid N, \text{Sig}_A)$$

4.7.2.6   Auth-Response processing

1. The merchant verifies the signature (Sig_A).
2. The merchant forwards the response and the acquirer's signature to

the customer as part of the Confirm message flow. The customer in turn verifies the acquirer's signature and the transaction is complete.

The 1KP protocol is simple and efficient for effecting electronic payments over open networks such as the Internet with minimal requirements for additional certification infrastructure. Its main weaknesses are the following:

- A customer authenticates himself to a merchant only using a credit card number and optional PIN as opposed to using digital signatures.

- The merchant does not authenticate herself to the customer or acquirer.

- Neither the merchant nor customer provide undeniable receipts for the transaction.

4.7.3   2KP

In 2KP, in addition to the acquirer, each merchant needs to possess a public-key pair and is required to distribute the public key contained in its certificate $CERT_M$ to both customer and acquirer. This enables the customer and acquirer to verify the authenticity of the merchant. We now describe the additions to the basic flows that are required in 2KP.

The starting information for each of the parties is as shown in Table 4.5. There are now three new elements in the Invoice:

1.   The merchant generates a random number V and creates a message digest $H(V)$. He adds $H(V)$ to Clear. (Note that Common now also contains $H(V)$). The inclusion of V in Confirm later acts as a receipt of proof to the customer that the merchant has accepted the authorization response.

Table 4.5   Starting Information

Actor	Information Items
Customer	DESC, CAN, PK_{CA}, $CERT_A$
Merchant	DESC, PK_{CA}, $CERT_A$, SK_M, $CERT_M$
Acquirer	PK_{CA}, SK_A, $CERT_A$

2. The merchant uses his secret key (SK_M) to sign the pair $H(Common)$ and $H(V)$ to produce Sig_M.

3. The merchant also includes his public key certificate $CERT_M$ so that the customer can verify the signature Sig_M.

The transaction message flow is shown in Figure 4.18. On receipt of the Invoice, the customer checks the merchant's signature Sig_M and generates a Payment message flow as before. The merchant appends the same signature Sig_M that he sent to the customer as well as his public-key certificate $CERT_M$ to Auth-Request. The acquirer checks the merchant's signature before authorizing the transaction. Finally, the value of V is sent in Confirm to the customer, who in turn computes $H(V)$ and verifies that this matches the value in Invoice.

The 2KP protocol satisfies all the requirements of 1KP as well as:

- The customer and the acquirer can verify the authenticity of the merchant due to the inclusion of the merchant's signature Sig_M and $CERT_M$.

- The merchant generates a random number V and includes a message digest of the number $H(V)$ in Common. He also signs the pair $H(V)$ and $H(Common)$ to form Sig_M. This signature and $H(Common)$ are verified by both the customer and the acquirer. The acquirer also signs

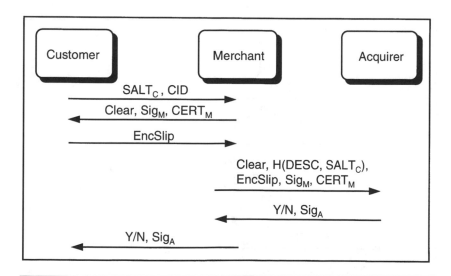

Figure 4.18   2KP protocol flows.

H(Common) in Sig$_A$. When the customer receives V as part of the Confirm message flow, he is able to verify that $H(V)$ contained in Sig$_M$ and Sig$_A$ matches $H(V)$ that he has computed. Also, no other party is capable of finding V as this would involve inverting a strong one-way function. In effect, the customer receives a receipt of the transaction that assures him that the merchant has received and accepted the payment.

4.7.4   3KP

In 3KP, all the parties possess public-key pairs and corresponding certificates. This allows for nonrepudiation of all protocol exchanges. The protocol is modified to have the customer send a certificate to a merchant, who forwards it onto the acquirer. We describe the additions that are required to the flows of 2KP.

As Figure 4.19 shows, the customer now sends his public-key certificate to the merchant as part of the Initiate message. As a part of the Payment, the customer sends his signature Sig$_C$ to the merchant, where Sig$_C$ is computed by encrypting EncSlip and H(Common). The merchant is able to verify the customer's signature as he already possesses the customer's certificate CERT$_C$. The merchant forwards Sig$_C$ as part of the Auth-Request to the acquirer, who verifies the signature in turn.

The starting information for each of the parties is as shown in Table 4.6.

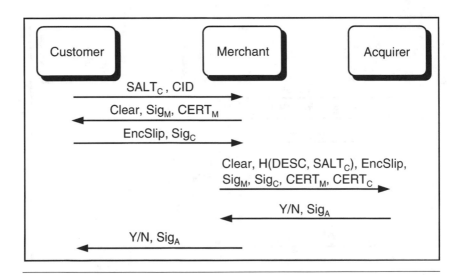

Figure 4.19   3KP protocol flows.

Table 4.6 Starting Information

Actor	Information Items
Customer	DESC, CAN, PK_{CA}, SK_C, $CERT_C$
Merchant	DESC, PK_{CA}, $CERT_A$, SK_M, $CERT_M$
Acquirer	PK_{CA}, SK_A, $CERT_A$

In 3KP, the customer's signature provides undeniable proof of the transaction authorization by the customer. This can be verified by both the merchant and the acquirer.

The *i*KP protocols provide varying degrees of protection depending upon the number of entities that possess public-key pairs. It is envisaged by the developers that 1KP will be the protocol used most in the short term, with 2KP and 3KP being phased in over a period of time.

4.8 Secure electronic payment protocol (SEPP)

SEPP [11] is a protocol developed by MasterCard in October 1995 for secure payment processing using bank card transactions over public networks and is based on 3KP (see Section 4.7). As Figure 4.20 shows public-key cryptographic techniques are used to ensure that message content is not altered during the transmission between originator and recipient. (Note that as in the *i*KP protocols, privacy of nonfinancial data is not addressed by SEPP.) Merchants are able to verify that a cardholder is using a valid account number. SEPP also provides a mechanism to prevent fraudsters from posing as legitimate merchants and "collecting" card data. In addition to defining the electronic payment protocol, SEPP also defines a certificate management system to control certificates supporting security services.

SEPP is the electronic equivalent of the paper charge slip, signature, and submission process. It assumes that the customer and merchant have already negotiated the price of the goods to be purchased out-of-band (e.g., through the WWW). SEPP takes input from the negotiation process (payment amount, order description, payment method, etc.) and causes payment to happen via a three-way communication among the cardholder, the merchant, and the acquirer.

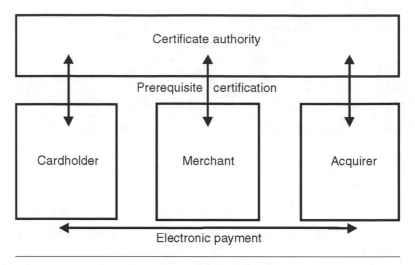

Figure 4.20   Overview of SEPP.

4.8.1   System architecture

The SEPP system is composed of a number of entities depicted in Figure 4.21, namely:

- *Cardholder:* An authorized holder of a bank card issued by an issuer who is registered to perform electronic commerce.

- *Merchant:* A merchant of goods or services and who accepts payment for them electronically.

- *Acquirer:* A registered financial institution that supports merchants by providing service for processing credit card transactions. The acquirer consists of an acquirer gateway and merchant registration authority. The acquirer gateway interfaces to the merchant system to support authorization and capture services to merchants. The merchant registration authority (MRA) enables the acquirer to securely receive, validate, and forward merchant certificate requests to the certificate management system and receive back certificates.

- *Certificate management system (CMS):* An agent of one or more bank card associations that provides for the creation and distribution of electronic certificates for merchants, acquirers, and cardholders. The CMS consists of one or more certificate authorities to provide a trusted, reliable certificate granting service to cardholders, merchants,

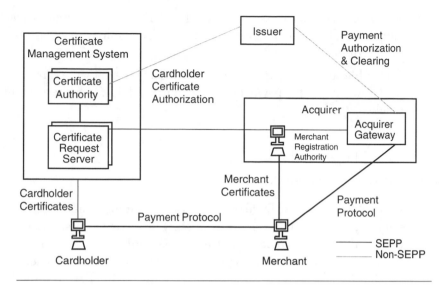

Figure 4.21   System overview.

and acquirers. It also contains certificate request servers that issue certificates to cardholders through the WWW and interfaces to the acquirer's MRA to provide merchant certificates. X.509 version 3 public-key certificates are specified.

4.8.2   Certificate management system

The CMS is implemented as a hierarchy of servers, each with its own cryptographic support. A certificate is used to bind the public key of a user to some uniquely identifying information (e.g., a customer's name or account number).

- A cardholder certificate binds the public key of a certificate holder to a specific account number and assures the merchant that a legitimate account number is provided in the transaction. In order to protect the cardholder's privacy a hashed (effectively encrypted) version of the account number is specified in the cardholder's public-key certificate. The cardholder passes her account number and a secret variable called a certificate code to an acquirer so that the acquirer can verify the hashed value contained within the cardholder's certificate.

- A merchant certificate assures the cardholder that the merchant is a legitimate MasterCard merchant (i.e., has a relationship with a MasterCard acquirer).
- The public key within an acquirer's certificate is used by the cardholder to encrypt the payment instruction, which includes the account number.

4.8.3   SEPP keys used

Several keys are used in SEPP, including the following:

- *Cardholder keys:* A cardholder requires a key pair for creating digital signatures during a payment transaction. The secret key is stored locally on disk in encrypted form using a password known only to the cardholder. The cardholder's public and secret key pairs are generated locally by a cryptographic device or software. In order to provide the maximum protection against compromise, the secret key is stored securely in tamper-proof hardware or protected with a password if it is stored on disk.
- *Merchant keys:* A merchant may either have one or two pairs of keys. One pair is required for creating digital signatures. The other pair is optional and is used for encryption of payment data sent from the acquirer back to the merchant, if the acquirer provides this option.
- *Acquirer keys:* Three key pairs are required by the acquirer gateway. The first is used to digitally sign receipts provided to the cardholder and merchant. The second is used for encrypting and decrypting payment data received from the cardholder. The third is used for signing renewal requests for certificates to be sent to the CMS.

The public components of each of the above key pairs are certified by the CMS.

4.8.4   Overview of payment process

SEPP assumes that the cardholder and merchant have been communicating in order to negotiate the terms of a purchase and generate an order. SEPP can be used in both interactive (e.g., WWW) and noninteractive modes (e.g., CD-ROM catalogue). In a noninteractive environment, the transaction details can be sent to the merchant via electronic mail.

SEPP defines six basic flows:

1. Purchase order with inline authorization;
2. Purchase order with delayed authorization;
3. Offline purchase order;
4. Capture;
5. Purchase order inquiry;
6. Error.

The following sections summarize the most important of these message flows.

4.8.5 Purchase order with inline authorization

This is the basic purchase order flow where the merchant performs an "online" authorization check. It is shown in Figure 4.22.

1. In the interactive message environment, a SEPP transaction starts when the cardholder sends an Initiate message to the merchant. This message is used to request the merchant to prepare an invoice as the first step in the payment process.

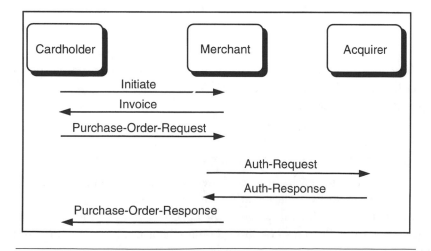

Figure 4.22   Purchase order with inline authorization.

2. The merchant responds with an Invoice message, which contains the amount of the transaction, merchant identification information, and data used to validate subsequent transactions in the sequence.

3. The cardholder responds by sending a PO-Request. It contains the payment instruction (PI) of the cardholder. The PI is encrypted such that it can be only read by the acquirer. This is necessary since the PI contains the cardholder's primary account number (PAN), which should not be revealed to the merchant.

4. The merchant then sends an Auth-Request to the acquirer.

5. The acquirer performs the following:

   • Authenticates the merchant;

   • Decrypts the PI from the cardholder;

   • Validates that the cardholder's certificate matches the account number used in the purchase;

   • Validates the consistency between the merchant's authorization request and the cardholder's payment data;

   • Formats a standard authorization request to the issuer and receives a response;

   • Responds to the merchant with a validated Auth-Response.

6. The merchant responds with a PO-Response indicating that either the merchant has received the purchase order request and the authorization request will be processed later, or the authorization response has been processed by the acquirer.

The cardholder can then (or at a later date) request a status of the purchase order by using a PO-Inquiry message. The merchant responds with a PO-Inquiry-Response message.

4.8.6   Purchase order with delayed authorization

This variation on the basic purchase order flow is shown in Figure 4.23. Here, the merchant chooses to delay authorization until after sending a response to the cardholder. The final message to the customer is a PO-Inquiry-Response rather than a PO-Response because the merchant has not yet completed the authorization. The Auth-Request and Auth-Response portion of flow is the same as in the previous case.

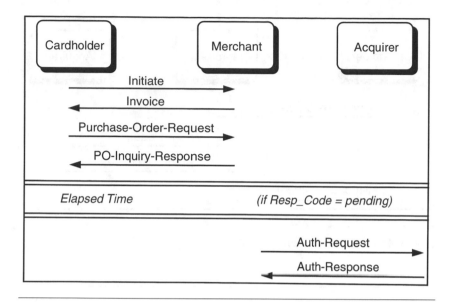

Figure 4.23   Purchase order with delayed authorization flow.

4.8.7   Offline purchase order

In the case of electronic mail transactions, the first message from the cardholder is a PO-Request. As Figure 4.24 shows, the PO-Response from the merchant is sent back to the cardholder via e-mail. The Initiate and Invoice messages are omitted.

4.8.8   Capture

A merchant uses the capture flow to request the credit card clearing system to transfer funds from the cardholder to the merchant. A capture flow may only occur after the authorization flow has been completed and if the purchase order was not captured as part of the authorization flow. The merchant must send the Capture-Request to the same acquirer to whom the Auth-Request message was sent. Figure 4.25 shows this dialogue.

SEPP supports three distinct modes of capture:

1. *Online capture combined with authorization.* The merchant may re-
    quest that payment be captured by the acquirer at the time authoriza-
    tion is obtained.

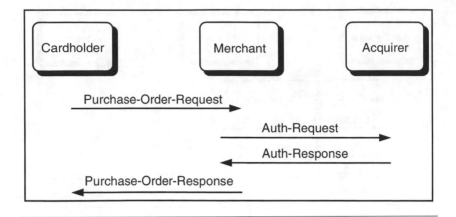

Figure 4.24   Offline purchase order flow.

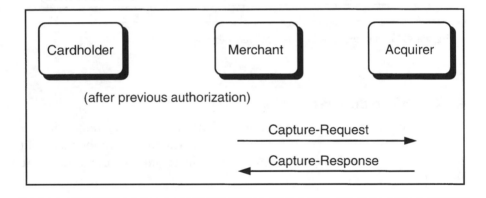

Figure 4.25   Capture flow.

2. *Deferred online capture.* The merchant may request payment capture separately from and subsequent to authorization.

3. *Offline capture.* The merchant may obtain payment through offline mechanisms that do not involve SEPP.

4.8.9 Security requirements

SEPP addresses a range of requirements for each party directly involved in the SEPP payment process.

4.8.9.1 Cardholder

- Unauthorized payments are impossible and cannot be charged to a cardholder's account without possession of the cardholder's account number and secret key.

- A cardholder can verify the authenticity/trustworthiness of the merchant.

- A cardholder receives undeniable proof of transaction authorization from the acquirer.

- A cardholder receives a receipt from the merchant that gives undeniable proof that the merchant received the payment authorization.

4.8.9.2 Merchant

- A merchant receives undeniable proof that the acquirer has authorized the payment transaction.

- A merchant also obtains undeniable proof that the cardholder has authorized the transaction.

4.8.9.3 Acquirer

- The acquirer obtains undeniable proof of transaction authorization by the cardholder prior to debiting the account.

- The acquirer obtains undeniable proof of transaction authorization by the merchant. It is impossible to authorize a payment transaction without the merchant's authorization.

Further work on SEPP has been abandoned in favor of the SET specifications as discussed in the next section.

4.9 Secure Electronic Transactions (SET)

The launch by the alliance comprising of MasterCard, Netscape Corporation, IBM, and others of the Secure Electronic Payment Protocol (SEPP) in October 1995 came within a few days of the launch by a VISA and Microsoft consortium of a different network payment specification called Secure Transaction Technology (STT). This led to an unfortunate situation where the two major credit card associations were each backing an independent solution for network payments.

For a number of months the two efforts proceeded in parallel, each developing separate reference implementations. Efforts were made to develop payment-method selection protocols that could accommodate both systems. Ultimately, good sense prevailed, and in January 1996, the companies announced that they would come together to develop a unified system that would be called Secure Electronic Transactions (SET).

Late in February of that year, two documents were issued, the first of which [12] gave a business overview of the protocols, and the second [13] of which gave more technical details. This was followed by a public comment period during which interested parties discussed the specifications, and identified flaws. Following this, a revised book 3 protocol description was released [14] that defines the production SET protocol.

Most significant organizations in the Internet payment industry have stated that they will support SET, and indeed, very shortly after the specifications were released, American Express—another payment card company with a global presence—stated that they would also adopt the protocol. Note, however, that the SET specifications at the time of writing are an interim standard, parts of which may change as the standardization work progresses.

The scope of the SET protocols was quite restricted from the outset. Firstly, it was intended only as a payment protocol. The specification documents make clear that protocols would be developed by other parties to address online shopping, price negotiation, payment-method selection, and other electronic commerce functions. SET would only come into play after the customer had decided what to buy, for how much, and that she wanted to pay with a payment card. Although not part of the standard, an appendix to the SET technical specification [13] does outline a method for "Interim Merchant/Cardholder Communication" that is likely to be influential in the absence of well-developed alternatives.

In a conventional MOTO credit card transaction, a cardholder forwards her details to the merchant who will then contact his (the merchant's) acquirer to obtain clearance for the payment. The acquirer can obtain this authorization from the institution that issued the card via a financial network operated by the card association (e.g., MasterCard or VISA). These private networks have existed for some time and have their own set of proprietary protocols operating on dedicated links with appropriate security mechanisms in operation. Thus an infrastructure of links and transaction-processing computer hardware exists to electronically authorize credit card payments. SET assumes the existence of such a facility and only specifies the subset of dialogues between the customer and merchant and between the merchant and an entity known as the payment gateway.

An overview of the payment process is shown in Figure 4.26. The card-

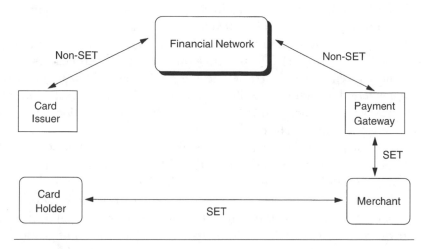

Figure 4.26 Phases of a credit card payment addressed by SET standards.

holder initiates a payment with the merchant using SET. The merchant then uses SET to have the payment authorized. The entity involved is called the payment gateway and it may be operated by an acquirer or could be some shared facility operated by a group of acquirers (or, indeed, the card association). The payment gateway acts as the front end to the existing financial network, and through this the card issuer can be contacted to explicitly authorize each and every transaction that takes place.

It is clear from the diagrams that SET is not intended to be a general-purpose payment protocol and is restricted to payment card or similar applications where parties will take on the role of buyer, merchant, or acquirer. It does not address transfer of funds from one individual to another and relies on the existing credit card infrastructure to effect the payment. The cardholder will see SET transactions on her credit card statement side by side with more conventional credit card payments, and the acquirer will see this as an extension of the current relationship he has with his merchant customers.

4.9.1   The SET trust model

Each of the parties that participates in a SET payment, with the possible exception of the cardholder, will be required to authenticate themselves at some point in the payment process. They will do this by using the private part of a public-key pair. For this to operate satisfactorily, the corresponding public keys must be certified by some trusted third party.

In SET, bindings between identities and their corresponding public keys are stored using certificates in X.509 version 3 format.

Figure 4.27 shows the format of such a certificate expressed in abstract syntax notation 1 (ASN.1). The principle purpose of this certificate is to bind the identity given by the *subject* field to the public key held in *subjectPublic-KeyInfo* where the binding is certified by *issuer*: the authority that applies the signature to the certificate. In SET, a hierarchy of certification authorities shown in Figure 4.28 will be used.

There will be a single root key for all entities using SET. This will sign the certificates of each of the brands (e.g., VISA, MasterCard, American Express, etc.) using a 2,048-bit key. Procedures are defined to change from one root key to another before the root certificate reaches the end of its validity period. Each of the brands will then either deal directly with member financial institutions in individual countries or they will delegate this to some kind of geopolitical organization (e.g., VISA Europe). The certificates issued by the brand CAs and those lower down in the hierarchy are all signed using a 1,024-bit key length, reflecting the less onerous security regime required at the lower levels.

If cardholder certificates are being issued, this function will be carried out by the card issuer. In the period leading up to the launch of SET, MasterCard had resolved not to do this, while VISA's policy was to require all cardholders to produce certificates when they engaged in a SET transaction. Payment gateways may be operated by an acquirer, who would already act as a merchant CA, but nevertheless, these gateways must be able to produce a certificate that has been signed by the payment CA before they can participate in a transaction.

SET also makes use of the *Extensions* field that became available in version 3 of the X.509 certificate definition. In particular, each certificate has a *Key*

```
Certificate ::= SIGNED { SEQUENCE {
                    version [0]Version DEFAULT v1,
                    serialNumber  CertificateSerialNumber,
                    signature  AlgorithmIdentifier,
                    issuer  Name,
                    validity  Validity,
                    subject  Name,
                    subjectPublicKeyInfo SubjectPublicKeyInfo,
                    issuerUniqueID   [1] IMPLICIT UniqueIdentifier OPTIONAL,
                    subjectUniqueID [2] IMPLICIT UniqueIdentifier OPTIONAL,
                    extensions  [3] Extensions OPTIONAL  }
```

Figure 4.27   The certificate definition in X.509 version 3.

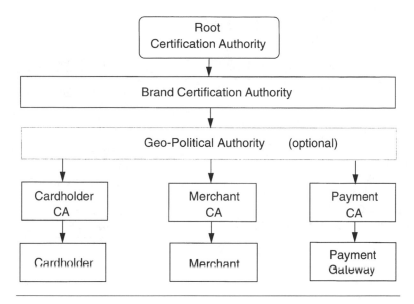

Figure 4.28 Certification authority hierarchy used in SET.

Usage Restriction field that specifies what tasks (e.g., signature verification, data encipherment, etc.) the key is approved for by the issuing CA. Cardholders are normally issued with a signature generation key certificate and they should not use the associated key pair for message confidentiality purposes.

The entities (cardholder, merchant, etc.) involved in SET transactions are identified in the certificates using an X.500 distinguished name. This is a collection of attributes that, taken together, uniquely identify the entity. Some examples of these attributes include country (c) and organization (o). Subdivisions of an organization can be identified by including one or more organizational units (ou) in the distinguished name. Normally, the last attribute used is the common name (cn), which would ordinarily give the individual name of an entity. In the case of SET cardholder certificates, neither the person's name nor the credit card number (often referred to as the primary account number or PAN) is shown in the certificate. Instead, a numeric quantity, computed by concatenating the PAN with a nonce as well as some fixed-character strings and computing the resulting hash, is used. This value is never regenerated, but is stored by the card issuer, and when a payment is attempted, the stored value is compared with the blinded account number contained in the request for payment authorization.

Figure 4.29 shows some examples of the kind of names that may be assigned to SET entities. The overall root of the hierarchy will be an organization

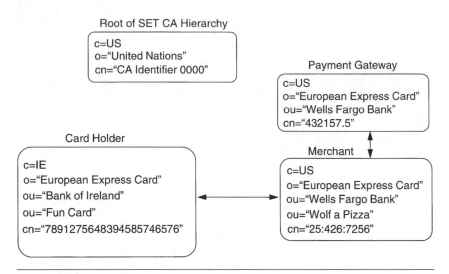

Figure 4.29   Some typical names assigned to SET entities.

that is at arms length from any of the card associations operating SET payment systems. The attributes specified in its name will be the country, the name of the organization, and a unique identifying string. Other examples shown in the figure are for a cardholder who has been issued with a "European Express Card" from the Bank of Ireland, where the local promotional name used is "Fun Card." The common name attribute is a blinded version of the card number. This cardholder is shown interacting with a merchant called "Wolf a Pizza," whose acquiring organization is the Wells Fargo Bank. The payment gateway is operated by the same financial institution.

4.9.2   SET message structure

The SET protocol consists of request/response message pairs, such as the PReq and PRes messages shown in Figure 4.30. In this section, the contents and flow of the messages required to complete a purchase transaction are presented. To allow interoperability, the messages are defined in a machine-independent format in the specification. This will allow clients produced by one software company to perform a SET transaction with a server developed by a completely different company.

Encryption is performed on parts of certain messages. This end-to-end solution allows information contained with the message to be selectively revealed to parties as required. For example, the financial data about a credit card

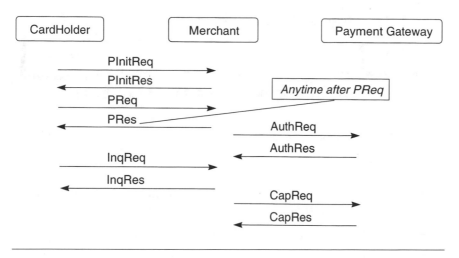

Figure 4.30   Steps in a SET transaction.

is not revealed to the merchant, and data about the purchased product is concealed from the acquirer. Point-to-point encryption of a connection link would not allow such selection to occur.

The messages needed to perform a complete purchase transaction (Figure 4.30) usually include

- Initialization (PInitReq/PInitRes);
- Purchase order (PReq/PRes);
- Authorization (AuthReq/AuthRes);
- Capture of payment (CapReq/CapRes);
- Cardholder inquiry (InqReq/InqRes) [optional].

These messages are not necessarily in the above order. The contents and function of each pair is now examined in turn.

4.9.3   Payment initialization (PInitReq/PInitRes)

The SET payment starts after the cardholder has been presented with a completed order form and approved its contents. The way in which goods are selected and presented in an order form is outside the scope of SET, but it is likely that shopping protocols will be designed to handle this.

The PInitReq message is sent to the merchant to indicate that the cardholder is ready to pay for the goods. As shown in Figure 4.31, it contains

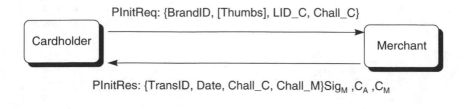

PInitReq: {BrandID, [Thumbs], LID_C, Chall_C}

Cardholder   Merchant

PInitRes: {TransID, Date, Chall_C, Chall_M}Sig$_M$,C$_A$,C$_M$

Figure 4.31   Initialization messages.

- Brand of card that will be used in the payment, such as VISA or MasterCard (Brand_ID);

- A local ID for the transaction (LID_C);

- Optional list of certificates (Thumbs) already stored by the cardholder software. This list consists of a thumbprint (SHA hash) of each certificate held;

- Challenge variable (Chall_C), which will be used in the merchant's response, to guarantee the freshness of the communication.

Upon receipt of the PInitReq, the merchant generates a globally unique ID that is combined with the LID_C to form the complete transaction ID (TransID). This is used to identify a specific purchase from other purchase messages received.

The merchant's response contains this TransID along with certificates and the current date. The cardholder's challenge is included along with a new merchant challenge (Chall_M). The certificates include those keys that are needed in the payment and that the cardholder doesn't already hold, such as the merchant and acquirer public keys.

Since the cardholder has now received an appropriate response to his challenge, he can be confident that the merchant is an accredited retailer.

4.9.4   Purchase order (PReq/PRes)

The purchase order messages fulfill the actual purchase by the cardholder from the merchant. It is the most complex message pair in the payment protocol. The cardholder sends two elements, the order information (OI) and payment instructions (PI), to the merchant, as shown in Figure 4.32:

- The OI holds data that identifies the order description at the merchant.

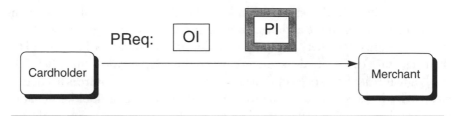

Figure 4.32 Purchase request.

- The PI contains the actual card data, purchase amount, and order and transaction identifiers. The PI is encrypted with the acquirer's public key so that the merchant cannot view its contents. It is forwarded to the acquirer later as part of the authorization.

4.9.4.1 Order information (OI)

The construction of the OI is shown in Figure 4.33. OIData consists of data from the initialization phase. The merchant challenge, Chall_M, is returned, demonstrating the freshness of the message to the merchant. ODsalt is a nonce that is used when creating a hash of the order description. By including this random nonce within the hash, dictionary attacks are prevented. That is, the nonce stops an attacker from guessing the hash value, H(OIData), by trying all possible combinations of dictionary words in the order description.

A dual signature is created using the hashes of OIData and PIData (the data

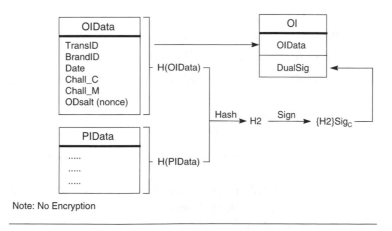

Figure 4.33 Construction of the order info (OI) element.

contents of the PI). The signature links OIData and PIData, which links the cardholder's order to the authorization payment instructions by showing that they were signed together. Anyone possessing either OIData or PIData and the dual signature can verify the signature without having to know the other. The dual signature is also a speed optimization since only one signature is needed instead of having to separately sign OIData and PIData. The cardholder signature certificate is also included with the signature so that the merchant can verify it.

4.9.4.2   SET dual signatures

While the dual signatures in SET are created in the normal way, as described in Chapter 3, a further optimization is applied. The result of XORing the hash of message 1 with the hash of message 2 is included with the signature. The signature can be verified with this value and either message 1 or message 2. This prevents having to include $H(M1)$ in one copy of the signature, and $H(M2)$ in the second copy of the signature when distributing to the two parties involved, as is normally the case. Instead, these values can be extracted from the XOR value and the single version of the dual signature verified. The following example clarifies this:

- Take two messages, M1 and M2.
- Create a dual signature in the normal way:
  $H2 = H(H(M1), H(M2))$. Then Sign H2.
- Normal dual signature:
  {H2}, Sig_X, $H(M1)$ for holder of M2.
  {H2}, Sig_X, $H(M2)$ for holder of M1.
- But now include $Y = H(M1)$ XOR $H(M2)$ in signature.
- SET dual signature: {H2}Sig_X, Y for all parties.
- The holder of M1 verifies the dual signature by extracting $H(M2)$ from Y:
  $H(M1)$ is first obtained by applying the hash algorithm to M1)
  $H(M2) = H(M1)$ XOR Y
- Having obtained $H(M2)$ from Y, the dual signature is validated in the normal way:
  $H(M1)$ and $H(M2)$ are concatenated, and the result then hashed.
  $H3 = H(H(M1), H(M2))$. The resulting hash, $H3$, should match $H2$ in the signature.
  $H3 = H2$ if signature valid.

The SET dual signature optimization allows the same signature material to be sent to both parties ($\{H2\}\text{Sig}_X$, Y), instead of having to replace Y with different values for each receiver. From the SET dual signature message, both parties can verify the signature that links message 1 and message 2 together.

4.9.4.3   Payment instructions (PI)

The PI is constructed as shown in Figure 4.34. Remember, the contents of the PI are never seen by the merchant, but are forwarded to the acquirer. The actual credit card data is included with nonces to defeat playback and dictionary attacks. The card data is protected by using extra-strong encryption as described in the following section. A hash of the order, $H(\text{Order})$, is included, which identifies the unique order the cardholder is referring to without giving away what that order is.

The same dual signature already created for OI is used as the signature on the PI. The PI is encrypted with the public-key exchange key of the acquirer. This prevents the merchant, or anyone else, from viewing its contents.

The payment request embodies the actual credit card payment from the cardholder's point of view. It is at the core of the SET payment protocol and once sent, the cardholder has shown an agreement to pay that cannot be easily reversed.

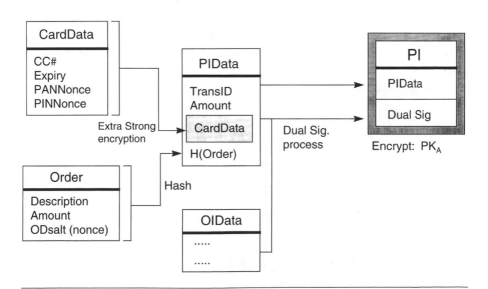

Figure 4.34 Construction of payment instructions (PI).

4.9.4.4 SET extra-strong encryption

Instead of encrypting with a symmetric DES key and then encrypting this symmetric key using RSA, the data is directly encrypted with RSA. This is illustrated in Figure 4.35 where extra strong encryption is used on the card data and is much stronger than the normal SET encryption.

4.9.4.5 Processing PReq

When the merchant receives a purchase request from a cardholder, the OI and PI parts are extracted. The merchant verifies the cardholder's dual signature on OI using the cardholder's certificate by traversing the certificate trust chain to the root.

Before sending a purchase response (PRes) to the cardholder, the merchant will normally perform the authorization and perhaps capture steps of the payment. Authorization and capture are described in the following sections. However, PRes may be returned before capture or before both capture and authorization. The option chosen will affect the contents of the messages.

If authorization is delayed, the merchant will return a purchase response indicating that the cardholder should inquire later about transaction status. The cardholder inquiry messages are described in Section 4.9.7.

When the merchant does send the purchase response to the cardholder, it will contain the transaction status and any result codes available. The message format is shown in Figure 4.36. The CompletionCode indicates whether the authorization or capture steps have been completed. Results contains the authorization or capture codes for the transaction if these steps have been performed. These codes were generated in the financial bankcard network to authorize and clear the transaction and may appear on the cardholder's monthly bill.

The purchase order messages form the actual purchase by the cardholder

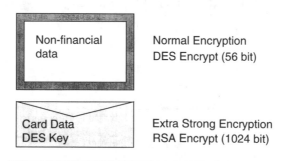

Figure 4.35   SET extra-strong encryption.

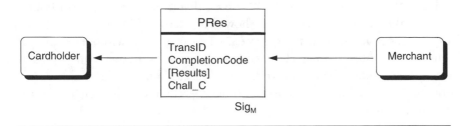

Figure 4.36 Merchant's purchase response message.

from the merchant. When the cardholder receives the merchant's response she knows that either the payment is complete or that the transaction is waiting to be processed by the credit card financial network.

4.9.5 Authorization (AuthReq/AuthRes)

This process allows the merchant to verify that the cardholder has credit for the purchase and to obtain permission to charge the transaction to her credit card. In the authorization request, the merchant sends data about the purchase, signed and encrypted to the acquirer. The PI from the cardholder is also forwarded in this request.

The data sent includes a hash of the order details as shown in Figure 4.37. If this matches the H(Order) present in the PI, the acquirer knows that the merchant and cardholder are in agreement about the ordered goods and purchase

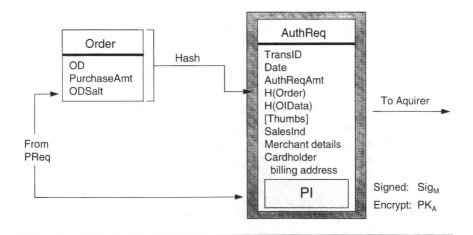

Figure 4.37 Requesting authorization of the purchase.

amount. The dual signature in the PI proves that it came from the cardholder. H(OIData) in the merchant request shows knowledge of OIData that is signed by the dual signature, showing agreement on the order data without revealing it. Thumbs is an optional list of relevant certificates held by the merchant to prevent the acquirer sending them in the response. The cardholder billing address (obtained outside the SET protocol) and other merchant details such as business type are also expected.

Both authorization and capture can be performed in a single request, known as a sales transaction. SalesInd is used to indicate if the merchant wishes to do this.

Upon receiving AuthReq, the acquirer decrypts the message parts, verifies signatures, and checks for consistency between the purchase details sent by the merchant and those in the PI. If the merchant's request (AuthReqAmt) is not the same as the PurchaseAmt, it is checked that this difference is acceptable to policy. Next, the acquirer obtains the authorization through the existing financial network as shown in Figure 4.38.

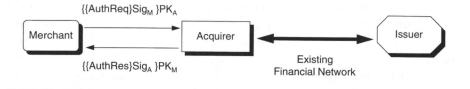

Figure 4.38   Obtaining authorization for a purchase transaction.

Having received a good authorization from the card issuer, an authorization response (AuthRes) is returned to the merchant with the authorization code from the issuer. Illustrated in Figure 4.39, it also contains a capture token, signed and encrypted, which is later used by the merchant to capture the payment. Only the acquirer can decrypt the token, keeping the capture data hidden from anyone else.

If capture was performed with the authorization (sales transaction), then the capture code and amount are returned instead of the capture token. Upon receiving a good authorization, a merchant can ship the goods purchased. A good authorization indicates that the card issuer has verified the card details and credit limit, and given the go-ahead for the purchase.

4.9.6   Capture of payment (CapReq/CapRes)

After processing an order, the merchant needs to request the payment previously authorized to be transferred to his account. The total payment for several

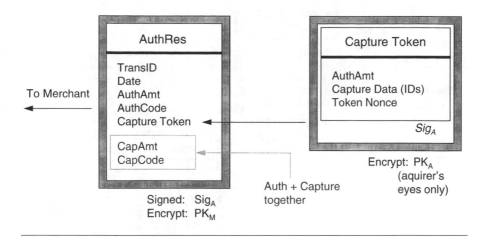

Figure 4.39   Authorization response with capture token.

authorizations can be captured in a single batch request as shown in Figure 4.40. A merchant might accumulate many capture tokens (from authorization) throughout the day and then request reimbursement for these at the end of the day.

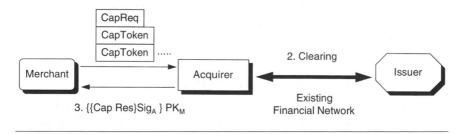

Figure 4.40   Capturing multiple authorized payments in a single request.

The contents of a capture request (CapReq) are shown in Figure 4.41. Many capture tokens from different transactions can be included in a single request for efficiency. For each token, the corresponding authorized amount and transaction ID are included. These should match the data encrypted within the capture token itself. CapID is just a unique value used to identify this capture from others. The request is signed and encrypted by the merchant.

After verifying the capture request, the acquirer credits the merchant's account. Transaction fees may be deducted at this stage. The capture response

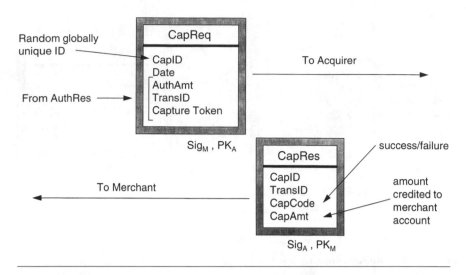

Figure 4.41   Capture request/response messages.

(CapRes), signed and encrypted, contains a success indication, the settled amount, and a capture code from the financial network.

After a successful capture, the merchant has received the actual payment of money from the cardholder's purchase. If the merchant has not already sent the purchase response to the cardholder, this is now done.

4.9.7   Cardholder inquiry (InqReq/InqRes)

The inquiry messages allow a cardholder to check the status of a transaction. An inquiry can be sent any time after the purchase request, and cardholders can only inquire about their own purchases. The inquiry can be performed several times for a single transaction.

The message contents are shown in Figure 4.42. The inquiry request contains the transaction identifier and includes a new challenge variable. This should be unique to each invocation, since the inquiry may be sent repeatedly. The inquiry is signed to prove that the request comes from the correct cardholder.

The inquiry response returned by the merchant is very similar to PRes. It contains the transaction status and any result codes (authorization or capture) available. Having received an inquiry response, the cardholder can be sure as to how a specific purchase with an accredited merchant is proceeding.

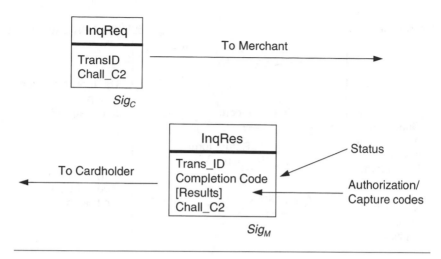

Figure 4.42 Inquiry request/response messages.

4.9.7.1 Cardholder registration

All parties involved in a payment need key certificates to send SET messages. When cardholders want to start using SET to make network payments, they must obtain a public key certificate from a certification authority (CA).

Every cardholder needs a signature certificate containing their public signature key so that messages signed by them can be verified. An encryption certificate, with a public-key exchange key, is optional since none of the SET payment messages sent to the cardholder are encrypted in the current version of SET.

The method for obtaining a CA signed certificate is outlined in Figure 4.43. Whether the cardholder is obtaining one certificate or multiple certificates, the procedure is much the same.

Certificates have an expiry date, which usually matches the credit card expiry date. The procedure for renewing certificates is also very similar to that shown. Similar certificate registration and renewal processes exist for merchants and acquirers.

The registration process starts when the cardholder sends a request (CInitReq) to the CA asking for:

- CA's key exchange certificate. This will allow later messages sent to the CA to be encrypted with its public-key exchange key. Clearly, to verify this certificate, all users must have a copy of the root public key.

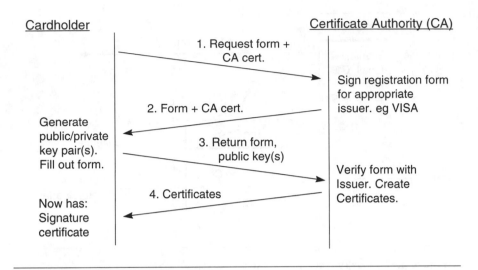

Figure 4.43 Cardholder registration.

- An electronic registration form from the cardholder's financial institution (issuer).

The contents of CInitReq are shown in Figure 4.44. The request type indicates whether the cardholder seeks a signature certificate, an encryption

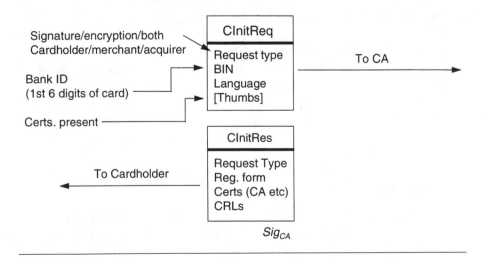

Figure 4.44 CInit request/response messages.

certificate, or both. The BankID (BIN) is the first six numbers on the card and uniquely identifies the issuing bank. The Language field is used to request the language on the returned registration form. A thumbprint (Thumbs) of current certificates held is also sent.

The CA's response (CInitRes) holds the appropriate registration form, the CA's certificates and those needed to verify them, and a list of relevant revoked certificates (CRLs), all signed by the CA.

The cardholder now validates the certificates by traversing the trust chain and removes any certificates listed in the revocation list. The cardholder can now be confident that she has received a valid registration form from an accredited certificate authority. The registration form is filled out and includes the credit card number and expiry date. In order to send this sensitive data to the CA, it is encrypted directly with the CA's public RSA key exchange key (SET extra-strong encryption).

The cardholder nonce (Nonce_CARD) will be combined with a CA-generated nonce (Nonce_CCA) at the CA to form PANNONCE. This nonce is used in the payment protocol (see Figure 4.34). H(Card data,PANNONCE) will also appear in the cardholder's certificates.

The cardholder signs the public keys that are to be certified and includes these with the registration form to construct the certificate request message (CertReq). The request is encrypted before sending it to the CA, as shown in Figure 4.45.

When the CA receives the certificate request, it authenticates the card with the issuing bank using an existing financial network. If the card data is valid, it will generate and sign certificates for the cardholder's public keys. The contents of these certificates are discussed in Chapter 3.

The certificate response from the CA (CertRes) contains the new certificates and the strongly encrypted Nonce_CCA, as shown in Figure 4.46. The cardholder verifies the certificates. She also combines the decrypted CA nonce (Nonce_CCA) with the cardholder nonce (Nonce_CARD) to form PAN-NONCE.

$$PANNONCE = H(\text{Nonce\_Card XOR Nonce\_CCA})$$

It can then be verified that H(CardData,PANNONCE), which forms the globally unique cardholder ID, appears in the new certificates:

$$\text{Unique Cardholder ID} = H(\text{CardData,PANNONCE})$$

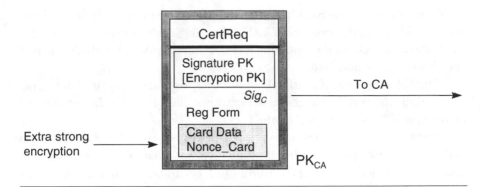

Figure 4.45   Certificate request message.

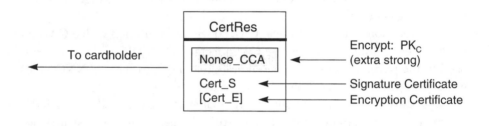

Figure 4.46   Certificate response message.

The cardholder now has the signature certificate required to make a purchase, and can start making credit card payments to SET merchants.

4.9.8   Developing SET applications

SET is exclusively a payment protocol. Supporting electronic commerce protocols such as those for shopping, price negotiation, payment selection, and information delivery will often need to be incorporated with a SET implementation to provide a useful electronic commerce application. Similarly, configurable, simple-to-use graphical user interfaces need to be provided so that the purchase steps in a SET transaction are transparent to the user. An application using SET will typically contain much more functionality than just the SET payment protocol alone, as shown in Figure 4.47.

In order to prevent every SET application developer having to implement SET for integration into the application, several SET implementations, APIs, and toolkits are available for this purpose. This has the advantage of allowing applications to be developed independently and yet use the same SET imple-

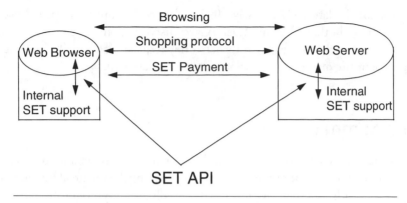

Figure 4.47 Integrating SET into end-user applications.

mentation. MasterCard and VISA provide a reference implementation of SET that is freely available for noncommercial use.

4.9.9   Evolution of the SET standard

Table 4.7 shows how the SET standard has evolved. The first live SET transaction was performed in Denmark on the last day of 1996 in an IBM pilot scheme. SET pilots are planned for around the world during early 1997 but it

Table 4.7   Progression of the SET Standard

Date	Documents Released
Jan. 1996	Press release announcing SET
Feb. 1996	Draft for Public Comment
	Book 1: Business Description (68 pg.)
	Book 2: Technical Specification (269 pg.)
June 1996	Draft for Testing
	Book 1: Business Description (71 pg.)
	Book 2: Programmer's Guide (431 pg.)
	Book 3: Formal Protocol Definition (135 pg.)
Aug. 1996	Book 3 revised and updated
	Book 3: Formal Protocol Definition (146 pg.)
Early 1997	Piloting activity begins

will probably be late 1997 or early 1998 before SET gains widespread use. In the meantime, both VISA and MasterCard discourage the use of credit cards over open networks such as the Internet. They request that a cardholder use the telephone or the mail to get a card number to a merchant.

4.10 Summary

In this chapter we have outlined a number of network payment methods using payment cards as the underlying method of achieving the financial transfer. The simpler methods, such as FV and CARI, involve no cryptography whatever, while SSL uses quite sophisticated cryptographic techniques to secure the link between customer and merchant. More complex three-way methods such CyberCash , iKP, and SEPP have laid the foundations for the SET protocol which, at the time of writing, is beginning to be deployed. It is expected that this protocol will supplant other schemes, and become the basis of all network transactions involving payment cards in the not too distant future.

REFERENCES

[1]   Information Technology Partners, *Collect All Relevant Information (CARI)*, Milford, CT, 1995, http://www.netresource.com/itp/cari.html

[2]   Sandberg, R., *The Sun Network Filesystem: Design, Implementation and Experience*, Sun Microsystems, Inc., 2550 Garcia Ave, Mountain View, CA 94110, 1983, http://www.sun.com/solaris/networking/nfsindex.html

[3]   Bagwill, R., et al., "Improving the Security of NFS," *Security in Open Systems -NIST Special Publication 800-7*, July 1994, http://csrc.ncsl.nist.gov/nistpubs/800-7/node148.html

[4]   Netresource, *Netresource Web Server*, http://www.netresource.com/itp/

[5]   Hickman, K., *The SSL Protocol*, Netscape Communications Corp., 501 E. Middlefield Rd., Mountain View, CA 94043, Feb. 1995, http://home.netscape.com/newsref/std/SSL.html

[6]   Kocker, P., A. Freier, and P. Karlton, *The SSL Protocol Version 3.0*, Netscape Communications Corp., March 1996, http://home.netscape.com/eng/ssl3/index.html

[7] Simon, D., *The Private Communication Technology Protocol*, Microsoft Corporation, April 1996, http://www.microsoft.com

[8] CyberCash, *CyberCash Web Server*, Reston, VA, 1996, http://www.cybercash.com/

[9] Eastlake 3rd, D., et al., *CyberCash Credit Card Protocol Version 0.8*, RFC 1898, Feb. 1996, ftp://nic.ddn.mil/rfc/rfc1898.txt

[10] Bellare, M., et al., "iKP - A Family of Secure Electronic Payment Protocols," *Proc. 1st USENIX workshop on Electronic Commerce*, New York, NY, July. 11–12, 1995, http://www.zurich.ibm.com/Technology/Security/extern/ecommerce/iKP.html

[11] MasterCard, *Secure Electronic Payment Protocol*, Oct. 1995.

[12] MasterCard and VISA Corporations, *Secure Electronic Transaction (SET) Specification - Book 1: Business Description*, June 1996, http://www.mastercard.com/set http://www.visa.com/

[13] MasterCard and VISA Corporations, *Secure Electronic Transaction (SET) Specification - Book 2: Programmer's Guide*, June 1996, http://www.mastercard.com/set http://www.visa.com/

[14] MasterCard and VISA Corporations, *Secure Electronic Transaction (SET) Specification - Book 3: Formal Protocol Definition*, Aug. 1996, http://www.mastercard.com/set http://www.visa.com/

Chapter 5

Electronic checks

PAPER-BASED PAYMENTS using a check, while still highly popular in the United States, have been falling out of favor in European countries. This process of decline has been encouraged by banks for two reasons. First, paper-based checks are expensive to process. They may involve the transport of the signed check all the way to the bank on which it is drawn before being able to determine that the payment can be made. The expense involved in the so-called *returned items* (bounced checks) means that the average cost per check is quite high. Second, the use of debit cards, where each transaction involves an electronic verification of the availability of funds, has all the properties of a check-based payment without the attendant disadvantages.

It is clear though, that there is a need for a check-like payment system where funds are transferred from the payer's bank account to the payee's bank account at the time the transaction takes place. From the banks point of view, it would be desirable to use existing interbank funds transfer networks as much as possible. This chapter will examine a number of electronic check schemes, some of which are stand-alone in technology terms, and others that make maximal use of the existing interbank infrastructure.

5.1 FSTC electronic check project

The Financial Services Technology Consortium (FSTC) [1] is a group of American banks, research agencies, and government organizations, formed in 1993, that have come together to assist in enhancing the competitiveness of the U.S. financial service industry. There are more than 60 members including Bank of America, Chemical Bank, and CitiBank. Staff from the member organizations come together to undertake technology projects in areas of common interest.

In the area of electronic payments, the consortium have two projects that are of interest. The first is concerned with defining an electronic check whereas the second is entitled "Electronic Commerce," and is primarily concerned with defining what new infrastructure will be required to support all forms of electronic commerce, including that involving electronic checks. The overall strategy of the group is to accommodate new forms of payment and commerce by a process of managed evolution from the methods in use today. This also involves making maximum use of, and causing minimum disruption to, the infrastructure that already exists.

5.1.1 Electronic check concept

As with its paper counterpart, the electronic check will contain an instruction to the payer's bank to make a payment of a specified amount to an identified payee. The fact that the check is in electronic form and is being conveyed across computer networks should allow more flexibility in the handling of the check. New services can be provided, such as the ability to immediately verify funds availability. Security can be enhanced by allowing digitial signature validation and check payments can more easily be integrated into electronic ordering and billing processes.

Figure 5.1 shows the overall concept. A payer would issue a check by assembling much the same information as is present on a paper check. It is assumed that users are enrolled in some kind of public-key-based identity scheme. This presupposes that some organization has issued these identities and is maintaining an appropriate certification infrastructure. At the time of writing, the FSTC has not addressed this issue. By varying the information included in the check, one can produce a variety of different payment types in addition to a conventional check. For example, changing the currency field could produce a traveler's check, whilst applying a bank's digital signature will yield a certified check.

In the FSTC architecture, all individuals capable of issuing electronic checks will be in possession of an electronic checkbook device based on some

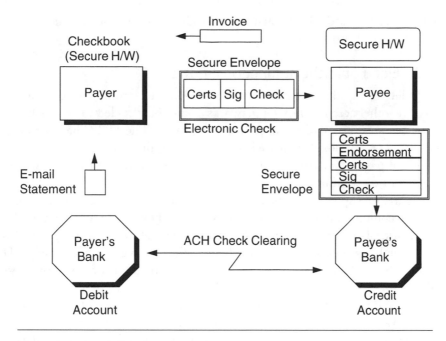

Figure 5.1 The FSTC electronic check concept.

form of secure hardware. The function of this device will be to securely store secret-key and certificate information as well as maintaining a register of what checks have been signed or endorsed recently. Figure 5.1 shows the check being transported to the payee in some kind of secure envelope. The form of this envelope is outside of the architecture and could be sent in a secure e-mail or in an encrypted interactive dialogue between the two parties.

The payee endorses the check when it is received, again making use of a secure hardware device of some sort before forwarding it to the payee's bank. Once it has reached this point, then the FSTC envisage the processing as being identical to that undergone by any paper check today. This means that the banks involved would clear the check using the normal automated clearing house (ACH) or electronic check presentment (ECP) methods.

In September 1995, a demonstration [2] of the FSTC electronic check concept was given that involved a purchase of an item from a merchant site on the Internet. The electronic check was transferred and funds moved from the buyer's bank account to the merchant's account across a conventional ACH network. The "checkbook" used was a secure hardware device, manufactured by Telequip Corporation [3] and called a "Smart Token." This device takes the form of a PC card (also known as a PCMCIA card) with an in-built crypto-graphic support processor.

5.1.2   Electronic check functional flows

The ability to rapidly move the information in an electronic check from one party to another across computer networks means that the electronic check may be used in a variety of different payment scenarios. The FSTC has identified four distinct scenarios[4] that are likely to be of importance.

The *deposit-and-clear* scenario is the first of these and mirrors the way in which most conventional paper checks are used.

Figure 5.2 shows the steps involved. The payer issues an electronic check signed in conjunction with her checkbook device. This is sent to the payee who endorses it, also using a secure hardware device before forwarding it to his bank. The bank will then clear the check with the payer's bank using ACH transfers. Steps 4 and 5 show the banks informing their customers of progress with "report" and "statement" steps. These are not key to the main message flow, and indeed could be paper reports posted out at regular intervals. One of the disadvantages of using the deposit-and-clear scenario is that all parties must have their networking and processing capabilities upgraded to deal with electronic checks, before a single payment can be made.

Figure 5.3 shows an alternative scenario referred to as *cash and transfer*. In this case, while the payee can accept checks electronically, his bank cannot. So in step 2, the payee cashes the check by presenting it to the payer's bank, specifying details of his bank account in the process. The payer's bank

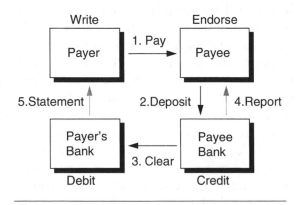

Figure 5.2   Functional flows in the deposit-and-clear scenario.

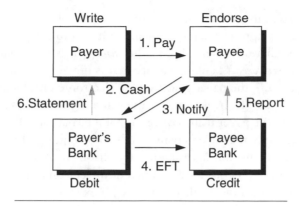

Figure 5.3 Functional flows in the cash-and-transfer scenario.

responds with a *Notify* message and then credits the payee's bank account using a conventional interbank electronic funds transfer (EFT).

The third scenario envisaged by the FSTC is referred to as the *lockbox* scenario. In this case, the electronic check is sent not to the payee, but to his bank. The destination account may be either the payee's primary bank account or a special-purpose account referred to as a lockbox, which is maintained by a bank or other third party on behalf of the payee. The lockbox facility corresponds to a service offered by U.S. banks to corporate clients when dealing with conventional paper-based checks.

Figure 5.4 shows the payee's bank clearing this in step 2 and sending

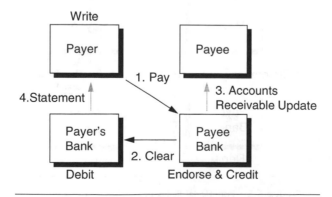

Figure 5.4 Functional flows in the lockbox scenario.

details to the payee in the form of an accounts receivable update. The transaction will ultimately appear in a regular statement sent to the payer.

The final scenario is referred to as the *funds transfer* scenario. It is very similar to the *direct credit* banking facility that is in widespread use today. As shown in Figure 5.5, the payer generates an electronic check and forwards it directly to her bank. The bank transfers the value to the payee's bank account, and debits that of the payer using conventional interbank EFT.

In this case, only the payer's bank needs to be equipped to process electronic checks, as all other flows are handled by existing bank-messaging systems.

The above four scenarios have outlined how electronic checks can be used as a payment method in ways that fit well with existing banking procedures. Nevertheless, banks wishing to take full advantage of the electronic check must provide some new infrastructure to handle this new form of payment. Once again, the emphasis in the FSTC is on causing minimum disturbance to the systems that are already in use.

5.1.3   Check-handling infrastructure

The changes that will be required in a bank's back office processing systems are under investigation by the electronic commerce project team within the FSTC. Their work has a much wider scope than simply the processing of electronic checks, and at the time of writing they had progressed to producing a document [5] detailing design considerations for an electronic payments infrastructure.

The starting point for this infrastructure is the existing set of interbank payment systems that are in place today. Figure 5.6 shows two banks, each

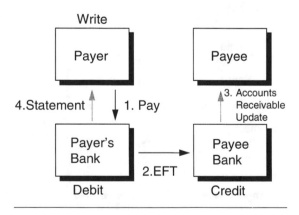

Figure 5.5   Functional flows in the funds transfer scenario.

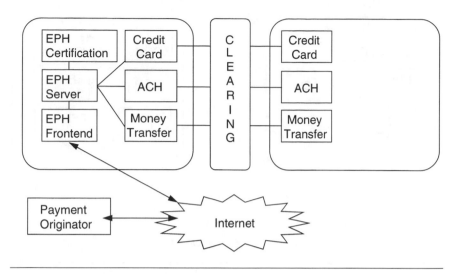

Figure 5.6   The interaction between the electronic payments handler (EPH) and existing payment systems.

equipped with systems for handling credit card transactions, ACH payments, and other forms of electronic money transfers. These systems connect to a variety of clearing networks to allow interbank transactions to take place. The FSTC group proposes that a new system, called the *electronic payments handler* (EPH), be added to those already in existence. This would be divided into a number of subsystems. The front end would interface to the Internet and communicate using its protocols. It would act as a secure line of defense for the EPH as a whole, being the only system that can be directly contacted by other machines on the public network. The core of the EPH system is the EPH server, which will allow many different forms of transactions to be made, including the processing of electronic checks. It would employ the services of the EPH Certification server, whose function is to issue certificates to customers of the bank and allow for their subsequent verification or revocation. The Certification server will also allow other banks' certificates to be verified, and the way the system is organized implies the existence of a banking certification hierarchy.

It is proposed that the EPH be introduced by banks in a phased manner, and Figure 5.6 shows the situation at phase 1. In this case, only the originator's bank is equipped with EPH subsystems and any communication with the other party's bank must take place through existing bank-clearing networks. In terms of the electronic check flows outlined above, this configuration would support

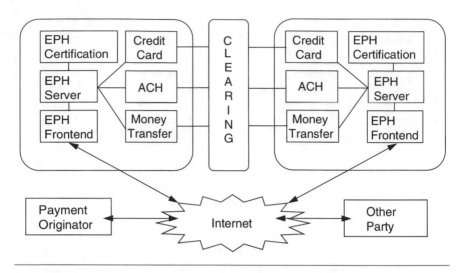

Figure 5.7 Phase 2 of EPH deployment.

the *cash-and-transfer* and *funds transfer* scenarios, but not the *deposit-and-clear* or *lockbox* situations.

In phase 2 of the deployment of the electronic commerce infrastructure, both banks involved in a transaction will be equipped with EPH systems, as shown in Figure 5.7. This configuration will allow all four electronic check flows to be carried out. The EPH systems at either bank can contact either party to the transaction to provide status information if required.

A third phase of EPH deployment is envisaged, but the extensions are concerned with interbank communication and have no bearing on the processing of electronic checks.

While the FSTC has been formulating a strategy for banks to deal with electronic checks, the research community has also been formulating systems that would allow check-like payments across computer networks. The following sections describe two of these.

5.2 NetBill

NetBill is a payment system developed at Carnegie Mellon University [6,7] that the developers claim is optimized for the selling and buying of low-priced information goods. The NetBill transaction protocol begins when a customer requests a quotation for a selected item and ends when a symmetric key is received for unwrapping the encrypted goods delivered during the goods delivery phase.

The participants in the system are shown in Figure 5.5 and consist of customers, merchants, and a NetBill server that maintains accounts for both customers and merchants. These accounts can be linked to conventional accounts in financial institutions. When a customer purchases goods her NetBill account is debited by the appropriate amount and the merchant's account is credited with the value of the goods. A customer's NetBill account can be replenished by transferring funds from her bank. Similarly, funds in a merchant's NetBill account are deposited into the merchant's bank account. NetBill guarantees that a customer pays for only the goods that she successfully receives. A NetBill transaction is similar to a check in that immediate transfers from one identified account to another take place at the time of purchase. The system does, however, lack the generality of a check in that one party must take on a merchant role for a payment to take place.

5.2.1 Protocol overview

NetBill provides transaction support through libraries integrated with different client-server pairs. The client library is called the *checkbook* and the server library is called the *till*. The checkbook and till libraries in turn communicate with the client and merchant applications, respectively. All network communication between the two is encrypted to protect against adversaries. The transaction protocol consists of a minimum of eight steps, shown in Figure 5.9.

Before invoking the NetBill protocol, a user will locate the information required from a server (e.g., a Web server). The NetBill transaction begins

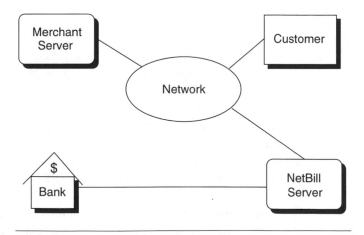

Figure 5.8 The NetBill concept.

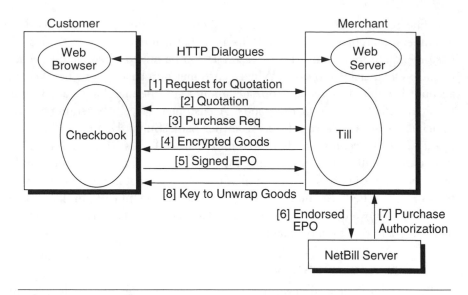

Figure 5.9   Transaction protocol.

when a customer requests a formal quotation from a merchant (Figure 5.9, step 1). There are provisions in the protocol to allow for negotiation of the standard listed price and for group/volume discounts and so forth.

The merchant, on receiving the request for a quotation, determines a price for the user and returns a quotation (step 2). If the customer accepts the price quoted, she instructs the checkbook to send a purchase request (step 3) to the merchant's till. Alternatively, the customer may configure her checkbook to send a purchase request automatically if the price is below a specified amount.

The till, on receiving the purchase request, fetches the goods from the merchant's application. It encrypts them with a one-time key and computes a cryptographic checksum on the result. The till then forwards the result to the customer's checkbook (step 4). The checkbook, on receiving the encrypted message, verifies the checksum. This gives the checkbook confidence that it has received the requested goods intact. Note at this point that the customer cannot decrypt the goods; neither has the customer been charged for them. The checkbook returns a signed electronic payment order (EPO) to the merchant's till (step 5).

At any time before the signed EPO is submitted, a customer may abort the transaction without danger of the transaction being completed against her will. The submission of a signed EPO marks the "point of no return" for the customer. Upon receiving the EPO, the till endorses it and forwards the endorsed EPO to the NetBill server (step 6).

The NetBill server verifies that the price, checksums, and so forth are in order and debits the customer's account for the appropriate amount. It logs the transaction and saves a copy of the one-time key. It returns to the merchant a digitally signed message containing an approval or failure message (step 7). The merchant's application forwards the NetBill server's reply to the customer's checkbook along with the key to unwrap the goods (step 8).

For transactions involving purchase of information goods, all NetBill transactions are atomic. In an ideal situation where only the above eight steps are involved, the NetBill server has to be contacted only once by the merchant. In the case of a dispute, a customer may contact the NetBill server directly. The intention of the designers was to keep the load on the NetBill server to a minimum, thus maintaining good response times.

5.2.2 Authentication procedure

In the course of a NetBill transaction, the parties involved identify themselves. The scheme used in NetBill is a modified version of the Kerberos scheme introduced in Chapter 3. The aim of the modifications is to retain the use of efficient symmetric encryption for the bulk of the traffic, but to decrease the Kerberos server dependency by allowing public keys to be used in certain parts of the protocol exchanges. The resulting scheme is called Public Key Kerberos [7,8].

In traditional Kerberos, if A wishes to communicate with B, a ticket must first be procured (T_{AB}) from a special-purpose server as well as an encryption key (K_{AB}) that will be used to secure the dialog with B. Although it contains K_{AB}, the ticket is not a secret quantity as it can only be decrypted by B. When A wishes to send a message to B, K_{AB} is applied to the data and, including the ticket, A sends the following:

$$T_{AB}, K_{AB} \text{[Message]}$$

When B receives this, he can extract K_{AB} from the ticket and unwrap the message. The message has been kept secret from eavesdroppers, and A has been satisfactorily authenticated.

The NetBill scheme differs from this in that before the communication takes place, A gets the Ticket (T_{AB}) not from a special-purpose server but directly from B in the following manner. A invents a symmetric encryption key, $K_{Challenge}$, and sends it to B in the following message:

$$K_{OneTime}[A, B, \text{TimeStamp}, K_{Challenge}], PK_B[K_{OneTime}], Sig_A$$

It is assumed that both A and B have access to each other's public keys in certificate form. This allows B to validate Sig_A if he wishes to ensure that the source of the message is indeed A. B then uses his private key to reveal $K_{OneTime}$, and thus gets access to the main portion of the message that contains the $K_{Challenge}$. B now constructs a normal Kerberos ticket, T_{AB}, and associated K_{AB}, and returns these to A encrypted with $K_{Challenge}$:

$$K_{Challenge}[T_{AB}, K_{AB}]$$

A invented $K_{Challenge}$ in the first place, and it was shared only with the holder of SK_B (i.e., B). When this message successfully unwraps, A recovers T_{AB} and K_{AB} in plaintext and knows that they were generated by B.

In NetBill, before a transaction occurs, the customer contacts the merchant in the above manner and establishes T_{CM} to be used in subsequent dialogues. Similarly, Merchant servers will establish tickets T_{MN} with the NetBill server and the customer will maintain a T_{CN} for communication (via the merchant) with the NetBill server. The period of validity of the ticket is configurable, but would potentially span many transactions.

5.2.3   Transaction protocol

The NetBill transaction protocol can be divided into three distinct phases. The first phase is where a customer requests a merchant for a quote for one or more identified products. This requires a minimum of two message exchanges or more, if the price must be negotiated. The second is the delivery phase, where the merchant sends encrypted goods to the customer. In the final phase, the customer sends a signed authorization to the NetBill server via the merchant, allowing the purchase to be completed.

5.2.4   Price request phase

When a customer wishes to make a purchase, the following message is sent to the merchant:

$$T_{CM}, K_{CM}[\text{Credentials, PRD, Bid, RequestFlags, TID}]$$

The merchant extracts K_{CM} from the ticket and uses this to unwrap the request for quotation. The most important elements of this are the product request data (PRD), which describes the goods required, and the bid, which is the price being offered by the customer. Other elements include the customers credentials, which specify any group memberships that may merit a discount,

RequestFlags, which give more information on the nature of the purchase, and a unique transaction ID (TID).

On receipt of this message, the merchant will compute a quotation for the goods and send the following message back to the customer:

$$K_{CM}[\text{ProductID, Price, RequestFlags, TID}]$$

The inclusion of the transaction ID (TID) links the quotation back to the original request made by the customer. In the response, the Price and Request-Flags refer to the terms that the merchant is offering rather than those requested by the customer, and the ProductID is a textual description that will appear on the customer's statement if the transaction is completed.

5.2.5   Goods delivery phase

When the price negotiation is completed, the customer accepts the merchant's offer by sending the relevant transaction ID, which signals to the merchant that the goods can now be transferred across the network to the customer:

$$T_{CM}, K_{CM}[\text{TID}]$$

The merchant generates a random key, K_{Goods}, which it uses to encrypt the information being purchased, and then sends the blinded product to the customer:

$$K_{Goods}[\text{Goods}], K_{CM}[SHA[K_{Goods}[\text{Goods}]]], \text{EPOID}$$

The customer can verify the integrity of the goods by applying the secure hash algorithm (SHA) to the goods and checking that it matches that computed by the merchant. She will not, however, be able to decrypt the goods until the payment is made. The electronic payment order ID (EPOID) is a quantity that will be used to uniquely identify this transaction in the NetBill database. It contains fields that identify the merchant as well as timestamp information.

5.2.6   Payment phase

The customer signals a commitment to make the payment by constructing an electronic payment order (EPO). This consists of two sections, the first of which contains details about the transaction and is readable by both the merchant and the NetBill server. The second part contains payment instructions and can only be read by the NetBill server. Since the customer is now encrypting data for the NetBill server, it is assumed that she has already authenticated herself and is in possession of an appropriate ticket, T_{CN}, and corresponding symmetric encryption key K_{CN}.

The transaction portion of the EPO includes the following fields:

- The customer's identity;
- The product ID and price specified in the merchant's quotation;
- The merchant's identity;
- A checksum of the encrypted goods.

The payment instruction portion of the EPO includes:

- A ticket proving the customer's true identity;
- The customer account number;
- A customer memo field.

To start the payment phase, the customer signs the EPO (by appending Sig_C) and sends it to the merchant:

$$T_{CM}, K_{CM}[EPO, Sig_C]$$

The merchant verifies the customer's signature, checks that the product ID, price, and goods checksum are in order before endorsing it and forwarding it to the NetBill server. The endorsement process involves concatenating the merchant's account number (MAcct), a memo field (MMemo), and the key used to encrypt the goods (K_{Goods}), and then signing the result with the merchant's private key to produce Sig_M. The quantity forwarded to the NetBill server is the following:

$$T_{MN}, K_{MN}[(EPO, Sig_C), MAcct, MMemo, K_{Goods}, Sig_M]$$

When the NetBill server receives the endorsed EPO, it unwraps the portion encrypted with K_{MN}, and performs checks on the customer's account. Assuming that the account is in good standing, it transfers the funds, and constructs a signed receipt as follows:

$$Receipt = [ResultCode, C, Price, ProductID, M, K_{Goods}, EPOID] Sig_N$$

The NetBill server includes some account status information with the receipt and sends the following to the merchant:

K_{MN}[Receipt], K_{CN}[EPOID, CAcct, Balance, Flags]

The merchant unwraps the receipt, keeps a copy, and re-encrypts it using K_{CM} before forwarding the message to the customer:

K_{CM}[Receipt], K_{CN}[EPOID, CAcct, Balance, Flags]

The payment has now been made, and the customer can extract K_{Goods} from the receipt and unlock the goods that were delivered earlier. The fields CAcct, Balance, and Flags give all necessary information on the post-transaction status of their NetBill account.

5.2.7   NetBill characteristics

NetBill aims to provide a total payment system, from price negotiation to goods delivery. In the basic scheme, a NetBill transaction requires eight messages to be exchanged. There are many variations within NetBill that allow, for example, the customer to hide her identity from the merchant, for price negotiation to take place, for limited spending authority to be given to others, and for disputes of all kinds to be settled.

All transactions must involve the NetBill server before they can be completed. In communications terms, this is a substantial overhead, especially when the value of the goods is low. The protocol has been designed to ensure that communication between the NetBill server and the other entities involved is kept to a minimum. Despite this, the NetBill server is the obvious bottleneck in the scheme. The smooth running of the system is dependent on the continuous availability of this central server, and since there is no easy way to distribute the load, this will put an upper limit on the number of parties that may participate in the payment system, making it inherently unscalable.

5.3   NetCheque

A second check-like system that is also based on the use of Kerberos [9] is the NetCheque payment system [10–13] developed at the Information Sciences Institute of the University of Southern California. NetCheque is a distributed accounting service consisting of a hierarchy of NetCheque servers (banks) that are used to clear checks and settle interbank accounts. This hierarchy allows for scalability of the system. It also allows users to select the bank of their choice based upon criteria such as trust, proximity, reliability, and so forth. Figure 5.10 depicts such a hierarchy.

A NetCheque account is similar to a conventional bank account against which account holders can write electronic checks. An electronic check is like a conventional paper check in that it contains the customer's signature. Unlike a paper check, it has to also be endorsed by the merchant before the check is paid.

The NetCheque system makes use of Kerberos tickets [13] for creating electronic signatures and endorsing checks. Kerberos is based on symmetric-key cryptography and is thus more computationally efficient than schemes based on public-key algorithms. A NetCheque consists of the following fields:

- Amount of the check;
- Unit of currency;
- Date;
- Account number;
- Payee(s);
- Signature of the customer;
- Endorsement(s) by the merchant and bank(s).

The first five fields of the check are in cleartext and are readable by the bearer of the check. The last two fields are verifiable by the bank against which the check was drawn.

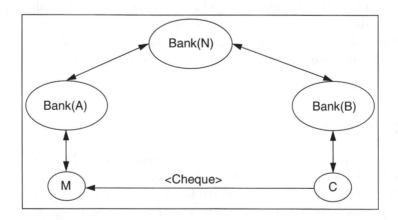

Figure 5.10   Hierarchy of NetCheque servers.

To write a check, a user generates the cleartext portion of the check. He obtains a ticket from a Kerberos server that is used to authenticate him to his bank (B) and allows him to share a session key (K_{CB}) with the bank. He then generates a checksum on the contents of the check and places it in an authenticator (Auth$_C$). He encrypts the authenticator with the session key that he shares with his bank and appends the ticket and the authenticator to the check:

$$Sig_C = [(Auth_C)K_{CB}, T_{CB}]$$

The ticket (T_{CB}) contains a copy of the session key (K_{CB}) and is encrypted with the *secret key* of the customer's bank (B). Figure 5.11 shows the exchange that takes place when a customer sends a signed check to a merchant.

The check can be sent to the merchant through electronic mail over an unsecure network, though in the interest of security it would be prudent to use an encrypted link. The latter requires that the customer obtain an additional Kerberos ticket for the merchant which enables him to share a session key with the merchant and encrypt the link between them.

On receiving a payment a merchant reads the cleartext part of the check and obtains a Kerberos ticket for the customer's bank (B) from a Kerberos server. The merchant generates an authenticator (Auth$_M$) endorsing the check in her name and for deposit into her account (see Figure 5.12). She appends the endorsement and the ticket to the end of the check. The merchant's signature (Sig$_M$) consists of:

$$Sig_M = \{(Auth_M)K_{MB}, T_{MB}\}$$

She then forwards the endorsed check to her bank (A) over a secure link. This can be done by obtaining a separate Kerberos ticket for her own bank (A) and using the shared session key to encrypt the link.

If the merchant and the customer both use different banks, then the merchant's bank sends an indication to the merchant that the check has been deposited for collection. If the check has to be cleared through multiple banks,

{Amt, Unit, Date, AccNo, M, Sig$_C$ }

C ⟶ M

Figure 5.11   Signing a check.

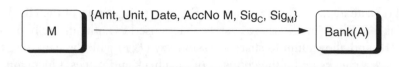

Figure 5.12   Endorsing a check.

each bank attaches its own endorsement to the check, similar to that of the merchant. Once the check has been cleared by the customer's bank, the attached endorsements can be used to trace back the path to the merchant's account and eventually credit her account for the same.

5.4 Summary

The earlier part of this chapter described the ways in which existing banking organizations can introduce a check-based payment system in a phased manner. This differs quite markedly from the NetBill and NetCheque systems designed within the academic research community. The latter are focused on electronic commerce applications where one party acts as a merchant selling goods whilst the FSTC electronic check is a much more general-purpose system. The use of secure hardware within the FSTC solution will limit its usefulness for online purchasing until such time as card reader hardware becomes commonplace on networked workstations.

As with any payment scheme, a major factor in its success is consumer acceptance. Any system backed by big-name banking organizations or indeed the banking industry as a whole will easily build consumer trust. Schemes that have originated in universities are unlikely to be adopted unless they can be taken up by financial organizations that consumers know and trust.

REFERENCES

[1]   Financial Services Technology Consortium, *About the FSTC*, 1995, http://www.fstc.org/about.html

[2]   Telequip Corporation, *FSTC unveils Electronic Checkbook for the Internet*, Nashua, NH, Sept. 21, 1995, http://www.telequip.com/092195.htm

[3]   Jones, M., and B. Schneier, "Securing the World Wide Web: Smart Tokens and their Implementation," *Proc. 4th International World Wide Web Conference*,

Boston, MA, Dec. 11-14, 1995, pp. 397-410,
http://www.w3.org/pub/Conferences/WWW4/Papers/330/

[4]   Financial Services Technology Consortium, *Electronic Payments Infrastructure:
Design Considerations*, 1995,
http://www.fstc.org/projects/commerce/public/epaydes.htm

[5]   Financial Services Technology Consortium, *FSTC Electronic Check Project
Details*, 1995, http://www.fstc.org/projects/echeck/index.html

[6]   Sirbu, M., and J. Douglas Tygar, "NetBill: An Electronic Commerce System
Optimized for Network Delivered Information and Services," *Proc. IEEE
Compcon '95*, San Francisco, CA, March 1995, http://www.ini.cmu.edu/netbill/

[7]   Cox, B., J. Douglas Tygar, and M. Sirbu, "NetBill Security and Transaction
Protocol," Technical Report, Carnegie Mellon University, 1995,
http://www.ini.cmu.edu/netbill/

[8]   Sirbu, M., and J. Chuang, *Public-Key based Ticket Granting Service in Kerberos*,
Carnegie Mellon University/Information Networking Institute, May 1996,
http://www.ini.cmu.edu/netbill/

[9]   Steiner, J. G., B. Clifford Neuman, and J. I. Schiller, "Kerberos: An
Authentication Service for Open Network Systems," *Proc. Usenix Conference*,
Dallas, TX, Feb. 1988, pp. 191-202,
http://nii.isi.edu/info/kerberos/documentation.html

[10] Clifford Neuman, B., and G. Medvinsky, "Requirements for Network Payment:
The NetCheque Perspective," *Proc. IEEE Compcon '95*, San Francisco, CA,
March 1995, http://nii.isi.edu/info/netcheque/documentation.html

[11] University of Southern California Chronicle, *The Check is in the E-mail*,
November 1994,
ftp://prospero.isi.edu/pub/netcheque/information/usc-chronicle-941107/
netcheque-usc-chronicle-941107.html

[12] Clifford Neuman, B., and G. Medvinsky, "NetCheque, NetCash, and the
Characteristics of Internet Payment Services," *MIT Workshop on Internet
Economics 1995*, Massachusetts Institute of Technology (MIT), Cambridge, MA,
March 1995, http://sansfoy.hh.lib.umich.edu/jep/works/NeumNetPay.html

[13] Clifford Neuman, B., "Proxy-Based Authentication and Accounting for
Distributed Systems," *Proc. 13th International Conference on Distributed
Computing Systems*, Pittsburgh, PA, May 1993, pp. 283-291,
http://nii.isi.edu/info/netcheque/documentation.html

Chapter 6

Electronic cash payment systems

IN CHAPTER 2, an analysis of current usage of conventional payment instruments showed that consumers make extensive use of cash. Depending on the country involved, somewhere between 75% and 95% of all transactions are paid in cash, even though the value of these transactions are for the most part quite low. It is difficult to pinpoint exactly what attributes of cash make it attractive, but they would undoubtedly include the following:

- *Acceptability:* Cash is almost universally acceptable as a form of payment, regardless of the transaction amount.

- *Guaranteed payment:* One of the reasons why it is so acceptable is that the physical handing over of the cash completes the transactions and there is no risk that the payment will not be honored at a later stage.

- *No transaction charges:* Cash can be handed from person to person, with no charges levied. There is no authorization required and, consequently, no communications traffic or charges.

- *Anonymity:* Many other forms of payment involve a paper trail linking either or both parties with the transaction. Cash allows transactions to take place anonymously. In addition to being attractive to criminals, this also has appeal for perfectly honest consumers that are worried about the ability of large organizations to monitor their movements and lifestyle.

Attempts to create an electronic cash payment method have focused in on subsets of the above attributes, but to date no system has managed to capture all of the above. In the following section, we examine the more influential systems that claim cash-like attributes.

6.1 Ecash (DigiCash)

DigiCash [1] is a company based in Holland and the United States that specializes in electronic payment systems and digital cash. Its founder, David Chaum, was one of the pioneers in the field, and has been called by some, "the father of digital cash." DigiCash has developed several different payment schemes that provide security and privacy using public-key cryptography. These include solutions for both open and private networks.

Ecash [2–4] was developed by DigiCash to allow fully anonymous secure electronic cash to be used on the Internet. It provides the privacy of paper cash with the added security required for open networks. It is an online software solution allowing payment for information, hard goods, and even pay-out services (where a client might receive back a payment as part of the service). Ecash is said to be fully anonymous because clients withdraw coins from a bank in such a way that the bank cannot know the serial numbers of those coins. The coins can be spent anonymously with a merchant, and even collusion between both the bank and merchant will fail to identify the spender.

Ecash coins worth real monetary value have been available on the Internet since October 1995, when the Mark Twain bank [5,6] of St. Louis, Missouri, started issuing them in U.S. dollars. Strong security is provided in the system through extensive use of both symmetric and asymmetric (public key) cryptography.

6.1.1 The Ecash model

The participants within the system are clients, merchants, and banks, as shown in Figure 6.1. Clients and merchants have accounts at an Ecash bank. Clients can withdraw coins against their account and store them in their Ecash wallet software that resides on their computer. The Ecash wallet software is known as

a *cyberwallet*. It stores and manages a client's coins, keeps records of all transactions, and makes the protocol steps appear as transparent as possible to the
client. The withdrawal protocol prevents the bank from being able to see the
serial numbers of the coins it is issuing.

A client can use the coins to later pay a merchant. At the time of purchase, the
merchant must forward the coins to the minting bank to ensure that they have not
already been spent. If the coins are valid, they will be deposited into the merchant's account. The merchant can then send the purchased goods or a receipt
to the client. A merchant can also make payments to a client using the same
procedure. This is useful for making refunds or providing pay-out services.

Currently, both client and merchant must have accounts at the same Ecash
bank. Coins obtained from one bank will not be accepted by another. As Ecash
becomes more widespread, it is likely that third parties might exchange coins
from different banks or the banks might provide this exchange themselves.
Interbank clearing may also become possible, although coins will still have to
be forwarded to the minting bank for verification.

6.1.2   Ecash coins

The electronic coins used within the Ecash system are unique in that they are
partly minted by the client before being signed by the bank. Each coin has a
serial number that is generated by the client's cyberwallet software. The serial
numbers are chosen randomly and are large enough so that there is very little
chance that anyone else will ever generate the same serial numbers. For example,
using a 100-digit serial number can guarantee this.

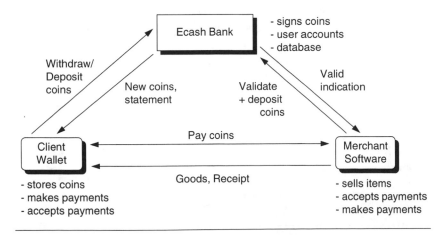

Figure 6.1 Entities and their functions within the Ecash system.

The serial number is blinded and sent to the bank to be signed. This is done using the *blind signature* protocol described in Chapter 3. The bank is unable to see the serial number on the coin it is signing. The method can be considered similar to putting the coin and a piece of carbon paper into an envelope. The envelope is sent to the bank where it is signed and returned to the client, as shown in Figure 6.2. The client opens the envelope and takes out the coin (unblinds it). The coin has now been signed. The carbon paper ensured that the bank's signature went through the envelope. The signature on the unblinded coin appears the same as any other normal digital signature. There is no way to tell from it that the coin was signed using the blind signature protocol.

6.1.3 Coin keys

However, there is a problem with this method. Since the bank cannot see what it is signing, how can a value be assigned to the coin? The value cannot be included with the serial number in the fields of the coin because the bank cannot see this. The client might assign a very high value and tell the bank that it is only a low-valued coin.

The problem can be solved by the bank using a different signature key for each coin denomination. The client informs the bank of the value it wants the blinded coin to be worth. The bank then signs the coin with the signature key representing this denomination and deducts that amount from the client's account. For example the bank might have a one-cent signature, a five-cent signature, a ten-cent signature, and so on. Figure 6.3 shows a coin worth 10 cents.

After the withdrawal process, a coin essentially consists of a serial number encrypted with the appropriate secret key of the bank. This acts as a signature:

$$\{Serial\#\}SK_{Bank's \ \$1 \ Key}$$

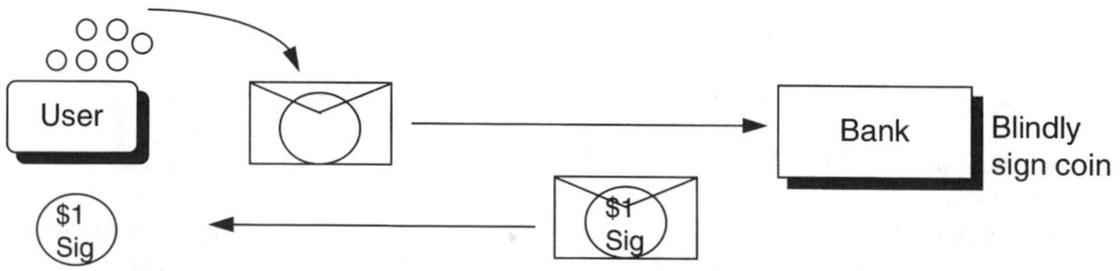

Figure 6.2 Blind signature analogy for withdrawing Ecash coins.

Figure 6.3   An Ecash coin worth 10 cents.

To allow the signature to be quickly verified (decrypted) an indication of which public key to use (*keyversion*) is usually included with a coin. For convenience, the plaintext serial number is also included:

$$\text{Coin} = \text{Serial\#, keyversion, }\{\text{Serial\#}\}\text{SK}_{\text{Bank's \$1 Key}}$$

Keyversion can be used to obtain other information about the coin, including its value, currency, and expiry date. This information is exchanged and stored during initial account setup with a bank, or again during withdrawal. The public keys needed to verify each different valued signature are also sent to the client at this time.

6.1.4 Double-spending prevention

Like other forms of electronic cash, Ecash coins are just pieces of data that can be copied. To prevent copied coins being spent repeatedly, this possible double spending must be prevented. Since the bank cannot see the serial numbers on the coins it issues, it cannot record these during a withdrawal. While providing full anonymity, this makes the bank's task of preventing double spending all the more difficult.

To ensure that a serial number is not spent twice, the minting bank must record every coin that is deposited back to that bank. A very large database of *all spent serial numbers* soon develops. A valid unspent coin must:

- Be signed, with any denominational signature, by the bank;
- Have an expiry date associated with it that is later than the present date;
- Not appear in the database of spent coins.

The third requirement can only be checked by the minting bank that maintains the database, and thus coins must be forwarded to it for online verification during a purchase, as shown in Figure 6.4.

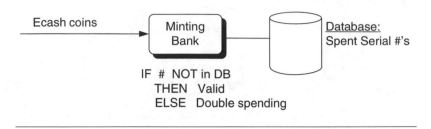

Figure 6.4   Preventing double spending of Ecash coins.

When a valid coin is accepted, it then becomes spent and its serial number is entered into the database. An attempt to spend the coin again should fail. Like many electronic cash schemes, Ecash coins can only be spent once.

Clearly, the size of the Ecash database could become very large and unmanageable. By using expiry dates with coins, the serial numbers of those coins can be removed after the expiry date. Coins that have expired will not be accepted as legal tender. The wallet software can automatically ensure that coins are returned to the bank before they expire. The bank host machine needs to have an internal scalable structure to cope with the size of the database. To further handle the problem of scalability, multiple banks, each minting and managing their own currency with interbank clearing, could be used. Even still, if a large number of people start to use Ecash regularly, the system may begin to show unacceptable delays and signs of overloading.

6.1.5   Withdrawing coins

Figure 6.2 shows an analogy of the blind signature protocol used to withdraw coins. The cryptographic protocol used is now examined. Ecash uses the RSA public-key algorithm. As described in Chapter 3, a public key consists of a modulus m ($m = p \cdot q$) and a number e (the public encryption key), in the RSA scheme. The secret key is a number denoted by d. To create key pairs for different denominations, different values of e and d are generated for the same modulus m.

To withdraw a coin the following steps occur:

1. The user's wallet software chooses a blinding factor r at random.

2. The serial number of the coin, serial#, is blinded by multiplying it by the blinding factor raised to the power of the public exponent ($e2$) for the requested denomination:

$$\text{serial\#} \quad \cdot \quad r^{e2} \quad (\bmod m)$$

Here, $e2$ is the public key for the 2-cent denomination key pair.

3. The bank signs the coin with its 2-cent secret signature key ($d2$):

$$(\text{serial\#} \; \cdot \; r^{e2})^{d2} \quad (\text{mod}\,m) \quad = \text{serial\#}^{d2} \; \cdot \; r^{e2 \cdot d2} \quad (\text{mod}\,m)$$
$$= \text{serial\#}^{d2} \; \cdot \; r \quad\quad (\text{mod}\,m)$$

The bank cannot see the serial# since it does not know r. The signed blinded coin is returned to the user.

4. The user divides out the blinding factor:

$$\frac{\text{serial\#}^{d2} \; \cdot \; r}{r} \quad (\text{mod}\,m) \quad = \quad \text{serial\#}^{d2} \quad (\text{mod}\,m)$$

The signed coin is what remains. This appears as a normal RSA signature (encryption with a private key):

$$serial\#^{d2} \quad = \quad \{serial\#\}SK_{\text{Bank's 2 cent Key}}$$

It cannot be linked to the withdrawal. In this way, *full anonymity* may be maintained.

Many coins of different denominations, specified by the client, can be obtained in a single withdrawal request. The request must be signed with the client's secret key, and the whole request is protected by encrypting it with the bank's public key (PK_{Bank}). This key is distinct from the public coin keys. The withdrawal request contains the unsigned blinded coins and an indication of the denominations required. Figure 6.5 shows the effective withdrawal request

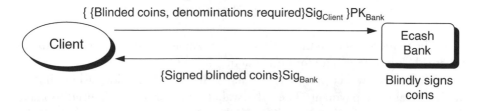

Figure 6.5   Messages used to withdraw Ecash coins.

without all of the implementation optimizations. A combination of both symmetric and asymmetric cryptography is used in the actual implementation for efficiency:

$$\{K_{Ses}\}PK_{Bank}, \{request, \{H(request)\}SK_{Client}\}K_{Ses}$$

For efficiency, the signature on a message consists of the request and a hash of the request encrypted with the signer's private key:

$$\{request\}Sig_X \ = \ \{request, \{H(request)\}SK_X\}$$

The symmetric algorithm that is currently used is triple-DES in CBC mode (see Chapter 3). The secure hash algorithm (SHA) is used to perform hashes.

After the bank has blindly signed the coins and debited the user's account, they are returned to the user. The withdrawal response is signed by the bank as shown in Figure 6.5. The message is not encrypted because only the client who knows the blinding factor can unblind the coins and later spend them.

6.1.6   An Ecash purchase

Once a client has Ecash coins stored in his cyberwallet software, he can spend these coins with a merchant. The client decides which item(s) to buy and places the order with the merchant. This might be done by submitting a form at a merchant's Web site. The initial shopping and ordering protocols are outside the scope of the Ecash protocols, but methods in which Ecash is integrated with the Web are discussed later.

Having received an order, the merchant sends a *payment request* to the client's cyberwallet. This message contains details about the order amount, the currency to be used, the current time, the merchant's bank, the merchant's account ID at that bank, and a description of the order:

$$payreq = \{currency, amount, timestamp, merchant\_bankID,$$
$$merchant\_accID, description\}$$

The request is sent in the clear, which might allow an eavesdropper to see what is being ordered and for how much.

The client's wallet presents the user with this information, asking if they wish to make the payment. The cyberwallet may also be configured to make payments automatically to specific merchants or for specific amounts. If the user decides to pay, coins valuing the requested amount are gathered from the wallet. The exact amount must be sent to the merchant because accepting change could compromise the user's anonymity (the merchant could record the serial numbers of the change and collude with the bank to reveal the user's identity). The cyberwallet will automatically assemble the correct amount and can withdraw new coins from the bank if more denominations are required.

6.1.7 Making the payment

The coins used in payment are encrypted with the bank's public key (PK_{Bank}) before they are sent to the merchant. This prevents them being stolen in transit and prevents the merchant being able to examine or tamper with them. The merchant forwards the coins to the bank to deposit them in her account. The payment message, sent to the merchant and later forwarded to the bank, consists of information about the payment and the encrypted coins:

$$\text{payment} = \{\text{payment\_info},\{\text{Coins}\}PK_{Bank}\}$$

The payment information includes details about the bank, amount, currency, number of coins, current time, and merchant IDs amongst other things:

$$\text{payment\_info} = \{\text{bankID,amount,currency,ncoins,timestamp,merchant\_IDs,}$$
$$H(\text{description}),H(\text{payer\_code})\}$$

The payment information is forwarded to the bank, along with the encrypted coins, during the merchant's deposit. A hash of the order description is included with the payment information. Since the merchant already knows the order, she can compare this value with a hash of her copy of the order, to verify that the client agrees on exactly what is being purchased. When the payment information is forwarded to the bank, it cannot know what is being purchased since only a hash of the order description is included.

6.1.8 Proving payment

Payer_code is a secret generated by the client. A hash of it, $H(\text{payer\_code})$ is included in the payment information so that the client can later prove to the bank, after the merchant has deposited the coins, that he made the payment. The bank will record that the merchant deposited a payment containing $H(\text{payer\_code})$. If the client reveals payer_code, the bank can be certain that the creator of payer_code (that is, the client) made the payment.

However, for this to work, the bank needs to be assured that *payment_info* was not tampered with between the time it left the client and the time it was deposited by the merchant into the bank. If it could be altered, the value of H(payer_code) could be changed. To prevent this, a hash of the payment_info is included with the coins before they are encrypted:

$$\{Coins, H(Payment\_info)\}\ PK_{Bank}$$

When the bank receives the payment, it will generate its own hash of the payment_info. If this matches the value encrypted with PK_{Bank}, which only it can decrypt, then it can be assured that the message was not altered. The full payment message is now:

$$payment = \{payment\_info,\{Coins,H(payment\_info)\}PK_{Bank}\}$$

The payer (client) remains anonymous, unless they decide later to prove the payment. The payee (merchant) is not anonymous as she must deposit the coins and she is identified in the payment information constructed by the client.

6.1.9   Payment deposit

Upon receiving the payment message, the merchant forwards it to the bank as part of a deposit request:

$$deposit = \{\ \{payment\}Sig_{Merchant}\ \}PK_{Bank}$$

The deposit may optionally be signed by the merchant and encrypted with the bank's public key. The bank checks that the coins have not been spent (double spending) and credits the merchant's account. An indication of success is returned to the merchant:

$$deposit\_ack = \{result,amount\}Sig_{Bank}$$

A similar deposit message format can be used by a client to return unspent coins to a bank.

Having received a good payment, the merchant may return the purchased item or a receipt to the client. If the merchant fails to do so, the client can prove that the payment was made and accepted by revealing the payer_code.

6.1.10 Integration with the Web

Figure 6.6 shows how Ecash is normally integrated with the Web at present. The client runs the cyberwallet software and a Web browser side by side. When

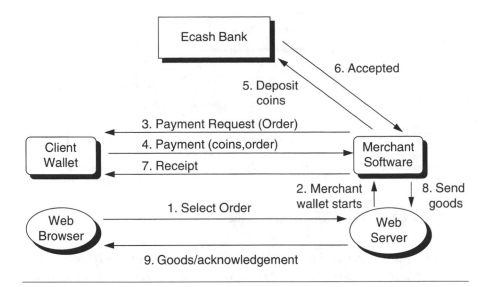

Figure 6.6 Using Ecash with the World Wide Web.

an order is selected from a merchant's Web page, the merchant's Ecash software is automatically started by means of a common gateway interface (CGI) script [7]. The CGI simply provides a means of running a program from a Web server and allowing it to pass back results through that server. The merchant software proceeds with the Ecash purchase as before. If the payment was successful, the item or purchase indication may be returned through the Web to the client's browser as shown (steps 8 and 9). This method has the advantage that it can be easily integrated with most Web browsers and servers.

6.1.11 Ecash in the mail

Ecash payments may also be made using electronic mail. The merchant still contacts the bank, through e-mail, to deposit the coins and prevent double spending before delivering the goods. The coins are protected in the same way as with the online protocol.

6.1.12 Transferring Ecash

User to user transfer of Ecash is possible, although the amount transferred still has to be forwarded to the bank for verification. The exchange uses the same protocols as with an Ecash purchase, as shown in Figure 6.7. The coins are forwarded through the payee to the bank where they are deposited. New coins worth the same amount are then returned to the payee. This is all done transparently

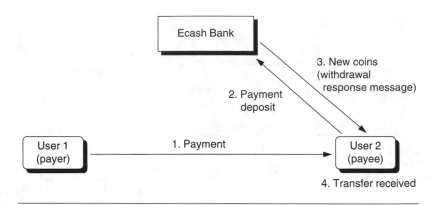

Figure 6.7   User to user transfer of Ecash.

by the software so that it appears that the new coins were received directly from the payer. Currently, as with merchant payments, both users must have accounts at the same Ecash bank in order to perform a user to user transfer.

6.1.13 Lost coins

If the network fails or the computer crashes during a payment transaction, coins might be lost. There is a mechanism available to recover the value of these lost coins. The client whose coins have been lost notifies the minting bank of this occurrence. The bank then sends the exact messages from the last n withdrawals to the client. Currently $n = 16$, so that all the signed blinded coins from the last 16 withdrawals are sent, as shown in Figure 6.8.

The client must still have the blinding factor used for these withdrawals; otherwise, the coins cannot be unblinded. The client's wallet will unblind all

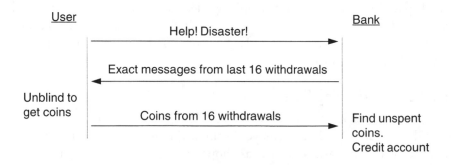

Figure 6.8   Recovering lost Ecash coins.

the coins and then deposit them into the client's account at the bank. It is necessary to deposit the coins because it will not be known which coins from the last 16 withdrawals have already been spent and which have not. The bank will check each coin deposited to see if it has already been spent or not. This is the normal verification to prevent double spending. The client's account will be credited the unspent amount. The value of any lost coins will have been recovered and the client can now withdraw new coins to spend.

6.1.14 Ecash and crime

There is a concern that fully anonymous electronic cash, like paper cash, will help to hide the identity of criminals. There are fears that it could be used for money laundering, tax evasion, bribes, black markets, and other such crimes.

With Ecash, only the payer (client) is anonymous. The payee (merchant) who receives a payment must deposit it into a bank account to validate the coins. The bank can monitor the deposits of suspected criminals. However, it would still be possible for a criminal to accept payments under the guise of a legal business. As described in an earlier section, it is also possible for a payer to prove to a bank that he made a payment. Thus, with the cooperation of the client who made the payment, the payee can be identified as accepting that payment.

While the person who receives a payment can be monitored, new coins that have been withdrawn are completely anonymous. The cryptographer Bruce Schneier described how to commit the "perfect crime" [8] and obtain such anonymous coins:

- An anonymous kidnapper takes a hostage.
- The kidnapper then prepares a large number of blinded coins. These are sent anonymously to the bank as a ransom demand.
- The bank signs the coins due to the hostage situation.
- The kidnapper demands that the signed blinded coins be published in a public place such as a newspaper or on television. This will prevent the pick up being traced. Nobody else can unblind the coins.
- The kidnapper can safely take the blinded coins from the newspaper or television and save them on computer. The coins are then unblinded and the kidnapper now has a fortune in anonymous digital cash.

6.1.15 Developing Ecash applications

DigiCash has produced a high-level application programming interface (API) for programmers developing applications that use Ecash as a payment method.

The Ecash software developer's kit [9] provides a library, in the C programming language that implements this API. It is available with source code for several popular platforms.

6.1.16 Magic Money

Magic Money [10] is another implementation of fully anonymous digital cash using blind signatures. It has many similarities with the Ecash system and was designed for experimental purposes by a group of cryptographic enthusiasts, known as cypherpunks, on the Internet. The source code is available in C and there is an example client program that can automatically accept and pay out Magic Money currency.

6.1.17 Remarks

An Ecash trial using a virtual currency called *cyberbucks*, was launched on the Internet in October 1994. By early 1996, over 30,000 participants had taken part in the trial and registration for new participants was closed. The Mark Twain Bank of St. Louis, Missouri, was the first bank to issue Ecash worth real monetary value (in this case, U.S. dollars). Since then, several other banks and Internet service providers have started issuing Ecash in various currencies.

Ecash provides secure, fully anonymous electronic cash for open networks. The Ecash software has been integrated with both the Web and e-mail. While payments as low as one cent are possible using Ecash, the computationally intensive cryptography, multiple messages, and database lookups prevent it from being used for efficient repeated micropayments. Also, the scalability of the system is perhaps limited by the cost of maintaining and searching a large database of all spent serial numbers during a purchase.

6.2 Project CAFE

The research that led to the Ecash product has continued. CAFE (Conditional Access for Europe) was a project funded under the European Community's ESPRIT program [11,12]. It began in 1992 and lasted for a duration of three years. The aim of the project was to develop a general system to administer rights to users (e.g., access to confidential data, entry to buildings, and so forth.) The most significant outcome of the project was the development of an advanced electronic payment system. The CAFE protocols are based on the idea of untraceable electronic cash proposed by David Chaum [13] and the concept of checks with counters as described in [14]. CAFE is thus a hybrid scheme in the sense that it offers all the benefits of anonymous electronic cash but at the same time lets the user sign checks up to a specified amount. Unlike other electronic payment schemes, the CAFE protocols allow for security of all parties involved in the system. Strong state-of-the-art cryptographic techniques are employed to protect all payment transactions, thus guaranteeing the security of the financial institutions. The use of tamper-resistant devices and observers ensures the security of the users of the system.

6.2.1   Goals of CAFE

CAFE is designed to be a universal, prepaid, offline payment system with multiparty security. The following are the salient features of the system:

- *Multiparty security:* Most existing systems provide *one-sided security* (i.e., the security of the financial institutions or money issuers from attack by fraudulent users). The designers of CAFE have found this to be inadequate to address the needs of users of electronic payment systems and designed the CAFE protocols around the idea of multiparty security. The security of each entity in the system is guaranteed without the need to trust a third party. This implies that each party must be able to trust the device that they are using. Also, procedures and algorithms used in the protocol must be open and available for inspection by all.

- *Offline payments:* There is no need for a payee (merchant) to contact a central database, usually maintained by an electronic currency issuer, at the time of purchase. This reduces the costs of maintaining/establishing a communications channel between the two.

- *Detection of double spending:* The CAFE protocols rely on tamper-resistant devices to provide the basic security of the system. If, however, under extreme circumstances the tamper resistance of a device is broken, then double spending can take place. The cryptographic protocols are designed such that double spending of electronic currency will be detected with a very high probability. This detection is achieved at a cost of maintaining a database of recently spent payment slips by the financial institutions.

- *Untraceable payments:* Under normal circumstances, payments cannot be linked to a user even if there is collaboration between the merchants and the banks. The identity of a user is, however, revealed if he double spends a payment slip. As with current banking procedures, the identity of the payee is not protected.

6.2.2   Architecture

The CAFE architecture is similar to most other payment systems in that there are three main participants in the protocols. They are the customers, merchants, and the financial institutions. We elaborate on the role of each briefly:

- *Payer:* A payer (customer) is equipped with a tamper-resistant device such as a smart card or an electronic wallet, which is used to store electronic currency and make payments.

- *Payee:* A payee (merchant) will receive electronic payments from customers in exchange for goods or services. She will deposit the payment with her bank (at a later stage) for clearance.

- *Bank:* A bank's role can be divided further into an *issuer/acquirer* of electronic currency. The issuer loads electronic money into a customer's account and ensures that the correct amount is debited from the customer's account. The acquirer accepts deposits from merchants and clears them through existing interbank clearing channels.

Figure 6.9 shows an overview of the protocol exchanges that take place between the various entities in the system.

6.2.3   CAFE devices

There are a number of tamper resistant secure electronic devices used in the CAFE system. These devices are used to store electronic money by the user, perform cryptographic operations and to make payments to merchants.

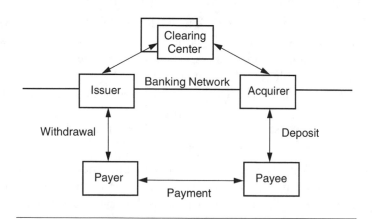

Figure 6.9   CAFE architecture.

- *Smart card:* This is the simplest of the devices used in the protocol. It is similar to a credit card and has an embedded microprocessor powered by an external source. All the information is stored on the chip, which also performs the cryptographic computations. It is referred to as the α (alpha) system.

- *Wallets:* A wallet consists of two parts that work in conjunction with each other. One part is known as an *observer* (see Chapter 3) and protects the bank's interests and the other is known as the *purse* and protects the user's interests. The purse includes a keyboard and a display. This further protects the user as he can enter his PIN on the purse and does not have to trust any third-party device. Furthermore, all communications between the wallet and the outside world are done exclusively through the purse, guaranteeing that the observer cannot divulge any secret information to the bank without the user's knowledge.

  1. *Two-button wallet* (α^+): The two-button wallet, as its name suggests, consists of a two-button keyboard and a digital display. The observer module is implemented as a smart card that also performs all the transactions. The purse monitors, verifies, and relays all communication from the smart card via an infrared interface to the payment terminal. The α^+ system is fully compatible with the α system.

  2. *Full wallet:* The full wallet (see Figure 6.10) has a full numeric keyboard and a display larger than that used in the α^+ device. The full keyboard allows the user to also enter amounts and PINs. The observer is implemented as a built-in smart card microprocessor. Unlike the smart card in the α system, the observer exclusively protects the interests of the bank. The wallet uses an adapted version of the protocols in the α system and ensures better privacy for the user. The full-wallet system is called the Γ (gamma) system and is compatible with the α and α^+ systems. In addition, it has a slot into which an α smart card can be inserted and money can be transferred.

6.2.4   Role of observers

Observers, or guardians as they are also known in CAFE, are devices implanted into a smart card to protect the interests of the financial institutions. They ensure the correctness of all transactions performed by the user. A user will not be able

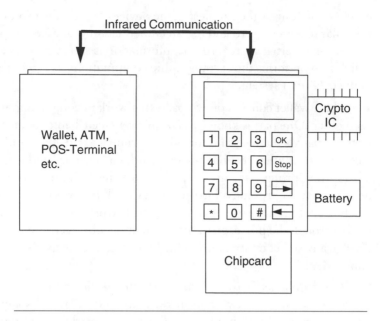

Figure 6.10   A full CAFE wallet.

to successfully complete a payment transaction without the cooperation of an observer. Also, genuine merchants will not accept payments that have not been authorized by a certified observer. An observer approves each payment in a manner similar to creating a digital signature. The form of this approval is such that one cannot obtain either the identity of the observer or the user from it.

6.2.5   Protocol overview

CAFE employs two types of security mechanisms to protect the system against attack. The first line of defense is the use of secure tamper-resistant devices to store cryptographic keys and to perform all cryptographic transactions. Protection against double spending is only guaranteed as long as the tamper resistance is not compromised. CAFE has a cryptographic fallback mechanism that allows the financial institutions to detect double spending of electronic currency (after it has been spent) and blacklist suspected users. The banks distribute these lists to all the merchants in the system.

6.2.6   Offline coins

The CAFE system uses the idea of offline coins first proposed in [15] as a fallback mechanism. At a very simple level, a CAFE offline coin is one where the identity of the payer is encoded into the coin number, which is constructed from two parts. When the coin is used in a payment transaction, the payer must reveal one part of the coin. If the same coin is used again, the user will have to reveal the second part of the coin. The coin is constructed in such a way that revealing a single part of the coin will not identify the payer, but if the coin is double spent, then the identity of the payer is revealed.

The following analogy will help to explain how the system works. The identity (I) of the user is encrypted with a one-time random number (P). The coin consists of two parts. The first part contains the encrypted identity $I \oplus P$, while the other part contains the key P. Each part is further encrypted with a commitment (encryption) scheme to produce $C(I \oplus P)$ and $C(P)$. In one payment transaction, the payer will have to open one of the commitments, which will be either $I \oplus P$ or P, which does not reveal the identity of the payer. However, if the other part is opened, then the identity of the payer will be found out. To detect such double spending, a bank maintains a database of all recently deposited coins and searches for corresponding pairs before clearing payment transactions. More efficient versions of the scheme are used in the actual system.

The concept of untraceable offline coins was proposed in [16] and is used as a starting point in the design of the α and Γ protocols. A *payment slip* in CAFE refers to a "k-spendable instrument" consisting of k parts, where each part can be spent once during a payment transaction. All signatures except signatures on payment slips are Schnorr signatures [17]. The Schnorr scheme proposes an efficient way to create digital signatures and minimizes the work to be done by the smart card. This is important since the 8-bit processor smart cards currently used in CAFE are rather limited. The scheme requires about 12 modular multiplication's for a single signature generation and most of the work can be done in the background (i.e., during the idle time of the processor).

6.2.7   The α protocol

The α (alpha) protocol refers to the set of protocols used by the smart card. There are a number of primitives, ranging from withdrawal of electronic currency to recovery of the value in lost cards.

6.2.7.1   Withdrawal

A payer usually only needs to communicate with the bank through a withdrawal session, which results in a number of blank electronic payment slips being loaded into his smart card. The bank keeps track of the balance in the card by means of a counter in the observer part of the smart card. The balance is updated during a withdrawal request and the corresponding amount deducted from the user's bank account. A withdrawal session consists of the following steps:

- The user's smart card sends the identity of his bank and information about his bank's public-key certificate to the terminal. This allows the terminal to connect to the correct bank and verify/update the bank's public-key certificate stored in the smart card.

- The card and bank then mutually authenticate each other through the terminal. The card generates a random number and sends it to the bank. The bank signs this with its secret key and returns the signature. The card verifies the signature using the public key of the bank. The card in turn authenticates itself to the bank by signing a random quantity sent by the bank. In addition, it also sends a snapshot of its currency table (counters). The bank verifies the signature.

- In order to ensure that the bank can identify double spending of payment slips, a public key (PK_{Id}) derived from the user's secret key (SK_{User}) is incorporated into the payment slips. To protect the identity of the user, the card blinds this value.

A payment slip consists of:

1. PK_{Blind}, which is a blinded version of PK_{Id}. This value also serves as a slip identifier.

2. Two auxiliary one-time public keys PK_1 and PK_2, which are not known to the bank.

Figure 6.11 shows the overall process of obtaining a blank payment slip from a bank. The user generates a payment slip and forwards the hash H(Payslip) of it to the bank. The bank creates a digital signature (Sig_{Bank}) on the forwarded hash. The signature binds the payment slip to the two one-time public keys PK_1 and PK_2. The user needs to only store the bank's signature on the card as all the other values can be regenerated by him at the payment stage. This allows for efficient storage of payment slips.

6.2.7.2 Payment

The payment transaction consists of the user filling in an amount into a blank payment slip together with the name of the payee, signed with the user's secret key. Figure 6.12 shows the steps involved in a payment transaction.

The protocol details are as follows:

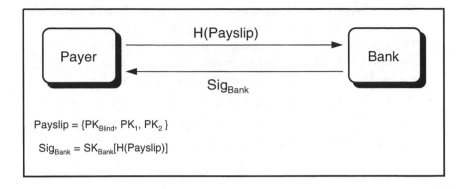

Figure 6.11   Generation of payment slips.

- A customer inserts her card into a merchant's (payment) terminal. The terminal tells the card the identity of the payee, the date, the amount to be deducted from the currency table, and so forth. This information is encoded by the card into the payment slip (M).

- The card regenerates the next payment slip to be used. This consists of generating the secret quantities and the one-time public keys. This is the most time-consuming part of the protocol and is usually done in the background while the payment parameters are being negotiated by the user and the merchant.

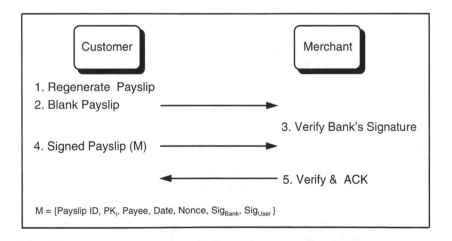

Figure 6.12   Payment transaction.

- The card sends the blank payment slip to the merchant, consisting of the bank's signature and the public keys needed to use the slip (PK_1, PK_2 where $i = 1$ or 2 depending on whether the slip is being used the first or second time). The payment slip is marked as being spent by the card even though the payment has not been completed yet.

- The terminal verifies the signature of the bank on the blank payment slip.

- The card prepares a message corresponding to the contents of the payment slip. It contains the following fields:

  1. The public keys of the payment slip PK_{Blind} (slip identity) and PK_i;
  2. Merchant ID;
  3. Date;
  4. Amount;
  5. Random string to ensure uniqueness of the message;

  The message is signed with the secret key of the user (SK_{User}) and the random strings used to generate the payment slip. This results in a digital signature Sig_{User}.

- The terminal verifies that the payment has the proper form. It does this in conjunction with the blank payment slip sent previously.

When the payment has been finalized, the terminal sends an acknowledgment to the card. The card updates its counters.

6.2.7.3   Deposit

On accepting a payment slip, the payee forwards it to the acquirer (at a later date) who in turn clears it through the existing financial clearing system. The acquirer:

- Verifies the contents of the payment slip and validates the bank's signature;

- Verifies that the payment slip has not been deposited previously.

- Looks for a matching pair PK_i in its database to verify that the corresponding part of the payment slip has not been spent previously.

If the first two conditions are fulfilled, the payee is entitled to be credited for the amount of the payment. A payee is responsible for checking all received payment slips against their local copies of the blacklist during a payment protocol. If a blacklisted slip is detected, the payee aborts the transaction. If a payee fails to check received payment slips against the blacklist, then he will have to accept responsibility for them as the clearing center will reject them. When the clearing center detects double spending, the payment slip will immediately be added to the blacklist.

6.2.8 The Γ protocol

The Γ (gamma) protocols are a modular extension of the α system. The Γ wallet consists of a purse that is capable of performing public-key cryptography. All communications between the observer and the outside world take place via the purse. This provides additional security for the user as the purse will blind/neutralize any communications that may disclose secret information about the user to the outside world. The Γ wallet is able to hold more payment slips than the α smart card. There is an onboard power supply which enables the wallet to compute intensive precomputations in the background. A user is also able to transfer a value from his Γ wallet to his α smart card. This feature is useful if the user does not want to carry his wallet around with him or only wants to carry a small amount on person.

6.2.9 Additional features

The basic CAFE system has the following additional features:

- *Multiple currencies:* The CAFE wallets have several "pockets" for different currencies. Like cash, the user may either exchange currency at the bank (lowering the amount in one pocket and increasing it another) or pay in nonlocal currency if the merchant accepts it.

- *Fault and loss tolerance:* If a user loses her wallet, the bank can recover the money from a backup and the deposit transcripts. This is done by regular backups during a withdrawal transaction. If a user wants to recover lost money, she reveals the identity of the payment slips stored after the last withdrawal. This enables the bank to track these payment slips.

6.2.10 Remarks

CAFE is an advanced payment mechanism that makes use of secure tamper-resistant devices such as smart cards and strong cryptographic protocols. It provides untraceable electronic payments and guarantees the security of all parties concerned. This feature is an important selling point for most consumers who are currently skeptical about the use of other payment systems that only provide for the security of the financial organizations.

6.3 NetCash

NetCash [18–20] is an identified online electronic cash system, for open networks developed at the Information Sciences Institute of the University of Southern California. It consists of distributed currency servers that mint electronic coins and issue these coins to users of the system, accepting electronic checks in payment for them. The system is *online* in that each coin must be verified as being valid and unspent by forwarding it to the minting currency server for verification during a purchase. Although the digital cash is *identified*, with each coin having a unique serial number, there is an exchange mechanism to provide *limited anonymity*. Anyone with valid coins can exchange them anonymously with a currency server for new ones.

NetCash is a macropayment system suitable for selling hard goods, information, or other network services. Users can both make and accept payments. It is a software-only solution, requiring no special hardware; both asymmetric and symmetric cryptography are used to provide the network security of the system and to limit fraud. All parties must have their own public/private key pair (PK_X,SK_X). The use of multiple currency servers allows the system to *scale*; that is, to handle the addition of users and usage without causing performance to significantly drop.

6.3.1 Framework/model

The NetCash system consists of buyers, merchants, and currency servers, as shown in Figure 6.13. Since there are multiple currency servers, a user might choose one that is geographically close and trustworthy. A currency server provides the following four services to its clients (buyers or merchants):

- Verifying coins, to prevent double spending;
- Issuing coins in return for payment by electronic check;
- Buying back coins, giving an electronic check in return;
- Exchanging valid coins for new ones, which thus provides some anonymity.

NetCheque [21–23] (see Chapter 5) is proposed to provide the electronic check infrastructure required to bring monetary value into and out of the

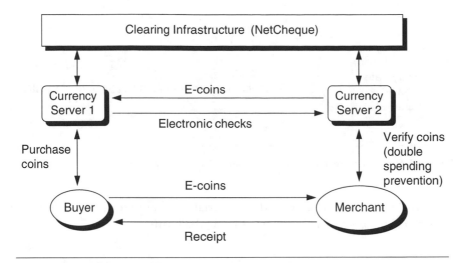

Figure 6.13   The NetCash system.

NetCash system. Not only can clients buy and sell NetCash coins in exchange for electronic checks, but NetCash servers can use electronic checks to settle debts between themselves.

When a buyer is making a purchase from a merchant, both parties may use different currency servers. The buyer may have bought coins from one currency server (CS1), but the merchant may want to verify these coins through her local currency server (CS2). Coins can only be ultimately verified by the currency server who minted them. CS2 will have to forward the coins received from the merchant to CS1 to be verified. In return for valid coins, CS1 will generate an electronic check for CS2. In turn, CS2 can either issue new coins to the merchant or send an electronic check in exchange for the valid coins minted by CS1. All the checks can be cleared through the NetCheque accounting and clearing infrastructure. While NetCheque is the clearing mechanism proposed, it is conceivable that any other similar electronic check scheme or clearing infrastructure could be used.

If CS2 indicates to the merchant that the coins were valid, a receipt and/or the purchased goods can be returned to the buyer. The structure of a NetCash coin and the protocols involved in making a basic purchase are now examined in turn.

6.3.2 NetCash coins

An *electronic coin* is a piece of data representing monetary value within an electronic cash system. NetCash uses *identified electronic cash*, where each coin

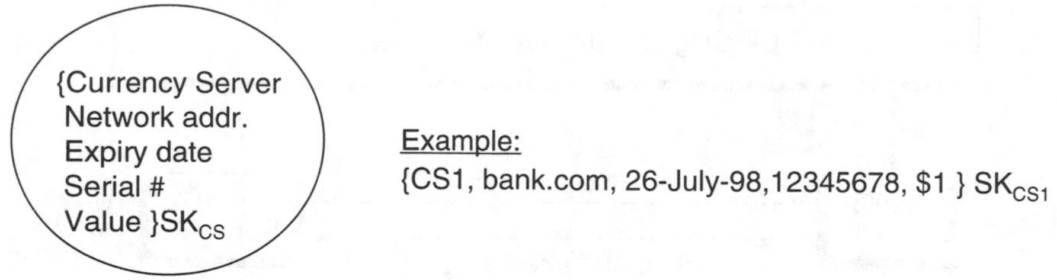

{Currency Server
Network addr.
Expiry date
Serial #
Value }SK$_{CS}$

Example:
{CS1, bank.com, 26-July-98,12345678, $1 } SK$_{CS1}$

Figure 6.14   Structure and example contents of a NetCash coin.

is minted by a currency server and has a serial number unique to that server. A NetCash coin, as shown in Figure 6.14, has the form:

$$Coin = \{CS\_name, CS\_addr, Expiry, Serial\#, Value\}SK_{CS}$$

Each coin is encrypted with the minting server's secret key (SK$_{CS}$). This forms a digital signature to show that it is authentic. In an actual implementation, to improve efficiency, the digital signature might be formed by taking a hash of the coin's fields and encrypting the result with the server's secret key. This would be more efficient than encrypting all the fields as above. The purpose of each field is now briefly explained:

CS_name: The name of the minting currency server. If CS_addr is invalid, this could be used to look up the current network address of the server in a public directory.

CS_addr: The network address of the minting currency server.

Expiry: The date on which a coin becomes invalid and will no longer be accepted as valid currency. The purpose of this is to limit the amount of serial numbers that must be remembered by a currency server to prevent double spending.

Serial#:   A unique identifier of the coin to the minting currency server.

Value: The amount the coin is worth.

6.3.3   Double-spending prevention

Since an electronic coin is just a piece of data, it is easy to copy it and try to spend it repeatedly. To prevent double spending, a currency server maintains a list of the serial numbers of every coin minted by it *in current circulation*.

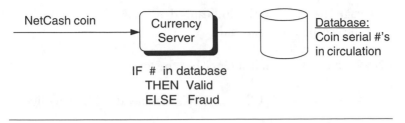

Figure 6.15   Preventing double spending in the NetCash system.

During a purchase, the payee will verify that the coins haven't been double spent by returning them to the minting server, as shown in Figure 6.15. The currency server checks that a coin's serial number is present in its database. If it is, the coin is valid. The serial number must then be removed from the database and the coin will be replaced with a new coin with a different serial number (or an electronic check). The new serial number will be recorded in the database and the coin will be returned to the payee.

A coin can be valid for one purchase only. If it was left in circulation, there would be no way of distinguishing it from one that had already been spent. If a coin's serial number does not appear in the database, then it has either been spent before and removed or it may have expired. Serial numbers that have expired may be removed from the database to limit its size and to allow serial numbers to be reused.

6.3.4   Coin transfer

Monetary value can be exchanged between individuals but, as with a basic purchase, the minting server will need to be contacted to prevent double spending. Where the individuals trust each other not to doubly spend the coins, coins could be transferred directly. Eventually, all coins will have to be returned to the minting server to be verified before they expire.

6.3.5   Certificate of insurance

Within NetCash, only currency servers are required to have a certificate, known as a *certificate of insurance*. It has two functions:

- A means of distributing the server's public key (PK_{CS}) securely, signed and verified by a trusted third party. This key is used to verify the signature on a coin and to encrypt messages sent to the server.

- It proves that a third party, called the Federal Insurance Corporation (FIC), is providing insurance for a currency server to produce and manage NetCash coins. It indicates that coins minted by this server can be accepted as legal tender.

A NetCash certificate of insurance has the form:

$$Cert \; = \; \{Cert\_ID, CS\_name, PK_{CS}, Issue\_date, Expiry\}Sig_{FIC}$$

The purpose of each field is as follows:

Cert_ID: A globally unique identifier of the certificate.

CS_name: The name of the minting currency server.

PK_{CS}:   The public key of the currency server.

Issue_date: The date from which the certificate is valid.

Expiry: The date the certificate expires and is no longer valid.

The certificate is digitally signed with the secret key of the FIC, which acts as a central certification authority (CA). Any buyers or merchants who contact a currency server directly need to obtain that server's certificate. The protocols for distributing certificates to buyers and merchants, and for initially obtaining a server certificate from the FIC are not defined for the NetCash system. Clearly, if the scheme is to be piloted, solutions for these problems will have to be found and implemented.

6.3.6   Basic purchase

To make a purchase using NetCash, a potential buyer first obtains coins from a currency server, buying them with an electronic check. While not discussed by the designers of the system, it is conceivable that an alternate mechanism, such as a credit card scheme, could be used to buy coins. Some of the purchased coins are then sent to the merchant in payment for an item. To protect against double spending, the merchant will verify the coins, either directly with the minting server or indirectly through a server of his choice. In exchange for valid coins, the merchant can receive new coins, minted by the server he contacted, or an electronic check. A signed receipt from the merchant, and possibly the purchased item, may then be sent to the buyer.

The steps involved in a basic purchase are shown in Figure 6.16 and are now explained in more detail.

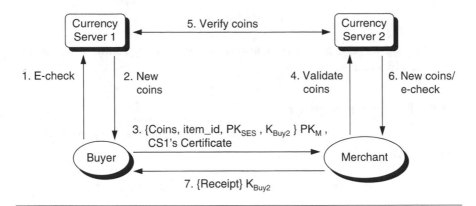

Figure 6.16   Making a purchase with NetCash.

6.3.7   Obtaining coins

The user sends an electronic check, along with a randomly generated one-time symmetric session key, encrypted with the server's public key to the server:

$$\{E\text{–check}, K_{Buyer}\}PK_{CS1}$$

The message can only be decrypted and read by CS1. The check should be such that it can only be spent once, so that replaying the message will achieve nothing. The server will return new coins to the buyer, encrypted with the session key K_{Buyer}:

$$\{\text{New coins}\}\ K_{Buyer}$$

The exchange with the server can be generalized so that either a check or coins can be exchanged with the server for either new coins or a check. Obviously, a check is never exchanged for another check. The generalized request becomes:

$$\{\text{Instrument}, K_X, \text{transaction}\}\ PK_{CS}$$

where *Instrument* is either an electronic check or coins, K_X is a session key generated by sender X (buyer or merchant), and *transaction* indicates whether new coins or a check are wanted in exchange. A successful reply is simply the desired instrument (coins or check), protected by the session key:

$$\{\text{Instrument}\}K_X$$

These messages can be used to anonymously exchange coins with a server as detailed in a later section.

6.3.8   Paying a merchant

The buyer sends a purchase request to the merchant, encrypted with the merchant's public key (PK_M):

$$\{\text{Coins, item\_id, } PK_{Ses}, K_{Buy2}\} PK_M, \text{ CS1's certificate}$$

The buyer must securely obtain PK_M before the purchase can take place. The designers suggest that this be done by sending the buyer's public key (PK_{Buyer}) to the merchant. The merchant can then safely send his public key (PK_M) to the buyer, encrypted with that buyer's public key (PK_{Buyer}):

$$\{PK_M\}PK_{Buyer}$$

This is not entirely safe since an attacker could intercept PK_{Buyer} and return a false merchant public key:

$$\{PK_{Attack}\}PK_{Buyer}$$

Payments can then be intercepted since they will be encrypted with the attacker's public key. A more secure means of distributing public keys, such as by using certificates, could be used to defeat this attack.

The fields of the purchase request have the following purposes:

Coins: The purchase amount in NetCash coins.

item_id: A means of identifying the item the buyer wishes to purchase.

PK_{Ses}:   A freshly generated public-key session key. After a successful purchase, this may be used to encrypt the purchased goods or to uniquely identify the buyer. If the buyer does not wish to remain anonymous to the merchant this could be the buyer's normal public key, PK_{Buyer}.

K_{Buy2}:   A freshly generated symmetric session key. This is used to

encrypt the response, and should be different than K_{Buyer} (used to obtain coins from the server).

The method for selecting goods and price negotiation are outside the scope of NetCash.

6.3.9 Verifying coins

The merchant verifies the signature on the coins using the server's certificate, which was included in the request. To verify that the coins haven't been double spent, the merchant forwards them, in this case indirectly, to the minting server (CS1) through his preferred server (CS2). An exchange request is used:

$$\{\text{Coins}, K_M, \text{transaction}\}\text{PK}_{\text{CS2}}$$

K_M is a symmetric session key generated by the merchant. CS2 in turn forwards the coins to CS1 for verification, accepting an electronic check in return (for valid coins). New coins minted by CS2, or a check, are then sent to the merchant, depending on which was requested in the transaction:

$$\{\text{New coins/check}\}K_M$$

Finally an encrypted receipt, signed by the merchant, is returned to the buyer:

$$\{\text{receipt}\}K_{\text{Buy2}}$$

where

$$\text{receipt} \;=\; \{\text{amount, transaction\_id, date}\}\text{Sig}_M$$

The signature on the receipt can be verified using the merchant's public key (PK_M). The delivery of the purchased item or service is outside the NetCash protocols. However, transaction_id, the receipt, and PK_{Ses} can be used for authentication and encryption when the item is delivered.

6.3.10 Providing limited anonymity

When a user buys coins from a currency server, the server could record the serial numbers on the coins it issues and to whom they were given. If the server later receives the coins back from a merchant, a record of the user's spending habits

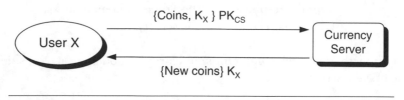

Figure 6.17   Exchanging coins anonymously with a currency server.

may be built. Since a user can select which server she deals with, she might choose one that she trusts not to keep such records. Even still, it would be more reassuring if there was a mechanism to guarantee some anonymity.

The *anonymous coin exchange* mechanism can be used to provide this limited anonymity. As shown in Figure 6.17, anyone can exchange valid coins anonymously with the minting server for new coins. The currency server will only know the network address of where the request is coming from. However, if all individuals are equipped with personal machines, a network address may be a good indication of where a transaction originated from. In this scenario, the transaction could be forwarded through another host, called a *proxy*, to conceal the originating network address. K_X is a temporary session key that does not identify the owner.

When coins are exchanged in this way, it might be the buyer or the merchant (as part of coin verification) who performs the exchange. At best, the currency server could maintain records matching the serial numbers of the old coins against the new ones. When the coins are eventually redeemed for a check, the server will know who initially bought the coins and who eventually traded them in, but not who held any intermediary coins. This prevents the server from keeping accurate spending profiles, provided the merchant doesn't collude with the server. However, by spending with a merchant who is known to always exchange coins for an identified check, anonymity may be limited.

Clearly, the anonymity provided is far less than some fully anonymous digital cash systems, such as Ecash, described elsewhere in this chapter.

6.3.11 Merchant anonymity

A merchant may remain anonymous to a currency server by using the anonymous exchange protocol to obtain new coins from the coins presented by a buyer. The buyer remains anonymous to the merchant, although the merchant will know the network address from which the buyer's requests originate. The merchant can be anonymous to the buyer provided he generates and distributes a temporary public-key pair instead of using PK_M for every purchase. This is perhaps not very practical since public keys take far longer to generate than symmetric ones, and this will delay the purchase. A receipt from an anonymous merchant is also of limited value.

6.3.12 Preventing anonymity

By refusing to exchange coins for new ones, and instead issuing named checks, a currency server can prevent its users from being anonymous. The server can know to whom it issues coins and from whom those coins are received back. Buyers and merchants may still remain anonymous to each other using the protocols described earlier.

6.3.13 Clearing

To reconcile balances (in the form of checks) between currency servers, it is proposed that each server have an account with a NetCheque accounting server (AS), as shown in Figure 6.18. When a currency server CS1 verifies coins with the minting currency server CS2 on behalf of a user, the currency server will always accept an electronic check in exchange for the coins. This ensures that a server only issues its own coins to users. At the end of the day, a currency server can present all checks collected that day from other servers or buyers to their accounting server, which will clear it through the NetCheque infrastructure. NetCheque is described in Chapter 5.

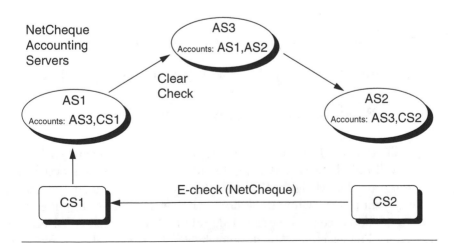

Figure 6.18 Using NetCheque to reconcile balances between servers.

6.3.14 Extensions

Two main extensions are proposed. The first aims to prevent merchant fraud by guaranteeing the buyer a valid receipt or a refund. Normally, there is no mechanism to prevent a merchant accepting a buyer's money and then never delivering the goods or a receipt. The second proposal covers *offline operation*, where a currency server does not have to be contacted at the time of purchase. Both extensions are now examined.

6.3.15 Preventing merchant fraud

To prevent merchant fraud, a coin is extended to have both user- and merchant-specific parts, valid only during specified time windows:

$$Coin \;=\; \{C_M, C_{Buy}, C_X\}$$

The basic idea is that the first part of the coin, C_M, can only be spent by the merchant. If the merchant spends this and does not honor the purchase, the buyer can obtain proof from the bank that the merchant was paid by using the second part of the coin, C_{Buy}. C_X, the third part, is a precaution that allows the coin to be spent by anyone if C_M and C_{Buy} are never used within their valid time windows.

Each of the three parts contains all the information present in a regular NetCash coin, such as the same serial number and value fields. These fields are identical in all three parts. However, the expiry field will be modified in each such that C_M is valid during the first time frame, C_{Buy} during the second, and C_X after that:

$$C_M \;=\{\text{CS\_name}, \text{CS\_addr}, \text{Serial\#}, \text{Value}, \text{Merchant\_info}, \text{time\_frame1}\}\text{SK}_{CS}$$

$$C_{Buy} \;=\{\text{CS\_name}, \text{CS\_addr}, \text{Serial\#}, \text{Value}, \text{Buyer\_info}, \text{time\_frame2}\}\text{SK}_{CS}$$

$$C_X \;=\{\text{CS\_name}, \text{CS\_addr}, \text{Serial\#}, \text{Value}, \text{time\_frame3}\}\text{SK}_{CS}$$

C_M will contain information pertaining to a specific merchant, including PK_M. C_M will only be accepted as legal tender by the currency server if the holder can prove knowledge of SK_M (which only the merchant should know) and the current time is within the validity window specified within the coin. The exact method used to prove knowledge of SK_M is not given in the NetCash specification. For example, though, knowledge of SK_M could be proved by encrypting a secret with PK_M and asking the merchant to decrypt it:

$$\text{SK}_M\,(\text{PK}_M\,(\text{Secret})) = \text{Secret}$$

Similarly, C_{Buy} will contain buyer-specific information, such as PK_{Buyer}, which can be used to authenticate the buyer if she tries to spend the coin during the second time window, when it is valid. The third part of a new coin, C_X, which is valid during a third time window, will not have any additional information or keys embedded in it. The time windows of the three coin parts do not overlap.

Figure 6.19 shows how a buyer can obtain and spend an extended coin to prevent merchant fraud. The buyer obtains the coin from a currency server in much the same way as before, except that dates for the coin's time windows (date_M, date_{Buy}) and the merchant's public key (PK_M) are included. The buyer must know who the merchant is, and have his public key, before the extended coins can be obtained. Another disadvantage is that the currency server will have to mint and sign all three parts of the coin when the buyer initially requests it.

C_M is valid during the first time window and is sent in payment to the merchant using the same protocol as for the basic purchase. The merchant validates the coin with the minting currency server as before, accepting new coins or a check in exchange. The merchant should then return a signed receipt to the buyer.

If no receipt or purchased goods are returned, the buyer will send C_{Buy} to the currency server during the second time window, as shown in Figure 6.20. The currency server checks whether C_M was spent during the first time window.

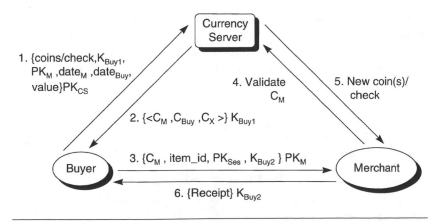

Figure 6.19   Preventing merchant fraud by using extended NetCash coins.

If it was, the server returns a receipt that includes the merchant's identity, his public key, and the value of the spent coin, all signed by the server:

$$\{\text{Merchant\_id}, PK_M, \text{amount}, \text{date}\}\text{Sig}_{CS}$$

The receipt proves that the merchant received and spent the buyer's money. It could also include the buyer's identity. If C_M was never spent, then the server will refund the value of the coin by returning a new coin. If neither C_M nor C_{Buy} are spent during their respective validity periods, C_X can be spent as a normal coin in the third time window.

6.3.16 Offline protocols

The extended coin with time windows, described in the previous section, can be used in an offline protocol. The buyer must know the merchant in advance and obtains the coin as shown in steps 1 and 2 of Figure 6.19. At any later time during the time window of C_M, the coin can be spent at the merchant. The merchant knows that the coin cannot already have been spent since it is specific to him and can only be spent by him within the first time window. However, he must check that a buyer did not already pay him using the same coin. Any time later within the first time window, he can redeem the coin with the currency server without fear of it already having been spent.

The actual length of the time windows is not discussed in the NetCash specification. If it is a very large value, then the buyer will have to wait a considerable amount of time before C_X can be spent if C_M and C_{Buy} are not used. Alternatively, if the time window is small, the merchant will have to verify the coins quickly and the benefits of an offline system will be lost. A time window length that balances out the opposing effects of these two scenarios should be chosen.

The designers also suggest that the basic NetCash protocol could be used with tamper-resistant smart cards. An observer within the smart card prevents

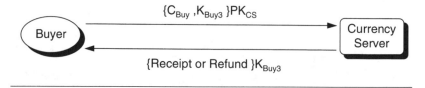

Figure 6.20   Obtaining a purchase receipt or refund during the second time window.

a buyer double spending coins and eliminates the need for online verification of coins with a server. Smart cards and observers are discussed in Chapter 3.

Finally, it has been suggested that other offline electronic cash schemes, such as those by Chaum [24], could be integrated with the NetCash framework. Chaum's scheme identifies an individual who double spends coins after the crime has occurred.

6.3.17 Remarks

NetCash provides a secure and reasonably scalable identified electronic cash system. Limited anonymity is possible and can be controlled. Use of strong cryptography and particularly public-key cryptography may make it computation-intensive and cause delays. Another drawback is that coins of different denominations may have to be obtained from a currency server to make an exact payment during a purchase.

6.4 CyberCoin

One cash-like system that has been in operation on the Internet since late 1996 is the CyberCoin [25] service operated by the same company who developed the CyberCash credit card service described in Chapter 4. The system is designed to be used where the value of a transaction is too low to be economically paid for by credit card.

The system shares similarities with an online electronic cash scheme. Customers buy CyberCoin cash from the CyberCash server, charging the amount to their credit card or bank account. The CyberCoin cash is stored in a special area of the CyberCash wallet, the same piece of software that can be used to make CyberCash credit card payments. When a user decides to pay a merchant, she forwards a payment message to the merchant who verifies it with the CyberCash server. If the transaction is successful, the merchant can deliver the goods to the user. The CyberCoin cash, having already been verified, can later be deposited into the merchant's bank account via the CyberCash server. The CyberCash wallet maintains a log of every transaction made. While a merchant will not know the consumer's identity, the CyberCoin system is not anonymous as the CyberCash server will have records of each user's transactions.

In the CyberCoin service, the electronic coin metaphor is a lot weaker. It is unlike tokenized systems, such as Ecash, where pieces of data (the electronic coins) represent actual monetary value. When a customer buys CyberCoin cash, an account is established with the CyberCash server. Making a payment is similar to authorizing an amount to be transferred from this account to the merchant's account. At some later time, value can be transferred between the CyberCash accounts and financial institutions linked to the server via the banking network.

CyberCoin is a proprietary system and the protocol details had not been published at the time of writing. However, Figure 6.21 shows the communications steps that take place. Setup messages using public-key cryptography are used to load a CyberCash wallet with CyberCoin cash and to set up symmetric key material. Similar messages must be used to transfer the value of any cash back into a real bank account, but this is not required just to verify a payment.

CyberCoin cash can be spent at any merchant and during a purchase transaction only symmetric-key cryptography is used. While this allows it to be more efficient for making small payments than Ecash or NetCash, a third party (the CyberCash server) must still be contacted during a transaction. Steps 1 to 4 show a user paying a merchant. Double spending is not possible, since real electronic cash, where tokens represent actual monetary value, is not being used. However a similar effort, involving less computation, is required by the merchant in verifying that the payment is valid (receiving authorization) with the CyberCash server.

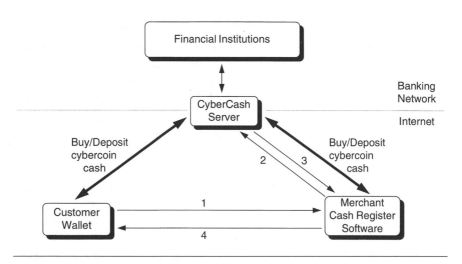

Figure 6.21 Communications steps in making a purchase with the CyberCoin system.

6.5 Mondex

As was the case with checks, the approach taken by researchers to electronic cash and that taken by the banking industry are quite different. The trend in banking has been towards the use of more sophisticated payment cards to effect payment in the retail context. A number of schemes have been tried out [26] that involve preloading a chip card with value that could then be spent at retail outlets. These schemes are generally referred to as *prepayment cards* and one of the more successful of them is the Mondex electronic cash card.

The concept of the Mondex card was developed at NatWest, a major U.K. banking organization, in 1990. The technology was developed with a number of manufacturers involved in the production of secure hardware, including Hitachi Corporation, and this led to a trial in 1992 involving 6,000 staff at a NatWest office complex in London. This limited trial was followed in July 1995 by a major public trial in Swindon, a town of some 190,000 inhabitants near London. In July 1996, a separate company, Mondex International, was formed to promote the technology through a series of trials in many different locations around the world.

The Mondex payment scheme relies on the use of a contact chip card, the core of which contains a chip based on a modified Hitachi H8/310 microcontroller. This is an 8-bit microprocessor with on-chip RAM, ROM, and EEPROM as well as a serial communications controller to allow it to converse with the outside world. The control program for the Mondex payment scheme is implemented in the ROM of this microcontroller and allows value to be transferred from one Mondex chip to another using a proprietary (and secret) chip-to-chip protocol.

To facilitate this value transfer, a number of Mondex support devices are available. The card is initially loaded by contacting a bank using either a Mondex automated teller machine (ATM) or using a specially adapted telephone. These access devices do not need to know how the chip-to-chip protocol works, but rather they incorporate an *interface device* (IFD) that contains a control processor that mediates in the dialogue between the card and the bank. At the bank, a form of money safe called a *Mondex value box* is installed. This is a hardware device that can hold large numbers of Mondex cards and acts as a store of value for dialogues with the issued card population. Transfers to and from the *value box* are monitored by a software system referred to as the *value control and management system*, and the movements will then be reflected in the bank accounts of the cardholders.

Figure 6.22 shows this process taking place. A Mondex card is inserted

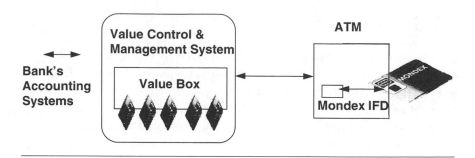

Figure 6.22   Loading a Mondex card with value.

into an ATM (or adapted telephone) whereupon chip-to-chip dialogues take place between the IFD and the card under the control of the ATM device. The Mondex IFD then establishes a dialogue with the bank. Once the cardholder's account number has been established, and the card identity verified, value is transferred from the cards in the bank's value box by chip-to-chip protocol to the destination chip residing in the card. The value control and management system will inform the bank's accounting systems to debit the cardholder's bank account for the amount.

Spending is a similar process, where retailers are equipped with a device called a *value transfer terminal*. Once again, this contains an IFD device that facilitates the transfer from the customer card to the retailer card. There is no need for an online dialogue with the bank to verify the transfer. At a later stage, the retailer may contact the bank, transfer the value to the bank's value box, and simultaneously have the amount credited to her account.

A wide range of other devices are available to assist in using the card. A keyring-sized reader can be used by cardholders to read how much money is stored in the card. A more elaborate device about the size of a pocket calculator allows individuals to move cash from one card to another. This device could of course be used to sell goods in a store but, being handheld, would be unsuited to over-the-counter transactions. Hardware is available to allow vending machines to be converted to accept the card, and a PC card device can allow Mondex cards to be attached to a workstation, and used for payment or money transfer across a network such as the Internet.

Little is publicly known about the security features [27] used in the protocol, but public-key technology of some kind is used to apply a form of signature to the messages moving from chip to chip. The card maintains a *purse narrative* that remembers the last 10 transactions in which the card took part and the retailer's hardware keeps records of the last 300 transactions [28]. This limits the anonymity of the system, which may be seen as a disadvantage by some card users. A strategy is in place that involves the Mondex card issuers periodically capturing transaction information in order to build a statistical sample of the transactions taking place. This measure is used in an attempt to detect fraud within the system at an early stage.

If a card is lost, the value stored in it cannot be recovered. The card, however, can be *locked* such that value cannot be transferred without entering a personal ID number (PIN) via a card interface device. If the card is subsequently found, a card ID can be read by the bank, allowing them to discover the owner.

Each card has two different security schemes available to it, one that is active and one that is dormant. Periodically, cards are instructed to activate the dormant system. As time goes on, new or renewed cards carry the dormant system as the new active system and carry a new dormant system. In this way, the Mondex security system can be constantly renewed without the need to change any of the interface devices.

As a protection against the use of the card by money launderers, each Mondex card has a position in a hierarchical *purse class* structure. This structure imposes rules on what other classes of card it can exchange value with and the associated maximum transaction value. Card issuers can ensure that high-value cards can only exchange value directly with the banking industry, ensuring that all such transactions produce an audit trail.

6.6 EMV cash cards

The Mondex scheme is not the only system to be advanced using smart cards to effect cash payments. Since 1994, EMV, a consortium consisting of Europay (a group of European card-issuing banks) together with the two major international credit card companies (MasterCard and VISA) have been working on common specifications for integrated circuit cards (ICCs), terminals to read the cards, and card applications. In June 1996, a three-volume specification was issued defining the physical, and electrical characteristics of the cards [29] and terminals, the architecture for a multi-application card reader terminal [30], and an application specification for handling credit/debit transactions [31]. No common specification was arrived at for an electronic purse application, but the specifications have meant that a population of card reader terminals can be deployed that can accommodate a number of different purse schemes independently.

Europay International was the first to launch a stored-value card, called the

CLIP Card, which makes possible a reloadable card that is capable of handling multiple currencies. This application was demonstrated in Seville, Spain in June 1996, and at the time of writing a number of European countries had announced intentions to launch CLIP-based payment schemes.

VISA International will use cards complying with the EMV specifications as the basis for their VISACash electronic purses. In addition to a reloadable card, a disposable version that comes loaded with a predetermined value is also available. These cards were first used in public trials at the 1996 Atlanta Olympic Games, and subsequently in many other locations around the world.

MasterCard International will market an electronic purse called Master-Cash, based on EMV secure hardware, and at the time of writing are collaborating with VISA and two major banking organizations to allow MasterCash and VISACash to run on the same hardware. This pilot project will take place in New York City.

The exact method of implementing the electronic purse is proprietary to each organization, and it is unlikely that convergence will be reached in this area for some time in the future.

6.7 Remarks

If usage patterns in electronic payments are to follow those in conventional commerce, there is no doubt that a cash-like method of payment will be in demand. It is difficult to isolate the exact reasons why users are attracted to cash, but anonymity is certainly among them. The Ecash and CAFE systems introduced early in this chapter have provided this using innovative cryptographic techniques. The NetCash system relaxes the requirement for anonymity, which makes the system considerably simpler.

Despite the fact that Ecash is in use in a number of areas throughout the world, the banking industry has yet to rally behind it in great numbers. This may be because the idea of total anonymity of the payment instrument causes some unease among the banking community. The CyberCoin system makes no attempt to provide anonymity and concentrates on making a system that is sufficiently lightweight that it can be used economically for small transactions. Mondex, on the other hand, while initially claiming to provide anonymity, subsequently proved to be maintaining a limited audit trail of the transactions that took place. The technical details of how EMV-based electronic purses work are not available in the public domain, but at least in the case of VISA-Cash a disposable version of the card is available, and this implies the possibility of anonymity. At the moment, however, since card readers are not typically part of a network workstation, these devices cannot be used for payments across a network. This means that for cash payments, the commercially available systems are Ecash, and cash-like payment methods such as CyberCoin.

REFERENCES

[1] DigiCash, *DigiCash Web Server*, 1996, http://www.digicash.com/

[2] DigiCash, *Ecash Web Server*, 1996, http://www.digicash.com/ecash/ecash-home.html

[3] DigiCash Press Release, *World's First Electronic Cash Payment over Computer Networks*, May 27, 1994, http://www.digicash.com/publish/pu_pr.html

[4] Wayner, P., "Digital Cash," *Byte*, Vol. 19, No. 10, Oct. 1994, pp. 126.

[5] Mark Twain Bank, *Mark Twain Bank Web Server*, St. Louis, MO, 1996, http://www.marktwain.com/

[6] DigiCash Press Release, *First Bank to Launch Electronic Cash*, Oct. 1995, http://www.digicash.com/publish/ec_pres3.html

[7] Sanders, T., et al., *The CGI Specification*, 1995, http://hoohoo.ncsa.uiuc.edu/cgi/interface.html

[8] Schneier, B., *Applied Cryptography: Protocols, Algorithms, and Source Code in C*, 2nd ed., New York, NY: John Wiley and Sons, Inc., 1996, p. 145.

[9] DigiCash, *Ecash Software Developer's Kit*, 1996, http://www.digicash.com/api/

[10] Product Cypher, *Magic Money Digital Cash System*, 1994, ftp://idea.sec.dsi.unimi.it/pub/security/crypt/code/MagicMoney.tar.gz

[11] Boly, J. P., et al., "The ESPRIT Project CAFE," *Computer Security -ESORICS '94, Third European Symposium on Research in Computer Security Proc.*, Lecture Notes in Computer Science, Vol. 875, 1994, pp. 217–230.

[12] Bosselaers, A., et al., "Functionality of the Basic Protocols," *Technical Report, ESPRIT Project 7023 (CAFE), Deliverable IHS8341*, Oct. 1995.

[13] Chaum, D., "Blind Signatures for Untraceable Payments," *Advances in Cryptology: Proceedings of CRYPTO '82*, Plenum, NY, 1983, pp. 199–203.

[14] Bos, J., and D. Chaum, "Smart Cash: A Practical Electronic Payment System," *Technical Report, CWI-Report: CS49035*, August 1990.

[15] Chaum, D., and Pedersen, T., "Wallet Databases with Observers," *Advances in Cryptology - CRYPTO '92, 12th Annual International Cryptology Conference Proc.*, Lecture Notes in Computer Science, Vol. 740, Berlin: Springer-Verlag, 1993, pp. 89–105.

[16] Brands, S., "Untraceable Off-line Cash in Wallets with Observers," *Advances in Cryptology - CRYPTO '93, 13th Annual International Cryptology Conference Proc.*, Lecture Notes in Computer Science, Vol. 773, Berlin: Springer-Verlag, 1994, pp. 302–318.

[17] Schnorr, C., "Efficient Identification and Signatures for Smart Cards," *Advances in Cryptology - CRYPTO '89 Proc.* Lecture Notes in Computer Science, Vol. 435, Springer-Verlag, 1990, pp. 239–292.

[18] Medvinsky, G., and B. Clifford Neuman, "NetCash: A design for practical electronic currency on the Internet," *Proc. First ACM Conference on Computer and Communications Security*, Nov. 1993, http://gost.isi.edu/info/netcash/

[19] Medvinsky, G., and B. Clifford Neuman, "Electronic Currency for the Internet," *Electronic Markets*, Vol. 3, No. 9/10, Oct. 1993, pp. 23–24, http://gost.isi.edu/info/netcash/

[20] Clifford Neuman, B., and G. Medvinsky, "NetCheque, NetCash, and the Characteristics of Internet Payment Services," *MIT Workshop on Internet Economics 1995*, Massachusetts Institute of Technology (MIT), Cambridge, MA, March 1995, http://sansfoy.hh.lib.umich.edu/jep/works/NeumNetPay.html

[21] Clifford Neuman, B., and G. Medvinsky, "Requirements for Network Payment: The NetCheque Perspective," *Proc. IEEE Compcon '95*, San Francisco, CA, March 1995, http://nii.isi.edu/info/netcheque/documentation.html

[22] University of Southern California Chronicle, *The Check is in the E-mail*, Nov. 1994, ftp://prospero.isi.edu/pub/netcheque/information/usc-chronicle-941107/ netcheque-usc-chronicle-941107.html

[23] Clifford Neuman, B., "Proxy-Based Authentication and Accounting for Distributed Systems," *Proc. 13th International Conference on Distributed Computing Systems*, Pittsburgh, PA, May 1993, pp. 283–291, http://nii.isi.edu/info/netcheque/documentation.html

[24] Chaum, D., A. Fiat, and M. Naor, "Untraceable Electronic Cash," *Advances in Cryptology - CRYPTO '88 Proc.*, Lecture Notes in Computer Science, Vol. 403, Berlin: Springer-Verlag, 1990, pp. 319-327.

[25] CyberCash, *CyberCash Web Server*, Reston, VA, 1996, http://www.cybercash.com/

[26] Harrop, P., *Prepayment Cards: The Electronic Purse becomes Big Business*, Financial Times Business Information, London, A Financial Times Management Report, 1991.

[27] Jones, T., *The Future of Money as it Affects the Payment Systems in the U.S. and Abroad*, Submission to the U.S. House of Representatives, June 1996, http://www.mondex.com

[28] Gilham, R., *Letter to Mr. Simon Davies of Privacy International in response to complaint on Mondex anonymity claims*, Area Trading Standards Officer, Bromley, U.K., June 1996, http://www.privacy.org/pi/activities/mondex/mondex_response.html

[29] Europay International S.A., MasterCard International Incorporated, and Visa International Service Association, *EMV '96 : Integrated Circuit Card Specification for Payment Systems*, June 1996, http://www.mastercard.com/emv/

[30] Europay International S.A., MasterCard International Incorporated, and Visa International Service Association, *EMV '96 : Integrated Circuit Card Terminal Specification for Payment Systems*, June 1996, http://www.mastercard.com/emv/

[31] Europay International S.A., MasterCard International Incorporated, and Visa International Service Association, *EMV '96 : Integrated Circuit Card Application Specification for Payment Systems*, June 1996, http://www.mastercard.com/emv/

Chapter 7

Micropayment systems

O F THE CONVENTIONAL PAYMENT INSTRUMENTS of cash, check, and card, the one most suited to low-value transactions is cash. Versatile as it is, it is limited in that no transaction can involve less than the value of the smallest coin (e.g., a penny). There are entire classes of goods and services where this poses a problem. Some examples include obtaining a quotation of the current price of a share on the stock market or making a single query of a database service. In conventional commerce, the solution to this has been to use a subscription mode of payment, where the buyer pays in advance and can avail of the product or service for a fixed period. While this ensures that the content provider can be paid for services rendered, it seals off what is in many cases a large customer base of people who may only wish to use a service very occasionally. It also restricts the ability of people to try out a service.

It is clear that the subscription model does not adequately solve the problem and that there is a need for a payment system that can efficiently transfer very small amounts, perhaps less than a penny, in a single transaction. This implies that communications traffic, which in itself costs money, must be kept to an absolute minimum. A system where the costs of conveying the payment

191

are greater than the payment itself is unlikely to succeed. In many of the payment systems covered in previous chapters, a merchant validated each payment by having a real-time dialogue with a server on the network representing the payment systems provider, either to check that funds are available, or to complete the payment. This represents a very high per-transaction overhead and must be eliminated in the design of a micropayment system.

The low value per transaction also means that the profit made on each transaction must also be small. For a server to be viable under these conditions, it must be able to process transactions at a high rate. This gives rise to a further requirement that micropayment systems must be able to make the payment verification inexpensively. If a server is taking appreciable time to do public-key encryption or decryption, then its throughput, measured in transactions, cannot be very great. Consequently, a successful micropayment system must not involve computationally expensive cryptographic techniques.

The electronic payment methods outlined in earlier chapters have involved systems that mirror the properties of conventional payment instruments already in existence. Micropayments, on the other hand, have not been available in conventional commerce, and their introduction opens up many new areas of business. One can envisage network users paying to consult an online encyclopedia, purchasing a single song from an album, ordering just the business pages from a selection of daily newspapers, and so forth. The remainder of this chapter will outline the most influential systems available in this new field of electronic commerce.

7.1 Millicent

Millicent [1,2] is a decentralized micropayment scheme developed by staff at Digital Equipment Corporation which is designed to allow payments as low as a tenth of a cent ($0.001) to be made. A Millicent payment can be efficiently validated at a vendor's site without need to contact a third party. This distributed approach, without any additional communication, expensive public key encryption, or off-line processing, allows it to scale effectively for repeated small payments.

The Millicent system uses a form of electronic currency called *Scrip*. Scrip can be thought of as the loose change you carry around in your pocket. It is fast and efficient to verify that it is valid, and if one loses a small piece of change by accident it is not of great concern. Scrip is *vendor specific* in that it has value at one particular vendor only. The security of the protocol is designed to make the cost of committing a fraud more than the value of a purchase. By using fast symmetric encryption the protocol can be both lightweight and secure.

7.1.1 The Millicent model

Figure 7.1 shows the three main entities in the Millicent system: *brokers, vendors,* and *customers.*

7.1.1.1 Brokers

A Millicent broker mediates between vendors and customers to simplify the tasks they perform.

Aggregating Micropayments
Typically, it might take a customer several weeks or months to make enough micropayments at a specific vendor to cover the cost of a standard macropayment financial transaction to that vendor. Thus it would not be efficient for a customer to buy *vendor scrip* (scrip that can be spent at a specific vendor only) from every vendor they wish to buy from. However, it is likely that a customer will make enough micropayments in total at different vendors to cover the cost of a macropayment transaction. A *macropayment* is a transaction capable of handling payments worth several dollars or more, such as those systems described in previous chapters.

One of the functions of the broker is to provide all the different vendor scrip needs of a customer in return for a single macropayment. In other words,

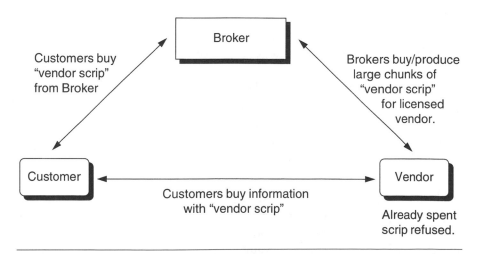

Figure 7.1 The Millicent model.

the broker sells vendor scrip to customers. The aggregation of the different vendor scrips justifies a macropayment transaction to purchase these pieces of scrip. A single vendor selling her own scrip would not normally justify this.

Replacing Subscription Services

In a subscription service, a vendor usually maintains account information for customers who have paid to use the service for a set length of time. Customers have to maintain account information for each different vendor. Vendors have to create, maintain, and bill accounts for possibly a large number of users. The Millicent broker frees both the customer and vendor from these tasks, replacing a subscription service with a pay-per-access micropayment system.

Selling Vendor Scrip

Brokers handle the real money in the Millicent system. They maintain accounts of customers and vendors. Customers buy vendor scrip for a specific vendor from their broker. The broker will have an agreement with each vendor whose scrip he sells. There are two main ways in which a broker gets the vendor scrip:

Scrip warehouse: The broker buys many pieces of vendor scrip from the vendor. The scrip is stored and then sold piece by piece to different customers.

Licensed scrip production: The actual broker generates the vendor scrip on behalf of that vendor. This is more efficient because:

- The broker doesn't need to store a large number of scrip pieces.

- The vendor does less computation since she doesn't have to generate the scrip herself.

- The license, which can be granted and sent across the network, is smaller to transmit than large chunks of scrip.

The license will allow the broker to only generate a specific amount of vendor scrip. The license should be enforceable through normal business practices. Brokers will typically be financial institutions or network service providers. They are assumed to be trusted by the other entities.

7.1.1.2   Vendors

Millicent vendors are merchants selling low-value services or information. A vendor accepts her own vendor scrip as payment from customers. The vendor can validate her own vendor scrip locally and prevent any double spending. The merchant sells vendor scrip at discount or a scrip-producing license to a broker. This discount or selling commission is how the broker profits from the scheme.

7.1.1.3   Customers

Users buy *broker scrip* with real money from their chosen broker, as shown in Figure 7.2. Broker scrip has value at that broker only. A macropayment scheme such as SET or Ecash could be used to initially buy the broker scrip. Using this broker scrip, the customer buys vendor scrip for specific vendors. The vendor scrip can then be used to make purchases.

7.1.2   Purchasing with Millicent

Initially, the customer buys some broker scrip using one of the macropayment systems, as shown in Figure 7.2. Typically, enough broker scrip to last a week might be bought, although more can be obtained at any time.

When a customer first encounters a new vendor, he must buy vendor scrip from the broker to spend at that vendor's site. Figure 7.3 shows a customer buying 20 cents of vendor scrip using the $5 of broker scrip purchased earlier. Both the new vendor scrip and change in broker scrip are returned. The same process will take place when a customer needs more vendor scrip, perhaps at the start of a new day.

The vendor scrip is sent to the merchant with a purchase request. The vendor will return a new piece of vendor scrip as change along with the purchased content. Remember, scrip is vendor-specific, and can be spent only at a particular merchant.

Figure 7.4 shows the customer buying from the *same vendor* again using the change. The customer already has valid vendor scrip for the vendor, so

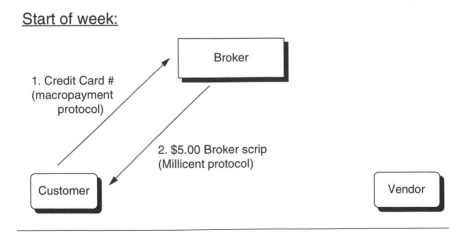

Figure 7.2   Buying broker scrip.

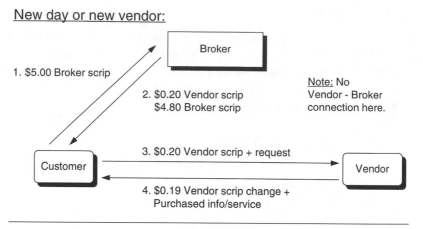

Figure 7.3 Purchasing from a vendor.

there is no need to contact the broker. Again, the scrip and purchase request are sent to the vendor who returns the item and the correct change. In this example the customer has bought an article costing 4 cents.

Repeated payments at a specific vendor are highly efficient in regard to network connections. If the customer already has valid scrip for that vendor, only a single network connection is required. Compare this with the number of network connections required in a secure macropayment scheme such as

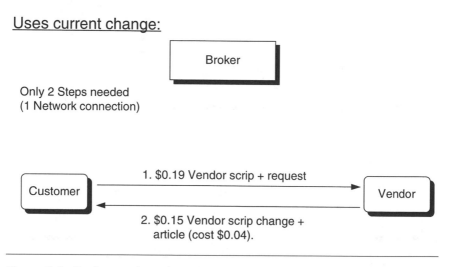

Figure 7.4 Further purchases from the same vendor.

SET or Ecash. This increased communications efficiency is provided at the cost of slightly relaxing the security, as discussed later.

7.1.3 Scrip

Scrip is a piece of data used to represent microcurrency within the Millicent system. Scrip has the following properties:

- A piece of scrip represents a prepaid value, much like prepaid phone cards, fare cards, or coupons.

- Scrip can represent any denomination of currency. Expected values range from one-tenth of a cent up to about $5, although there is no defined upper or lowerbound limits.

- The security of scrip is based on the assumption that it is only used to represent small amounts of money.

- It is vendor-specific and thus has value at one vendor only.

- It can be spent only once. Double spending will be detected locally by the vendor at the time of purchase.

- It can be spent only by its owner. A shared secret is used to prevent stolen scrip being spent, as discussed in Section 7.1.11.

- Scrip cannot be tampered with or its value changed.

- It is computationally expensive to counterfeit scrip. The cost of doing so outweighs the value of the scrip itself.

- Scrip makes no use of public-key cryptography. It can be efficiently produced, validated, and protected using a one-way hash function and limited symmetric cryptography.

- Scrip cannot provide full anonymity. It has visible serial numbers that could be recorded and traced. Some limited anonymity could be maintained by buying broker scrip using an anonymous macropayment system.

7.1.4 Scrip structure

Figure 7.5 shows the data fields that make up a piece of scrip. The purpose of each is now briefly examined:

Vendor: Identifies the vendor at which this scrip has value.

Value: Specifies how much the scrip is worth.

ID#:   A unique identifier of the scrip, much like a serial number. It is used to prevent double spending of the scrip.

Cust_ID#:   An identifier used to calculate a shared secret (customer_secret) that is used to protect the scrip and any scrip issued as change. Cust_ID# need not have any connection to the real identity of the customer, but it must be unique to every customer. Scrip issued as change will have the same Cust_ID# as the original scrip used to make the payment.

Expiry: The date on which the scrip becomes invalid. Used to limit the ID#s that must be remembered by a vendor to prevent double spending.

Info: Optional details describing the customer to a vendor. They might include the customer's age or country of residence. Such information could assist the vendor in making a sales decision on such matters as selling adult material and the levying of sales tax. The exact fields used, if any, will depend on an agreement between the brokers and vendors.

Certificate: The certificate field prevents the scrip being altered in any way and proves that it is authentic (but not already double spent). In this sense, it acts as a digital signature, although it is not created or validated using asymmetric key cryptography.

7.1.5   Scrip certificate generation

When a piece of scrip is generated the certificate field is created as a signature or "certificate of authenticity" for that scrip. The certificate is really a stamp of

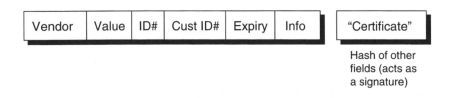

Vendor	Value	ID#	Cust ID#	Expiry	Info	"Certificate"

Hash of other
fields (acts as
a signature)

Figure 7.5   Scrip data fields.

approval that cannot be forged and that prevents any of the scrip's fields being altered.

It is created by hashing the other fields of the scrip with a secret, as shown in Figure 7.6. Only the vendor (or trusted broker) who mints the scrip will know this secret, which is called a *master scrip secret*. The vendor will maintain a list of many different master scrip secrets, numbered from 1 to N, for the purpose of minting scrip. Which master scrip secret is used with a particular piece of scrip depends on some part of the scrip's ID#. As a simplified example, if the last digit in the ID# was 6, then master scrip secret 6 might be used.

Since the certificate is the product of a one-way hash function, such as MD5, it prevents the scrip's fields from being altered successfully. Any change will result in a recomputed certificate not matching the original one. Only the party who knows the master scrip secret can generate scrip. Thus the scrip certificate prevents both tampering and counterfeiting.

7.1.6 Scrip validation

At the time of purchase, a vendor must be sure that the scrip she is accepting is valid. It must be

- Authentic scrip produced by the vendor or licensed broker;
- It must not have been already spent (double spending).

The merchant recalculates the certificate and compares it with the scrip certificate from the customer. This is shown in Figure 7.7. Both certificates will match if the scrip has not been tampered with.

7.1.7 Preventing double spending

To prevent double spending, the vendor checks that the ID# has not already been spent. The vendor maintains bit vectors (data structures where one bit is used to represent each ID#) corresponding to the issued serial numbers (ID#s) to keep track of spent scrip. Vectors covering ranges that have been fully spent or expired can be discarded. This will allow the vendor to keep the database of valid scrip ID#s in memory, which will speed up transactions.

7.1.8 Computation costs

Table 7.1 shows the computations required in a Millicent purchase. Compared to macropayment systems examined in earlier chapters, accepting a Millicent micropayment is cheap and efficient.

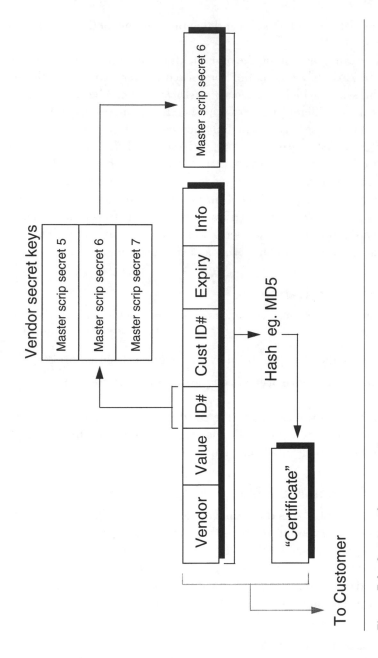

Figure 7.6   Scrip certificate generation.

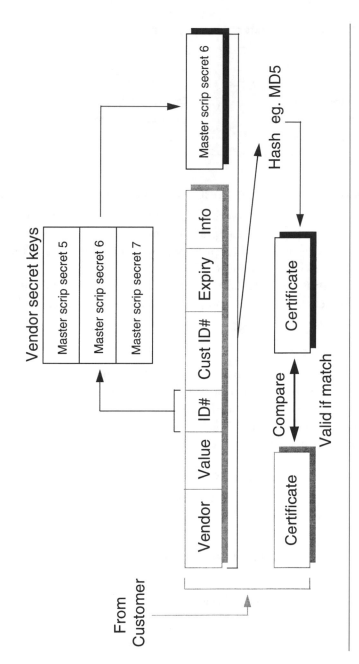

Figure 7.7 Validating scrip at the time of purchase.

Table 7.1   Computational Costs of Accepting Scrip

Action	Cost
Recalculate certificate	One hash function
Prevent double spending	One local ID# database lookup (in memory)
Making purchase across network	One network connection

7.1.9   Sending scrip over a network: The Millicent protocols

When sending scrip over a network, different levels of efficiency, security, and privacy may be required. For example, on an internal network within an organization, there may be little need for privacy or security. However, on the public network these may be more important.

There are three main Millicent protocols that provide different levels of these requirements. Table 7.2 compares their characteristics. Each is now examined in turn.

7.1.10   Scrip in the clear

In the simplest protocol, the customer sends the scrip unprotected across the network to the vendor. The vendor will also return the purchased content and change in the clear. No network security is provided in this protocol. An attacker can intercept the scrip or the change and use it himself. Remember, the stolen scrip can only be spent at one particular vendor.

7.1.11   Encrypted network connection

To prevent scrip being stolen, and to prevent an eavesdropper gaining any information from the transaction, the network connection can be encrypted.

Table 7.2   Characteristics of the Three Millicent Protocols

Millicent Protocol	Efficiency Ranking	Secure	Private
Scrip in the clear	1	No	No
Encrypted connection	3	Yes	Yes
Request signatures	2	Yes	No

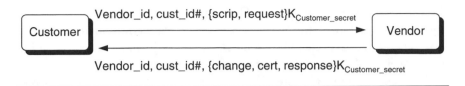

Figure 7.8   Purchase using encrypted network connection.

This can be done using a shared symmetric key, called the *customer_secret*, between the customer and vendor. The customer_secret is used to secure the communications channel using an efficient symmetric algorithm such as DES, IDEA, or RC4. Figure 7.8 shows a purchase using the customer_secret to encrypt the network connection. The protocol is both secure and private.

Scrip cannot be stolen and an eavesdropper cannot see the purchase or scrip details. Vendor_id and Cust_id# are sent in the clear in both messages so that the recipient can calculate customer_secret. The next section describes how the customer_secret is generated. The original scrip certificate is included in the response to show that it is the correct response to the request.

7.1.11.1   The customer_secret

Figure 7.9 shows how the customer_secret is generated when the scrip is created. It is formed by hashing the customer identifier with another secret,

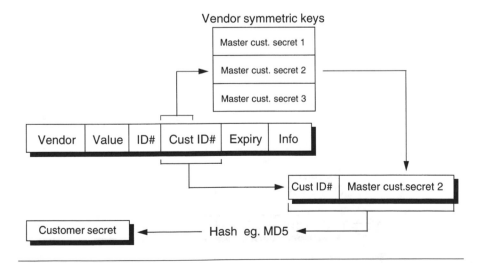

Figure 7.9   Generating a customer_secret.

called the *master_customer_secret*. Only the vendor (or trusted broker) will know this secret. As with the master_scrip_secret, the vendor maintains a list of many different master_customer_secrets, numbered from 1 to N. Part of the Cust_ID# is used to select the master_customer_secret.

The vendor can recalculate the customer_secret at any time from the piece of scrip. The customer must also obtain the customer_secret. It is returned to the customer when the vendor scrip is purchased from a broker, as shown in Figure 7.10. To protect the customer_secret as it passes from broker to customer, the transaction could be performed using a secure non-Millicent protocol. Alternatively, a secure Millicent transaction could be used, where a customer_secret exists for the broker scrip being used by the customer. The customer_secret would be used to encrypt the connection in much the same way as in Figure 7.8. The customer_secret for the broker scrip must be obtained using a secure protocol outside the Millicent system.

Table 7.3 summarizes the purpose and usage of the three different types of shared secret used in Millicent.

7.1.12 Request signatures

A fully encrypted network connection might be more than is required, especially if privacy is not important. A third Millicent protocol removes the encryption but maintains a level of security that prevents scrip being stolen.

The customer_secret is used to generate a *request signature* instead of being used for encryption. It is similar to the certificate field of a piece of scrip in that it is a hash of other fields. The request signature is generated by hashing the scrip, customer_secret, and request together, as shown in Figure 7.11. It is created by the customer and sent along with the scrip and request to the vendor. This is shown in Figure 7.12.

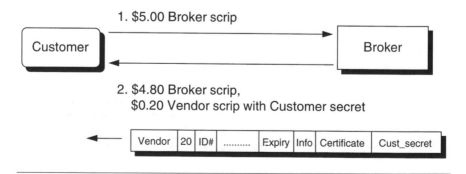

Figure 7.10   Buying vendor scrip.

Table 7.3 Secrets used in Producing, Validating, and Spending Scrip

Secret	Shared by:	Purpose
Master_scrip_secret	Vendor, minting broker	Prevents tampering and counterfeiting of scrip. Used to authenticate scrip.
Customer_secret	Customer, Vendor, minting broker	Proves ownership of the scrip. May be required to spend the scrip.
Master_customer_secret	Vendor, minting broker	Derives the customer_secret from customer information in the scrip.

The vendor verifies the request signature by recomputing it, as shown in Figure 7.13. Remember, the vendor can compute the customer_secret using the scrip and a master_customer_secret (Figure 7.9). If the request has been tampered with, then the two request signatures will not match and the vendor will refuse to process the transaction.

For a valid request, the vendor returns the purchase reply, change in scrip, and a reply signature. The reply signature is generated in the same way as the request signature, using the same customer_secret. The change cannot be

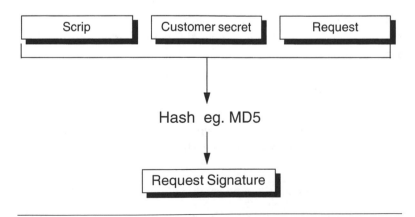

Figure 7.11 Generating a request signature.

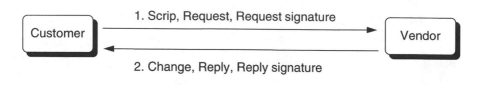

Figure 7.12   Purchase using a request signature.

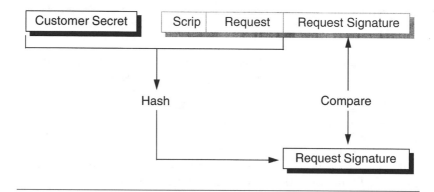

Figure 7.13   Vendor verifies the request signature.

stolen by an attacker because it cannot be spent without knowledge of the customer_secret. This is because without the customer_secret, a valid request signature cannot be calculated, and the merchant will refuse the transaction.

Thus, while an eavesdropper can see all parts of the transaction (no privacy), the purchase request cannot be altered and the scrip cannot be stolen. Security has been provided more efficiently than using encryption, but at the cost of losing the privacy.

7.1.13 Performance

It is desirable that both vendors and brokers can process a large number of transactions a second in order to make small micropayments viable. Initial tests of a Millicent implementation on a Digital AlphaStation 400 4/233 [1] produced the following results:

- 14,000 pieces of scrip can be produced per second.
- 8,000 payments can be validated per second, with change scrip being produced.

- 1,000 Millicent requests per second can be received from the network and validated.

The bottleneck appears to be in handling the network connection, which in this case was TCP, the transport protocol used on the Internet. Thus Millicent is capable of handling the maximum number of micropayment purchases that can be received from the network per second.

7.1.14 Millicent with the Web

Millicent is well suited for paying for Web content. The Millicent protocol can be implemented as an extension to the Web's HTTP protocol. A software implementation consists of a user wallet, a vendor server, and a broker server.

Since Millicent supports small micropayments, users may not be so tempted to steal or copy content worth only a cent. The designers feel that users will consider it foolish to steal if the price is already so low.

7.1.15 Extensions

Millicent can securely handle transactions from a tenth of a cent up to a few dollars. This makes it suitable for micropayments, such as paying for information content, database searching, or access to a service. However, it could also be used with a broad range of other applications that may or may not involve payments, both on the Internet and private networks. These might include

Authentication to distributed services: Scrip could be used to provide Kerberos-like authentication (see Chapter 3) for access to network services. At the start of the day, a user obtains authentication scrip from a broker. This authentication scrip is then used to buy scrip for access to particular network services. Access is dynamically provided based on a user having scrip for that system.

Metering usage: Millicent could be used with accounting and metering applications inside private networks. The organization will act as a broker, with employees as the customers. The vendors will be the servers to which the employees have access.

Usage-based charges: Millicent could be used for per-connection charges for such services as e-mail, file transfer, Internet telephone, teleconferencing, and other online services. However it would not be efficient enough for packet-level charging for these services.

Discount coupons: Further fields could be added to scrip to provide discounts for certain content. For example, having bought the first half of an article, the change scrip could contain a discount for buying the second half of the article, provided it was bought the same day with that scrip.

Preventing subscription sharing: By using scrip to access a prepaid subscription service, sharing of that subscription account can be prevented. The scrip acts as an access capability to the service, with the scrip change giving access the next time. However, trying to gain access with an already used piece of scrip (such as shared scrip would be) will fail.

7.1.16   Summary

Millicent is an efficient, lightweight, flexible micropayment system. It can support multiple brokers and vendors and can be extended for use with many applications. Lightweight message digest functions provide a security level suited to small micropayments, and Millicent significantly reduces communication for multiple accesses to the same vendor within a short time. A public trial of the Millicent system was scheduled for the summer of 1997.

7.2 SubScrip

SubScrip [3] is a simple micropayment protocol designed for efficient *pay-per-view* payments on the Internet. It was developed at the University of Newcastle, Australia, and is a *prepaid system* with no need for user identification.

In essence, it works by creating temporary prepaid accounts for users at a specific vendor. The user makes micropayment purchases from the vendor against this account. Since the account is temporary and prepaid, it does not carry the normal overhead associated with subscription services. The system does not require its own billing or banking hierarchy. Instead, any existing macropayment scheme, such as SET or Ecash, can be used to make the initial payment to a vendor to set up the prepaid account.

As with Millicent, the level of security is relaxed due to the low value of the transactions. The designers aimed to make the expense necessary for a successful attack much higher than the financial gain possible. In its basic form, no encryption is used at all.

7.2.1 Basic SubScrip

SubScrip uses techniques similar to some of Millicent's features to achieve a very low transaction cost. As with Millicent, a micropayment can be verified locally by a vendor without the need for any online clearance with a third party. Similarly, there is an initial overhead associated with making a payment to a new vendor. Both systems are optimal for repeated payments to the same vendor over a short time period.

7.2.2 Establishing a temporary account

However, unlike Millicent, SubScrip does not use a broker to mediate between users and merchants. Instead, an existing macropayment scheme takes over this role. A user chooses a macropayment scheme that a vendor can accept. The user makes a payment large enough to cover the macropayment transaction costs to that vendor, as shown in Figure 7.14. This payment will typically be of a few dollars and is used to set up a *temporary account* at the merchant.

In order to make micropayment purchases against the temporary account, the user needs some type of account identifier. Within the SubScrip system, this account identifier is called a *SubScrip ticket*. The merchant returns a SubScrip ticket to the user to access the new account.

7.2.3 Providing anonymity

A SubScrip merchant need not know the identity of a user he is dealing with. The anonymity provided will depend on the anonymity of the macropayment system used to initially pay a vendor. If a nonanonymous system is used, the merchant can link the name to the temporary account set up, and track all payments made against that account. With an anonymous system, the merchant will only know the network address that the customer's requests are coming from. Both the customer and merchant will have to agree on the same macropayment protocol to use.

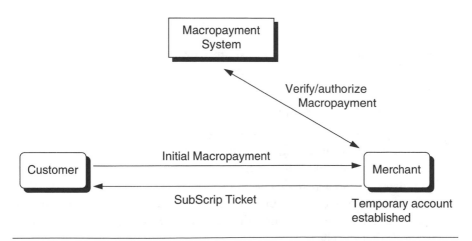

Figure 7.14 Establishing a SubScrip account with a vendor.

Figure 7.15   A SubScrip ticket.

7.2.4   A SubScrip ticket

A SubScrip ticket is the special account identifier used to authenticate the account owner to the account maintained at a vendor site in order to make a micropayment purchase. It is valid only at one particular merchant. As shown in Figure 7.15, it consists of the following fields:

Acc_ID: An account identifier that uniquely identifies the account at a vendor. It is chosen so that it is hard for an attacker to guess a valid account identifier. A large random number can be used.

Val: The amount of money remaining in the account at the vendor.

Exp: The date on which the account will expire. This limits the number of accounts that must be maintained by a vendor.

The merchant maintains a database of valid account IDs with the amount and expiry date of each account. Knowledge of the account ID is the only way to gain access to the account. The SubScrip ticket does not actually have value itself and is therefore not an electronic coin. However, without it, the prepaid value at the merchant cannot be accessed. The problem of lost or stolen tickets is discussed in Section 7.2.9.

SubScrip value is *transferable* to another user. This is done by giving that user the valid ticket for the account balance at a specific vendor.

7.2.5   A SubScrip purchase

To make a purchase, the user sends the SubScrip ticket to the vendor, who verifies that it is valid by checking the database, as shown in Figure 7.16. The micropayment amount is deducted from the account balance. A new random account identifier and a matching ticket with the new balance, is then generated for the account and returned to the user along with the purchased information or service. The user stores the new ticket, along with the address of the merchant, for further purchases.

It is not possible for users to commit fraud by altering the value or expiry

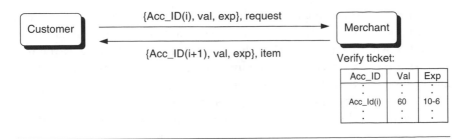

Figure 7.16   Purchasing with a SubScrip ticket.

fields on their SubScrip ticket. This is because these fields are included in the ticket for the user's information only. The database of accounts maintained by the merchant will always have the real account balances and expiry dates.

7.2.6   Security and privacy

The SubScrip tickets are sent in the clear, with no encryption used during a purchase. An eavesdropper can see exactly what is purchased and for how much in a transaction. The amount remaining in the user's account at the vendor can also be clearly seen from the new ticket returned. No privacy can be provided by the protocol in this form.

It is possible for an eavesdropper to obtain a valid account ID as a new ticket is returned to the customer as change. A stolen ticket could be spent by an attacker, and when the user next tried to spend it, it would already be invalid. An active attacker could also intercept a valid ticket being sent to the merchant as a purchase request. Once a valid ticket reaches the merchant, it is invalidated, and the attacker would have to prevent this ticket or a retransmission of it reaching its destination to successfully steal it.

The SubScrip designers accept the possibility of fraud in these ways. They feel that since a SubScrip ticket is only valid at one particular merchant, the amounts involved do not warrant the possibility of large-scale fraud. They consider the lightweight limited security to be adequate for normal pay-per-view micropayments.

7.2.7   Protected SubScrip

To provide increased security, at the cost of lowering the computational efficiency, a protected SubScrip protocol using public-key cryptography is proposed.

When a customer first buys a temporary SubScrip account at a merchant, the customer's public key PK_C, is also forwarded. The merchant stores this public key with the account ID in the account database. Whenever the merchant sends a new ticket for this account to the customer, it is encrypted with that customer's public key, as shown in Figure 7.17.

The ticket is not encrypted as it is sent from the customer to the merchant. The designers feel that it is unlikely that an attacker will go to the trouble of preventing the ticket reaching its destination (where it will be invalidated) in order to steal it.

7.2.8   Refunding SubScrip

Another proposed extension is to allow customers to convert unspent tickets back to real money. This would be done by sending the ticket to the vendor, who would pay the remaining account balance to the user using an existing macropayment system. A system in which any user can accept payments, such as electronic cash systems, will have to be used for this purpose. Credit card systems cannot do this. The cost of the macropayment transaction may have to be covered by the merchant by charging a fee for this service.

7.2.9   Lost tickets

A user might lose a ticket through an unsuccessful transmission or a software failure. An implementation of the merchant software might record the delivery addresses of users. Lost account IDs could then be recovered by sending the delivery address and approximate time of last access to regain the account.

In conclusion, SubScrip provides a lightweight, efficient, account-based micropayment system with limited security. It reduces the overhead required to maintain a complete subscription database and allows for some anonymity.

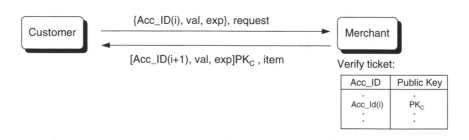

Figure 7.17   A protected SubScrip purchase.

7.3 PayWord

PayWord [4] is a credit-based micropayment scheme designed by Ron Rivest (MIT Laboratory for Computer Science, MA, USA) and Adi Shamir (Weizmann Institute of Science, Rehovot, Israel). The scheme aims to reduce the number of public-key operations required per payment by using hash functions, which are faster. Table 7.4 gives some estimated figures comparing the number of public-key and hash operations, and network connections, that can be performed per second on a typical workstation. Fast hash functions and symmetric-key cryptography are more suitable for micropayments, where speed is important, than the slower public-key cryptography used in many macropayment schemes.

PayWord uses *chains of hash values* to represent user credit within the system. Each hash value, called a *payword*, can be sent to a merchant as payment. A payword chain is vendor-specific and the user digitally signs a *commitment* to honor payments for that chain.

Brokers mediate between users and vendors and maintain accounts for both. They vouch for users by issuing a *PayWord certificate* allowing that user to generate paywords. They redeem spent payword chains from vendors, transferring the amount spent from the user's account to the vendor. It is not necessary for both a vendor and user to have an account at the same broker.

As with other micropayment schemes security is relaxed to increase efficiency. While some fraud is possible, parties that continue to abuse the system can be detected and removed.

Table 7.4 Comparison of Computational Speed of Cryptographic and Network Operations on a Typical Workstation

Operation	No. Per Second
Public-key signature (1,024-bit RSA)	2
PK signature verification (1,024-bit RSA)	200
One-way hash evaluation (MD5/SHA)	20,000
Network connection (TCP, Internet)	1,000

7.3.1   PayWord user certificates

Since PayWord is a credit-based scheme, vendors need some assurance that users will honor their payword payments. A *PayWord certificate* authorizes a user to generate payword chains, and guarantees that a specific broker will redeem them. Brokers and vendors do not need PayWord certificates in the PayWord scheme.

Users obtain a certificate when they initially set up an account with a broker, as shown in Figure 7.18. A macropayment scheme or credit card payment could be used to pay money into the account. The certificate will typically have to be renewed every month. This limits fraud by ensuring that users who have overdrawn accounts will not be issued with a new certificate, which would allow them to continue generating paywords.

A PayWord certificate is of the form:

$$C_U = \{B, U, A_U, \mathrm{PK}_U, E, I_U\} SK_\mathrm{B}$$

The certificate is signed by the broker (B). The certificate fields have the following meaning:

B Identifies the broker who issued the certificate. Paywords accepted from the user (U) will only be redeemable at this broker.

U Identifies the user who is authorized by this certificate to generate payword chains.

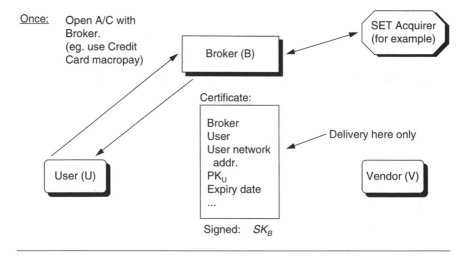

Figure 7.18   Obtaining a PayWord user certificate.

A_U The user's delivery address. This could include an Internet host address, e-mail, or mailing address. To limit fraud, items purchased by the user should only be delivered to this address.

PK_U The user's public key. Used to verify the user's digital signature on a commitment to a new payword chain.

E The date the certificate expires.

I_U Optional information. This could include credit limits per vendor, user-specific details, or broker details.

In order to verify a broker's signature on a certificate, a vendor must securely obtain that broker's public key, PK_B, in some way. How this is done will be specific to an implementation and is not discussed in the PayWord scheme.

Since identified certificates with a user identifier and address are used, no anonymity is provided.

7.3.2   Revoked certificates

A broker might maintain blacklists of certificates that have been revoked, much like the certificate revocation lists in SET. A user's certificate would be revoked if their secret key was lost or stolen, as this would allow others to generate payword chains under their name. It is the responsibility of a vendor to obtain any revoked certificate lists from a broker.

7.3.3   PayWord chains

A *payword chain* represents user credit at a specific vendor. It is a chain of hash values. Each payword (hash value) in the chain, has the same value, normally one cent. Other values are also possible as described in the next section. To generate a new payword chain, the user performs the following steps, as illustrated in Figure 7.19:

1.   Decide on the length, N, of the chain. A payword chain of length 10 will be worth 10 cents if the payword value is 1 cent. The chain value should be greater than the amount one is likely to spend at a vendor that day. Unused paywords in a chain can be safely discarded. Since they represent user credit, no value is lost.

2.   Select a *random number*, W_N.

3.   Perform N repeated hashes of W_N. Each hash value forms one payword. MD5 could be used as the hash function.

4.   The final chain will be: $\{W_0, W_1, W_2, \ldots, W_N\}$.

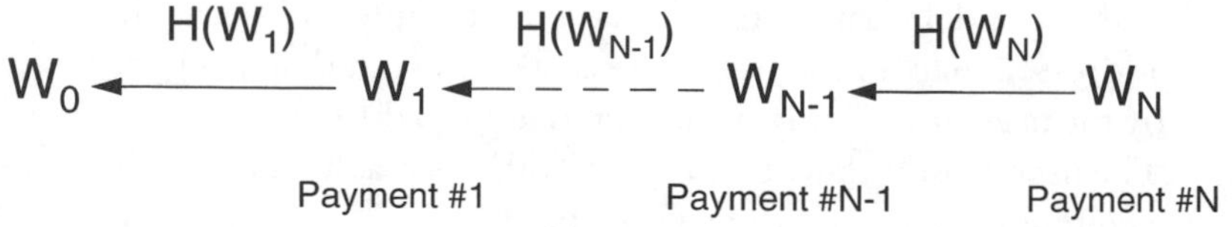

$$W_0 \xleftarrow{\quad H(W_1) \quad} W_1 \xleftarrow{\quad H(W_{N-1}) \quad} - - - - W_{N-1} \xleftarrow{\quad H(W_N) \quad} W_N$$

Payment #1   Payment #N-1   Payment #N

Figure 7.19   Generating a payword chain.

7.3.4   Commitment to a PayWord chain

Since PayWord is a credit-based scheme, the vendor and broker need to know who the spent paywords belong to so that the user's account can be charged appropriately. The user is authenticated by signing a *commitment* to a payword chain. The commitment will authorize the broker to redeem any paywords from the committed chain. It allows the vendor to be confident that they will be paid for paywords accepted from the user.

A commitment to a payword chain has the form:

$$\text{Comm} \quad = \quad \{V, C_U, W_0, E, I_{\text{Comm}}\} \, \text{SK}_U$$

The commitment is signed with the user's secret key. The fields have the following purpose:

V The vendor at which the committed payword chain is valid. A payword chain is vendor-specific.

C_U The user's payword certificate, as described earlier. Used to verify the user's signature and to verify authorization from a broker.

W_0 The root of the payword chain. Identifies the chain and allows paywords to be verified as belonging to that chain.

E The date on which the commitment expires. This limits the length of time both users and vendors need to store information about the state of a payword chain.

I_{Comm} Additional information. This could contain the length, N, of the chain. It could also define the value of a payword. Typically, each payword will be worth one cent, but other chain values might also be useful. The upper limit to the value of a payword will depend on the risk a vendor or broker is prepared to accept. The broker might recommend an upper limit within a user's certificate. Paywords with value greater than $1 may have too much risk associated with them.

7.3.5 Spending PayWords

When users encounter a vendor from whom they wish to purchase goods, they generate a new payword chain and a commitment. The commitment is then sent to the vendor, as shown in Figure 7.20, to show the user's intentions of spending paywords there.

To make a one-cent payment, the user then sends the first payword (W_1) to the vendor. This is verified, as shown in Figure 7.21, by taking the hash of the payword W_1. If the payword is valid, the hash should match the root of the chain (W_0) found in the commitment. This works because only the user could possess the valid W_1 payword. It is computationally difficult to generate a value that would hash to W_0 due to the nature of one-way hash functions. Thus, even knowing W_0, an attacker or a cheating vendor cannot generate valid paywords in the chain.

To make a further one-cent payment, the user will send W_2. The vendor then compares the value obtained by taking the hash of W_2, $H(W_2)$ to the previous valid payword (W_1) received. If W_2 is valid, then the values will match, as shown in Figure 7.22.

Figure 7.20 Paying a vendor with paywords.

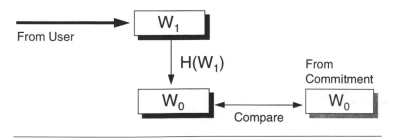

Figure 7.21 Verifying the first payword.

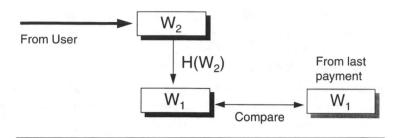

Figure 7.22   Verifying further payments.

7.3.6   Variable-size payments

Payments of values greater than one cent can be made by sending paywords further down the chain, without having sent skipped-over paywords. For example, to make a three-cent payment after having spent W_2, the fifth payword, W_5, can be sent. This is shown in Figure 7.23. The actual payment message consists of a payword and its index into the chain:

$$P = (W_i, i)$$

This allows the vendor to know how many hashes should be performed. In this example, the vendor must perform three repeated hashes on W_5. The user's name may also have to be included in the payment message to allow the vendor to identify the user, depending on implementation details. The vendor is responsible for recording the last valid payword in a chain accepted from a user.

The broker does not need to be contacted during a payment. The paywords can be quickly verified locally by the vendor. After the initial commitment, the actual size of the payment message, P, sent is small, which further improves communications efficiency. As with many electronic payment systems, there is no guarantee that the purchased item will be delivered by the vendor.

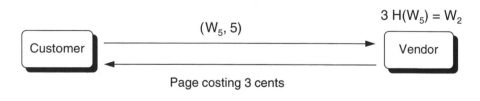

Figure 7.23   Making a payment greater than one cent.

Users maintain unspent paywords until they have finished spending at the vendor or until the commitment for that payword chain has expired. A vendor should keep each user's commitment and last valid payword received. Even after redeeming a spent chain, the vendor should retain a commitment that has not expired to prevent replay attacks.

7.3.7 Redeeming spent PayWords

To receive payment a vendor redeems payword chains with the appropriate broker, perhaps at the end of each day. For each chain, the vendor must send the following, as shown in Figure 7.24:

- The signed user commitment for that chain;
- The highest indexed payword spent.

The broker verifies the highest payword, W_L, by performing L hashes on it. The value obtained must match W_0 in the user's commitment if W_L is valid. If the user's signature and W_L are valid, the broker debits the spent amount from the user's account and pays the vendor.

7.3.8 Computational costs

The efficiency of the PayWord system is summarized below:

Broker:
- One signature/user/month (C_U);
- One signature verification/user/vendor/day (*Commitment*);
- One hash per payword spent.

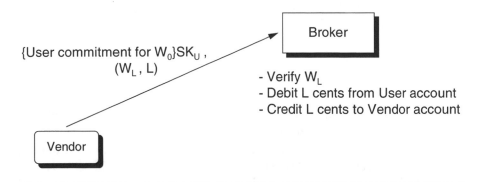

{User commitment for W_0}SK_U ,
(W_L , L)

Broker

- Verify W_L
- Debit L cents from User account
- Credit L cents to Vendor account

Vendor

Figure 7.24 Redeeming paywords with a broker.

Vendor:
- Two signature verifications/user/day (*Commitment* and C_U);
- One hash per payword spent.

User:
- One signature/vendor/day (*Commitment*);
- One hash per payword constructed.

Only the user needs to perform the computation-intensive public-key signature online, and then only once per vendor per day. Signature verifications are less computation-intensive (see Table 7.4) and are also kept to a minimum. Hash functions are computationally cheap and are performed once per payword by all parties. The broker could perform certificate generation and payword redemption offline for efficiency. PayWord is most efficient for repeated micropayments to a specific vendor.

7.3.9   Extensions

It may be desirable to be able to use paywords of different values at the same merchant within a short space of time. This could be done by extending the commitment to contain the roots of several different chains. The paywords would have different values in each separate chain, and these values would be specified in the commitment. The payment message would then have to identify which payword chain was being used as well as the payword index.

A commitment could be used as a simple electronic check to make a macropayment. Instead of including the root of a payword chain, the commitment would specify the amount to pay the vendor. The commitment, like an electronic check, is signed by the user.

7.3.10 Remarks

PayWord minimizes communication costs for a payment transaction. Unlike the Millicent system, a broker does not have to be contacted for a new vendor payment nor is there any need for scrip change or the returning of unused vendor-specific scrip to the broker. However, PayWord's credit scheme provides more opportunity for user fraud than Millicent, especially if a user's secret key is compromised.

7.4 *i*KP micropayment protocol

The authors of the *i*KP [5] suite of protocols have developed a credit-based micropayment scheme that can be used in conjunction with 3KP but does not depend on it for making micropayments (Section 4.7 provides a detailed account of the *i*KP protocol). The scheme is based on the creation of a chain of hash values [6,7] using a one-way function. A strong one-way function (F) is such that given a value (x) it is easy to compute $F(x)$. But given a value (y), it is computationally infeasible to find x such that $y = F(x)$. Using such a one-way function F, a customer chooses a random value X and computes a chain of hash values using the following:

$$A^0(X) = X$$

$$A^{i+1}(X) = F(A^i(X))$$

The values $\{A^0, ..., A^{n-1}\}$ are referred to as *coupons*. These coupons enable the customer to make n micropayments of fixed value (val) to a merchant. The customer forwards A^n to the merchant together with the value (val) per coupon and the total number of coupons n using an arbitrary macropayment system. The micropayments are performed by successively revealing $\{A^{n-1}, A^{n-2}, ..., A^0\}$ to the merchant. The merchant can verify this in turn as it is he that possesses A^n.

$$A^n(X) = F(A^{n-1}(X))$$

For example, say $n = 100$. The customer releases the coupon A^{99} for the first item to be purchased. The merchant can verify this as $A^{100}(X) = F(A^{99}(X))$. The customer releases subsequent coupons $\{A^{98}, A^{97}, ...\}$ for each additional payment made to the merchant.

7.4.1 μ-3KP protocol

The basic payment model used is the same as in 3KP. It consists of a customer (C), a merchant (M), and an acquirer gateway (A), each of which possesses a public-key pair. This provides for verification of the authenticity of each of the participants and nonrepudiation of messages between them. Figure 7.25 shows the message flows that are used in the initial authentication of a customer to a merchant which binds that customer to a specific hash chain. This is done by sending a Credit-Request message signed with the secret key of the customer.

Once the merchant has obtained authorization for the customer from the acquirer, the customer can start making micropayments. Note that, as before, the customer and merchant agree upon the description and value of the goods prior to initiating the μ-3KP protocol.

The merchant accumulates the coupons deposited by the customer until the last coupon in the chain is reached or until the merchant is satisfied that he has accumulated enough coupons to warrant sending a Clear-Request to the acquirer. (Note that there is no maximum lifetime for coupons). There is a trade-off between clearing intermediary coupons, in which case he may suffer from multiple clearing charges and waiting for all coupons to be deposited by a customer, whereby the merchant may lose some amount of interest. The merchant receives a Clear-Response message back from the acquirer indicating whether the payment has been accepted or rejected.

There are two possible behavior patterns that may be observed among users of micropayment protocols:

- Customers that engage in repeated micropayment transactions with a merchant (e.g., downloading multiple Web pages from a server);

- Customers that engage in a single transaction with a particular merchant.

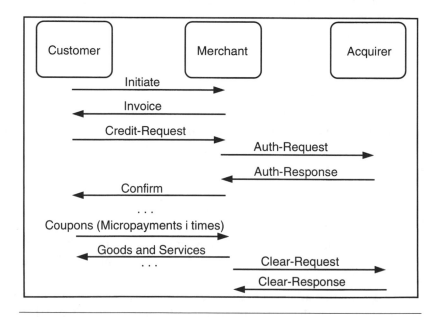

Figure 7.25   Framework of μ-3KP protocol.

The latter requires a trusted third party (TTP) such as a broker to accumulate the micropayment transactions from a number of users and forward it to the merchant to make the protocol economically feasible.

7.4.2 Repeated micropayments

In circumstances where a customer is going to have a long-term relationship with a merchant it is economically feasible to establish a direct macropayment relationship with that merchant. The customer chooses the "root" of the hash chain X. She calculates a chain of hash values (n coupons) $\{A^0, A^1, \dots, A^n\}$ using a one-way function such as MD5 or SHA. She then initiates the μ-3KP protocol for credit verification from the merchant.

Before taking a detailed look at the protocol exchanges, we explain the meaning of the various quantities exchanged by the entities in the system (see Table 7.5). These individual quantities are usually combined to form composite fields, as shown in Table 7.6.

The basic message flows, depicted in Figure 7.25, are as follows:

- *Initiate:* The customer initiates the payment transaction by sending to the merchant her identity (CID), the root of the chain of hash

Table 7.5   Individual Quantities Occurring in μ-3KP

Item	Description
CAN	Customer's account number (e.g., credit card number)
ID_M	Merchant ID. Identifies merchant to acquirer
TID_M	Transaction ID. Uniquely identifies the transaction
DESC	Description of the goods. Includes payment information such as credit card name and bank identification number
$SALT_C$	Random number generated by C. Used to randomize DESC and thus ensure privacy of DESC on the M to A link
$NONCE_M$	Random number generated by a merchant to protect against replay
DATE	Merchant's current date/time
Y/N	Response from card Issuer. YES/NO or authorization code
R_C	Random number chosen by C to form CID
CID	A customer pseudo-ID that uniquely identifies C. Computed as CID = $H(R_C, \text{CAN})$
V	Random number generated by merchant and used to bind the Confirm and Invoice message flows
V'	Second random number generated by the merchant and used to bind the Auth-Request and Clear-Response message flows

Table 7.6   μ-3KP Composite Fields

Item	Description
Common	Information held in common by all parties, A^n, n, val, ID_M, TID_M, DATE, $NONCE_M$, CID, $H(DESC, SALT_C)$, $H(V)$, $H(V')$
Clear	Information transmitted in the clear, ID_M, DATE, $NONCE_M$, $H(Common)$, $H(V)$, A^n
SLIP	Payment Instruction, n, val, $H(Common)$, CAN, R_C
EncSlip	Payment Instruction encrypted with the public key of the acquirer, $PK_A(SLIP)$
$CERT_X$	Public-key certificate of X issued by a CA
Sig_A	Acquirer's signature in response to Credit-Request message flow, $SK_A[H(Y/N, H(Common))]$
Sig'_A	Acquirer' signature in response to a Clear-Request message flow, $SK_A[H(Y/N, Sig_A, V', A^{n-i})]$
Sig_M	Merchant's signature, $SK_M[H(H(Common), H(V)]$, $H(V')$
Sig_C	Cardholder's Signature, $SK_C[H(EncSlip, H(Common))]$

values (A^n), the value of each coupon (val), the total number of coupons in the chain (n), a random number ($SALT_C$), and her public-key
certificate ($CERT_C$). This information is sent to the merchant in
cleartext.

- *Invoice:* The response from the merchant contains the merchant's
  identity (ID_M), the transaction identifier to uniquely identify the transaction, the date, and a nonce. These fields are transferred as part of
  Clear. The merchant and customer share some information such
  as the amount and description of the goods, which is known as
  Common. The merchant creates a message digest on Common and
  a random number (V). He forms a digital signature (Sig_M) on the
  two digests and includes this in the Invoice. This allows the customer to verify that she and the merchant agree on the details of the
  transaction.

- *Credit Request:* The customer sends a request to the merchant that
  contains the total number of coupons (n), the value of each coupon
  (val), and the customer's account number in SLIP. The SLIP is encrypted with the public key of the acquirer to form EncSlip. The customer then forms Common and creates a message digest on it. This
  should match the one sent by the merchant in Invoice. She creates a

digital signature on EncSlip and H(Common) to form Sig_C. The customer sends EncSlip and Sig_C to the merchant.

- *Authorization Request:* This is a request from the merchant to the acquirer to authorize a payment transaction. The merchant creates a digital signature Sig_M. He forwards Clear, the randomized hash of the goods description ($H(\text{DESC}, \text{SALT}_C)$), the encrypted slip (EncSlip), the signature of the customer (Sig_C) and his own signature (Sig_M) to the acquirer. The actual transfer of money is initiated at a later date using the Clear-Request message flow.

- *Authorization Response:* The acquirer sends a signed response that contains a positive or negative indication. A positive response gives the merchant guarantee of the customer's credit limit.

- *Confirm:* The merchant forwards the acquirer's signed response to the customer as well as the first random number V. The inclusion of V in Confirm proves to the customer that the merchant has accepted the authorization response.

- *Micropayments:* The customer can then make multiple micropayment transactions until such time that she has purchased all the goods that she requires or has exhausted her supply of coupons for the merchant. The customer may have to supply the transaction identifier (TID_M) with each micropayment so that the merchant can associate a coupon with a particular hash chain.

- *Clear-Request:* The merchant asks the acquirer to perform a payment. In our case, it consists of a number of micropayments. When the merchant receives the last coupon in the chain (A^0) or decides that he needs to deposit the coupons (A^j) collected so far, he composes a Clear-Request message. He calculates the total payment due, which is $n - j$ times the amount of each coupon (val), and sends this along with the last coupon (A^{n-j}), the second random number (V'), and the signature of the acquirer (Sig_A). He sends the Clear-Request message to the acquirer. The acquirer can verify the hash chain and processes the request as a regular iKP transaction. The amount to be cleared may be different from the amount authorized.

- *Clear-Response:* This is a signed response from the acquirer to the merchant indicating whether the payment transaction was successful or not. It contains a positive or negative response as well as a digital signature (Sig'_A) on the second random number (V'), the total number of coupons (A^{n-j}), and the acquirer's previous signature (Sig_A).

Figure 7.26 shows the detailed message exchanges that take place when making repeated micropayments to the same merchant.

7.4.3 Nonrepeated micropayments

In many cases, when a user is initially browsing a merchant site she may make one or a small number of micropayment transactions. This may not warrant the overhead of establishing a macropayment context between the customer and the merchant. In such circumstances a TTP in the form of a broker is introduced who acts as an intermediary and collects micropayments on behalf of merchants from customers. The volume of transactions processed by the broker is large enough for a macropayment context to be established between the broker and the merchants. The protocol steps are as follows:

- The customer establishes a micropayment relationship with the broker. She also establishes a shared session key with the broker (K_{CB}). The latter is not part of the μ-3KP protocol.

- When the customer wants to make a purchase from a specific merchant, she sends a coupon $A_{CB}^i(X)$, the name of the merchant (M), and the description of the goods (DESC) (see Figure 7.27). In the context

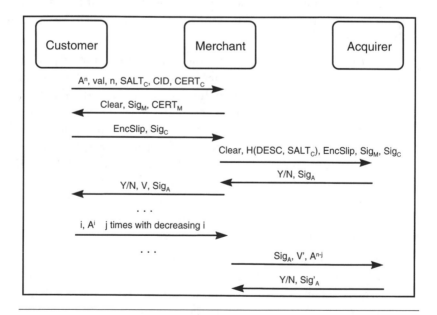

Figure 7.26 μ-3KP protocol.

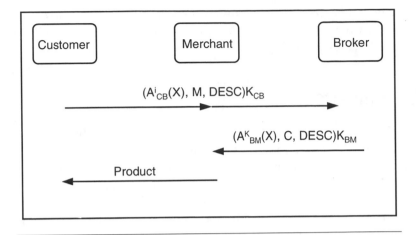

Figure 7.27 Nonrepeated micropayments.

of the WWW, the DESC could be a URL. The fields of the message are encrypted using a previously established session key shared between the customer and the broker.

- The broker translates the customer's coupon into a coupon for the merchant A_{BM}^k (X) and adds the customer's name and the description of the requested goods. He encrypts the fields of the message with the session key shared between himself and the merchant. The encrypted message is either sent directly to the merchant or to the customer, who transparently forwards it to the merchant.

- The merchant sends the goods to the customer.

Using a broker as an intermediary provides no additional security gains. It does, however, simplify the transaction complexity at the merchant's site as the merchant-broker relationship will usually be a longer lasting one than one with individual buyers. Therefore, more micropayments can be performed per macropayment relationship.

7.4.4 Remarks

The μ-3KP protocol aims to provide all the benefits of a micropayment system with the added security of nonrepudiation of messages between all entities involved in the process. The initial authentication of a customer to a merchant requires a number of message flows, which adds to the overall cost of the transaction. The protocol also requires the establishment of a full certification hierarchy. Compared to other micropayment protocols, the μ-3KP protocol seems to be an expensive option.

7.5 MicroMint

MicroMint [4] is a second micropayment scheme designed by Ron Rivest and Adi Shamir who also developed the PayWord scheme. It is based on a unique form of identified electronic cash that requires no public-key cryptography. MicroMint coins can be spent efficiently *at any vendor* without the need to contact a bank or broker for verification at the time of purchase.

The security level provided is less than that of PayWord, but allows MicroMint to be more efficient for micropayments made to many different vendors. While some small-scale fraud is possible, large-scale fraud is designed to be computationally difficult.

7.5.1   The MicroMint model

Within the MicroMint system, coins are minted by a broker, who then sells them to users, as shown in Figure 7.28. A broker might maintain user and vendor accounts that can be settled using a macropayment scheme. A user can spend the coins at any vendor. Double spending is possible since no

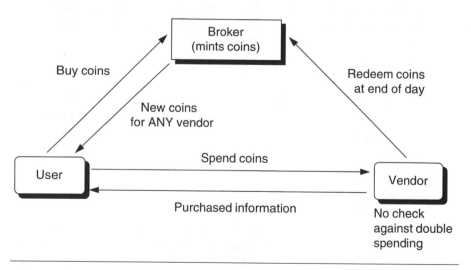

Figure 7.28   Entities within the MicroMint system.

check is performed to see if a coin has already been spent, at the time of purchase. However, a broker records which coins were issued to a user. Double spending will be detected, after the fraud, at the end of the day when vendors redeem spent coins with a broker. User's whose coins are repeatedly double spent will be *blacklisted* and expelled from the system. Fraud prevention is discussed later in more detail.

7.5.2 MicroMint coins

In macropayment electronic cash schemes, such as Ecash and NetCash, an electronic coin is usually digitally signed by the bank to show that it is authentic. However, to sign and verify every coin in this way in a micropayment scheme would be too computationally expensive. Instead, MicroMint adopts a scheme that makes it very computationally difficult for anyone except the broker to mint valid coins. However, it is quick and efficient for anyone to verify a coin.

A MicroMint coin is a *k-way hash function collision*. A one-way hash function or message digest maps a value x to a value y of specified length, as described in Chapter 3:

$$H(x) = y$$

A hash function collision occurs when two or more different values of x map to the same value of y:

$$H(x_1) = H(x_2) = y$$

It is usually hard to generate two values that map to the same value of y (two-way hash function collision).

A k-way hash function collision occurs when k different input values map to the same output value of y:

$$H(x_1) = H(x_2) = H(x_3) \ldots . = H(x_k) = y$$

If k is set equal to 4 ($k = 4$), a MicroMint coin will be a four-way hash function collision, as shown in Figure 7.29.

Each coin is worth one cent, and the coin, C, consists of the four input values that collide to the same value y when the hash function is applied:

$$C = \{x_1, x_2, x_3, x_4\}$$

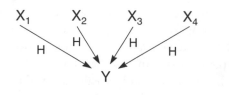

Figure 7.29   A four-way hash function collision.

7.5.3   Verifying a coin

A coin can be easily verified by:

- Performing four hashes on each x_i to obtain the same y value:

$$H(x_1) = H(x_2) = H(x_3) = H(x_4) = y$$

- Ensuring that each x is different. Otherwise, the x values could be set to be the same value, and they would then obviously map to the same y value.

- Verifying a coin only proves that a coin is authentic. It cannot be used to detect double spending. To do this, the broker needs to maintain a copy of each coin already spent to check against.

7.5.4   Minting coins

To mint a coin involves finding multiple values of x that hash to the same value of y. Within MicroMint, each value of x is restricted to be the same length (m bits). The hash function used will define the length of y (n bits). The hash function will map every x value onto some y value ($H(x) = y$). Since y is n bits long, there are 2^n possible y values.

The procedure can be thought of as throwing a ball (x) into one of 2^n bins (y values). When four balls ($k = 4$) land in the same bin, a valid coin has been minted, as shown in Figure 7.30. This is because four different values of x (four different balls) have hashed to the same y value (landed in the same bin).

Balls are thrown at random and cannot be aimed at a specific bin. That is, we don't know what y value a certain x value will hash to before we perform the hash function. If there are many bins (a large value of n), then many balls will have to be thrown before four will happen to land in the same bin. When this happens, the first valid coin has been minted. The computational costs of minting coins is discussed in the next section.

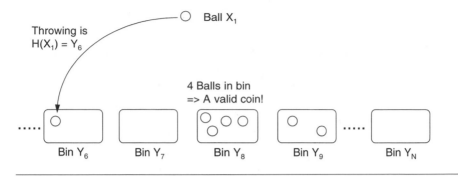

Figure 7.30 MicroMint coin minting analogy.

It takes less throws to mint the next coin because many of the bins will already have some balls in them. Thus it is computationally expensive to mint the first coin, but minting more coins after that becomes progressively cheaper. This makes it difficult for an attacker to economically forge coins. The broker can buy special hardware to perform the hashing, and by minting a large number of coins will be able to produce coins cheaply, much like a real world mint.

7.5.5 Computational Costs

The number of hashes (throws) needed on average to produce the first coin (*k*-way collision) is

$$T = 2^{n(k - 1)/k}$$

where n is the length in bits of the hash value y. The value k is the number of x values that must hash to the same y value to produce a coin.

Putting $k = 4$ (4 balls per coin), $n = 48$ (2^{48} bins), then

$$T = 2^{48(4-1)/4} = 2^{36}$$

To generate the first coin therefore requires 2^{36} or approximately 69 billion ($6.9 \cdot 10^{10}$) throws.

By throwing c times as many balls as T, there will be on average c^k coins (*k*-way collisions) produced, so cT hash operations produces c^k coins. Therefore, to generate approximately 1 billion ($1.0 \cdot 10^9$) coins, let $c = 178$, $k = 4$, and

$$c^k = 178^4 = 1.00 \cdot 10^9 \text{ (1 billion coins)}$$

The number of hashes required will be

$$cT = 178 \cdot 2^{36} = 1.22 \cdot 10^{13} \text{ hashes}$$

For a billion coins, this comes out as:

$$\frac{1.22 \cdot 10^{13}}{1.0 \cdot 10^9} \quad = \quad 12,232 \text{ hashes per coin}$$

Only 12,232 hashes on average are required to generate a valid coin. This illustrates how after an initial large investment the broker can economically mint coins. The time taken to generate coins will depend on the hash function used, the number of coins required, and other parameters discussed in later sections. The designers suggest some possible current technology that could be used to form the special broker hardware needed in their paper [4].

7.5.6 Multiple coins per bin

The broker should only produce a maximum of one coin from each bin. If more than k balls fall into the same bin, several coins could be made from subsets of the values in the bin. For a bin with five x values, possible coins include

$$C_1 \quad = \quad \{x_1, x_2, x_3, x_4\}$$

$$C_2 \quad = \quad \{x_1, x_2, x_3, x_5\}$$

$$C_3 \quad = \quad \{x_1, x_2, x_4, x_5\} \text{ and so on.}$$

However, an attacker who obtains any two of these coins can generate the other coins produced from this bin. The value C_3 can be produced knowing C_1 and C_2, for example. For this reason, only one coin should be produced from each bin.

7.5.7 Coin validity criterion

Using special hardware, a broker will be able to calculate a very large number of hashes in a short time period when minting coins. However, to remember the value of each ball and the bin it landed in will require substantial storage space.

To reduce this requirement without having to reduce the number of hashes performed, part of the coin's hash value y can be required to match a specific pattern. If there is no match, the coin can be discarded as invalid. When coins are being verified by vendors or users, this additional validity requirement will also have to be checked.

A hash value y is divided into two parts, the high-order bits a and the low-order bits b:

$$y \;=\; a,b$$

The broker chooses a value z that is equal in length to a. The choice of z could be random, and should be kept secret while the coins are being minted. For the coin to be valid, a (the high-order bits of y) must match z:

$$a \;=\; z \text{ for a good coin.}$$

Those values of x that do not map to a y value that satisfies this criterion can be discarded, and their values need not be stored. By varying the length of a (the part of y that must match a pattern z), the broker can control the number of thrown balls that will have to be remembered and that will become valid coins. However, as the storage requirement decreases, less coins will be produced for the same computational effort. Therefore, more computation will have to be performed to produce an adequate number of coins.

7.5.8 Preventing forgery

A broker takes the following steps to prevent large-scale forging of coins:

Special hardware: The broker invests in hardware that gives a computational advantage over attackers. The hardware might consist of special-purpose chips that can compute hash values quickly. The broker can ensure that good hash values (y) require many computations to discover by increasing the length of a ($y = a, b$) required to match some pattern z.

Short coin validity period: Coins are given a short lifetime of one month. This gives an attacker less time to try and compute valid coins. Unused coins are returned to the broker at the end of each month.

Early minting: The broker will start minting coins a month ahead of their release. Coins for use in June will be minted during May. The broker has much more time than an attacker to mint coins.

Coin validity criterion: The broker will reveal a new coin validity criterion at the start of the month when the new coins are released. Forged coins cannot be generated until this is known. The coin validity criterion can either be the value z, which the hash values must match, or it could define H to be a new hash function and keep z the same.

Different bins (y values): The broker does not compute all possible coins, only enough for that period's needs. It is likely that some forged coins may map to different bins than those used by the broker. By remembering the bins used by that batch of coins, a broker can detect forged coins coming from other bins. A bit array (an indexed list of 0's or 1's), with one bit (a single 0 or 1) for each bin (y value) can be used for this purpose. To record a bin y as having been used, a 1 is placed at position y in the array. Those bins that were not used will have a 0 at the appropriate index in the array.

$k > 2$: If coins are two-way collisions, it is easier to compute valid coins. The value of k should be greater than 2. Putting $k = 4$ seems to work well in theory.

Extensions: Further extensions are possible to make forgery more difficult. These are discussed in Section 7.5.11.

7.5.9   A MicroMint purchase

A purchase simply consists of sending the coin(s) along with the purchase request to a vendor, as shown in Figure 7.31. Since each coin is worth one cent, the exact amount required can be paid, and no change is necessary.

No encryption is used within MicroMint and the communications channels are not secure. Coins can be stolen and intercepted in any of the steps shown in Figure 7.28. If this is a problem the user/broker and vendor/broker communications can be encrypted using agreed-upon encryption keys. How this is done is an implementation issue and details are not provided in the MicroMint scheme. The encrypted solution is not suitable for the communications link between a user and an unknown vendor. It would require expensive public-key encryption and certificates to secure the link. Instead, the MicroMint coins can be extended to become user-specific, as described in Section 7.5.11. This makes the spending of stolen coins more difficult.

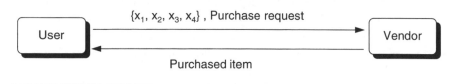

Figure 7.31   A MicroMint purchase.

7.5.10 Double spending

No check is performed at the vendor against double spending. If the coins are valid, the purchased item is returned. However since MicroMint offers *no anonymity*, the broker will detect doubly spent coins only when the vendor redeems them. Both user fraud and vendor fraud are possible. Vendors might try to redeem coins already spent at other vendors. The broker may not be able to distinguish whether a user or vendor is committing the fraud.

The broker records the user to whom coins are issued and the vendor from whom those coins are received back from, then keeps track of how many doubly spent coins are connected with each user or vendor. *Repeat offenders* are blacklisted and denied further access to the system. The designers feel that some small-scale double spending is acceptable. They propose that a broker not pay a vendor for an already spent coin. This might discourage cheating vendors from selling already spent coins.

7.5.11 Extensions

A number of extensions and variations are proposed to increase the security and usefulness of the basic MicroMint scheme. These include:

Hidden predicates: By only allowing certain balls (x values) to become part of a valid coin, forgery can be further limited. The x value must have certain properties initially known only to the broker. These properties, called *hidden predicates*, can be announced by a broker after the coins have been released. Unless all the x values that make up a coin obey these hidden predicates, the coin is not valid. Since the broker will know what the hidden predicates are when the coins are minted, it is not necessary to waste time calculating the hash of an x value that does not obey them.

A hidden predicate might require that a low-order bit of x be equal to some function of the higher order bits. It should be difficult to work out from examples. A broker could define a series of hidden predicates on a month's coins and reveal a new one each day. Valid coins would obey the required predicate, while many forged coins might not. A vendor can verify that a coin is valid by checking that it obeys the predicate published by the broker.

User-specific coins: Coins can be related to the identity of a user. A vendor can then check to verify that the person spending the coins is the correct user linked to those coins. This ensures that stolen coins cannot be spent by most users.

One way of implementing this is to assign each user to a small user group. The broker will give a user U of that group coins that hash to the group identity:

$$h2 \left(\text{Coin}\right) = h2(U) = \text{GID}$$

where Coin $= (x_1, x_2, x_3, x_4)$ and h_2 can be a different hash function than that used for validating coins. The user's identity U should also hash to the group identity. A vendor can authenticate a user U and check that the GID of the coins matches the user's group.

Vendor-specific coins: To reduce the chance of fraud, coins can be constructed so that they may be redeemed by a small group of vendors only. This may prevent vendors selling already spent coins to other vendors or users. To create vendor-specific coins involves a more complicated method than user-specific coins, where the definition of what forms a coin is made more complex.

Coins for multiple months: It is possible for the broker to mint some of the coins for several different months at the same time. The process can be done at a lower computational cost than minting for one month alone. Since the broker can now effectively mint coins faster, the process can be slowed down by making them harder to mint. This can be done by increasing the length of the hash value y and the validity criterion z.

To concurrently mint coins for several months, the broker decides on different values of the validity criterion z for upcoming months. A new value of z will be announced each month as new coins are released. When minting, if a ball turns out to be a good ball for one of the months, by meeting the criterion for any month, then it is stored. This will result in coins for several different months being minted simultaneously.

Different-valued coins: Coins could be worth different values, according to predicates on the x values. These predicates might be announced at the start of the month and could be verified by anyone.

Unlike some of the other micropayment schemes examined, MicroMint is optimal for small payments at many different vendors. It proposes a unique form of identified electronic cash suitable for micropayments. No public-key cryptography is required, but as a result double spending is possible.

7.6 Micropayments summary and analysis

The concept of a micropayment emerged in 1995, and very quickly a diverse range of schemes had been introduced. Some of these, such as Millicent, have been designed specifically to cater for the new form of payment, while others, such as $\mu - i\text{KP}$, have been designed as an add-on to an existing macropayment scheme. As we have seen, these make use of some novel cryptographic techniques, including the use of fast message digest algorithms to authenticate a message and the use of economies of scale in coin minting.

A key feature of micropayments is to minimize the communications necessary during a transaction and to reduce the number of computation-intensive public-key operations. Millicent uses no public-key cryptography and is optimized for repeated micropayments to the same vendor. Its distributed approach allows a payment to be validated, and double spending prevented, without the overhead of contacting a third centralized party online during a purchase. With payments as low as one-tenth of a cent being feasible, it appears to be one of the best candidates for general-purpose micropayments. Its only drawback is that seamless successive payments to multiple vendors is hindered by having to contact a broker for every new party encountered.

SubScrip is similarly optimized for repeated micropayments to the same vendor. However, use of a macropayment to set up a temporary account at a vendor will force the user to spend an adequate amount at that vendor to justify this overhead. It is more suited to replacing short-term subscription services or making micropayments to a regularly visited vendor.

PayWord improves on Millicent and SubScrip by removing the need to contact a third party when making a payment to a new vendor. The need to return some form of change, as with the Millicent and SubScrip schemes, is also eliminated. However, PayWord is a credit-based scheme where a user's account is not debited until some time after a purchase. This provides more opportunity for fraud since a large number of purchases can be made against an account with insufficient funds. The use of user certificates with public-key operations also adds some computational overhead.

The *i*KP micropayment scheme is unique in that it offers two different solutions: one for repeated payments with the same vendor, and the other for single payments to different vendors. However the requirement of a full certification hierarchy and several message flows for a transaction make it less efficient than other schemes.

Finally, MicroMint uses a new form of identified electronic cash to provide a system optimized for micropayments to many different vendors. While it is the most efficient scheme for making these unrelated payments, small-scale fraud is easily possible. Double spending is not prevented, although it will be detected after the fact. Combined with the high computational requirements needed by a broker to mint coins, it is not likely to be adopted in the near future.

At the time of writing, no large-scale trials have yet been undertaken with any of these schemes, so it is not yet clear what systems will endure. As the demand for a feasible and efficient micropayment system increases, it is likely that more schemes and solutions will be proposed. It is clear, however, that whatever system is successful, the micropayment concept will radically alter the nature of network commerce over the coming years.

REFERENCES

[1]   Glassman, S., et al., "The Millicent Protocol for Inexpensive Electronic Commerce," *Proc. 4th International World Wide Web Conference*, Boston, MA, Dec. 11–14, 1995, pp. 603–618, http://www.research.digital.com/SRC/millicent/

[2]   Manasse, M., "The Millicent Protocols for Electronic Commerce," *Proc. 1st USENIX workshop on Electronic Commerce*, New York, NY, July 11–12, 1995, http://www.research.digital.com/SRC/millicent/

[3]   Furche, A., and G. Wrightson, "SubScrip - An efficient protocol for pay-per-view payments on the Internet," *Proc. 5th International Conference on Computer Communications and Networks (ICCCN '96)*, Rockville, MD, Oct. 16–19, 1996, http://www.cs.newcastle.edu.au/Research/afurche/subscrip.ps

[4]   Rivest, R., and A. Shamir, *PayWord and MicroMint: Two Simple Micropayment Schemes*, May, 1996, http://theory.lcs.mit.edu/~rivest/RivestShamir-mpay.ps

[5]   Bellare, M., et al., "iKP - A Family of Secure Electronic Payment Protocols," *Proc. 1st USENIX workshop on Electronic Commerce*, New York, NY, July 11–12, 1995, http://www.zurich.ibm.com/Technology/Security/extern/ecommerce/iKP.html

[6]   Lamport, L., "Password Authentication with Insecure Communications," *Communications of the ACM*, Vol. 4, No. 11, Nov. 1981, pp. 770–772.

[7]   Merkel, R., "A Certified Digital Signature," *Advances in Cryptology -CRYPTO '89 Proc.*, Lecture Notes in Computer Science, Vol. 435, Berlin: Springer-Verlag, 1990, pp. 218–238.

Chapter 8

Payment systems— Prospects for the future

The only way to successfully predict the future is to invent it.

Alan Kay

IT IS CLEAR from the discussion in Chapter 2 that effecting payment for goods and services in conventional commerce is carried out in many diverse ways that differ in popularity from one country to another. Electronic payment techniques have reflected this diversity, and for each conventional payment method, there is an electronic counterpart. We have classified these methods into four major categories—card, check, cash, and micropayments—and have described the more important existing and proposed systems. It is clear that a certain degree of convergence will occur in the industry where systems that address the same user needs will compete and that one will emerge as the victor.

One can expect, however, that just as in conventional commerce, users will require a range of payment methods with at least one (and probably more) system from each of the above categories being widely supported. A recognition of this fact is the existence of the Joint Electronic Payment Initiative (JEPI) [1], an industry consortium that has come together to define a set of protocols and interfaces that can support the use of a wide variety of payment methods for network commerce. Similar support for a range of payment methods will be provided by the European electronic commerce project SEMPER (Secure Electronic Marketplace for Europe) [2].

In the area of payments by card (credit, debit, and charge), it seems clear that the industry has converged on the Secure Electronic Transactions (SET) method of effecting payment. SET has its roots in some of the other systems that are covered in Chapter 4 and these are of interest from a historical perspective. Systems that make no use of cryptography, such as First Virtual, may continue to find uses where the supporting infrastructure needed for SET is unavailable. Since credit card payments based on SET will be widely deployed from 1997 onwards, it is likely that this will account for the bulk of Internet payments in the short to medium term.

Progress in the area of electronic checks has been considerably slower. The research and academic community has advanced a number of schemes that provide check-like payment instruments, but industry efforts have concentrated on simpler schemes involving small-scale extensions to the paper-based check-processing system. At the time of writing, no specification of this is available. This implies that widespread deployment of the system will not happen for some time. However, because few extensions are needed to the backbone infrastructure, a system like that envisaged by the Financial Services Technology Consortium (FSTC) could be deployed quite quickly. In cases where a check payment is being made from a customer to a merchant, an equivalent transaction could be made using SET with a debit card, and this method may supplant check payments that are made in this context.

Electronic cash has also suffered from a lack of convergence. The "father of electronic cash," David Chaum, originated the cryptographic techniques used to produce electronic coins that could be spent in an anonymous fashion. This work has been carried through in the research world by the CAFE project and in the commercial world by Ecash. Although Ecash is in use in a small number of locations around the world, the banking industry as a whole has not rallied behind it. Instead, the focus has been on electronic purse systems such as Mondex or EMV Cash cards. These schemes depend on the use of chip cards, and thus can only be used in a situation where a card can be physically inserted into the merchant's card reader, or where payers have card-reading hardware incorporated into their network workstation. Although the availability of such hardware is rare today, an industry group called PC/SC (Personal Computer/Smart Card) [3] has been formed that has plans to make smart-card interfaces a standard equipment item on low-cost workstations. Until this occurs, Ecash and similar software-based systems are the only workable solution for networked cash payments.

The advent of micropayments has heralded a completely new form of commerce that hitherto has not existed. It will take some time for awareness of this technique to filter through to the major producers of electronic content, but this is likely to be followed by an explosion of activity in this area. A number of schemes have been described in Chapter 7, none of which has yet undergone extensive piloting. Which system or systems succeed in this area is still very much an open question.

In Chapter 2, we gave an overview of the size and structure of the current conventional payment systems market. Clearly, if electronic methods were to supplant even 1% of conventional payments, it would represent an enormous industry worldwide. The unstoppable growth of the Internet and the tidal wave of electronic commerce that follows in its wake indicates that they will capture considerably more than 1%. It is this impetus that will continue to inject dynamism into the industry in the years to come.

References

[1] CommerceNet and the World Wide Web Consortium, *The Joint Electronic Payment Initiative (JEPI)*, 1996, http://www.commerce.net/work/taskforces/payments/jepi.html

[2] Abad Peiro, J., N. Asokan, and M. Waidner, *Payment Manager -Overview*, SEMPER Activity Paper 212ZR054, March 1996, http://www.semper.org/info/212ZR054.ps

[3] Microsoft Press Release, *PC/SC Workgroup to Develop Open Technology for Integrating Smart Cards and Personal Computers*, Redmond, Washington, Sept. 10, 1996, http://www.smartcardsys.com

About the Authors

Donal O'Mahony received B.A., B.A.I., and Ph.D. degrees from Trinity College, Dublin, Ireland. After a brief career in industry at SORD Computer Systems in Tokyo and IBM in Dublin, he joined Trinity College as a lecturer in computer science in 1984. He is co-author of *Local Area Networks and their Applications*, published by Prentice-Hall in 1988. At Trinity, he coordinates a research group working in the areas of networks and telecommunications. Within this group, projects are ongoing in a wide range of areas including electronic commerce, network security, and mobile communications technology. Dr. O'Mahony has acted as an independent consultant to government and private industry organizations across Europe on a wide variety of projects involving strategic networking issues. His e-mail address is Donal.OMahony@cs.tcd.ie

Michael Peirce graduated with a B.A. (Mod) in computer science from Trinity College, Dublin. His final-year dissertation concerned the design of a new scalable anonymous electronic payment mechanism for the purchase of goods and services on the World Wide Web. The results of this work were published in the *4th International WWW Conference* in December 1995. He has acted as the maintainer of a highly popular WWW page on electronic payment since 1994. He regularly co-presents tutorials on network payment systems and digital cash to international audiences. Currently he is working as a researcher in the area of mobile communications, with the Networks and Telecommunications Research Group (NTRG) at Trinity College, Dublin. His e-mail address is Michael.Peirce@cs.tcd.ie.

Hitesh Tewari earned his bachelor's and master's degrees in computer science from Trinity College, Dublin. His M.Sc. thesis was in the area of electronic payment systems and made use of secure cryptographic protocols in association with control information to check key usage by individuals. He is currently working as a researcher at Trinity College in the area of mobile data communications systems and is pursuing a Ph.D. His e-mail address is Hitesh.Tewari@cs.tcd.ie.

Index

Recent Titles in the Artech House Computing Library

Internet and Intranet Security, Rolf Oppliger

Managing Computer Networks: A Case-Based Reasoning Approach,
Lundy Lewis

*Metadata Management for Information Control and Business
Success,* Guy Tozer

Multimedia Database Management Systems, Guojun Lu

Practical Guide to Software Quality Management, John W. Horch

*Practical Process Simulation Using Object-Oriented Techniques and
C++,* José Garrido

Risk Management Processes for Software Engineering Models,
Marian Myerson

*Secure Electronic Transactions: Introduction and Technical
Reference,* Larry Loeb

Software Process Improvement With CMM, Joseph Raynus

Software Verification and Validation: A Practitioner's Guide,
Steven R. Rakitin

Solving the Year 2000 Crisis, Patrick McDermott

User-Centered Information Design for Improved Software Usability,
Pradeep Henry

For further information on these and other Artech House titles,
including previously considered out-of-print books now available
through our In-Print-Forever® (IPF®) program, contact:

Artech House	Artech House
685 Canton Street	46 Gillingham Street
Norwood, MA 02062	London SW1V 1AH UK
Phone: 781-769-9750	Phone: +44 (0)20 7596-8750
Fax: 781-769-6334	Fax: +44 (0)20 7630-0166
e-mail: artech@artechhouse.com	e-mail: artech-uk@artechhouse.com

Find us on the World Wide Web at:
www.artechhouse.com